TRUTH, JUSTICE, &
A NICE WHITE COUNTRY

by

GREG JOHNSON

Counter-Currents Publishing Ltd.
San Francisco
2015

Cover image:
Léon Frédéric, *Les âges de l'ouvrier*, 1895–1897, central panel
Musée d'Orsay

Cover design by
Kevin I. Slaughter

Published in the United States by
COUNTER-CURRENTS PUBLISHING LTD.
P.O. Box 22638
San Francisco, CA
94122 USA
http://www.counter-currents.com/

Hardcover ISBN: 978-1-935965-91-6
Paperback ISBN: 978-1-935965-92-3
E-book ISBN: 978-1-935965-93-0

Library of Congress Cataloging-in-Publication Data

Names: Johnson, Greg, 1971- author.
Title: Truth, justice & a nice white country / by Greg Johnson.
Other titles: Truth, justice, and a nice white country
Description: San Francisco : Counter-Currents Publishing Ltd., 2016. |
   Includes bibliographical references and index. | Essays orginally from the
   Counter-Currents/North American New Right webzine.
Identifiers: LCCN 2016004328 (print) | LCCN 2016016890 (ebook) | ISBN
   9781935965916 (hardcover : alk. paper) | ISBN 9781935965923 (pbk. : alk.
   paper) | ISBN 9781935965930 (ebook) | ISBN 9781935965930 (E-book)
Subjects: LCSH: White nationalism. | White supremacy movements. | Ethnic
   relations--Political aspects. | Ethnicity--Political aspects.
Classification: LCC HS1610 .J65 2016 (print) | LCC HS1610 (ebook) | DDC
   305.809--dc23
LC record available at https://lccn.loc.gov/2016004328

CONTENTS

TRUTH, JUSTICE, &
A NICE WHITE COUNTRY

The North American New Right advocates *ethnonationalism*: the idea that the best way to preserve and promote peace, racial and cultural diversity, and the general welfare of the world is to create racially and culturally homogeneous homelands for every distinct people.

We think such arrangements are best for all peoples, but we are most interested in the welfare of our own race, the white race, since it is the only human race threatened with simple biological extinction. For this reason, we also call ourselves *White Nationalists*, since we are concerned primarily to preserve the white race in all of its genetic and cultural diversity.

But aren't there higher concerns than the preservation of the white race? What about humanity? What about global biodiversity? What about the welfare of the world as a whole? My answer is simple: preserving whites contributes to these larger goals in two ways. First, we are *part* of the world. But beyond that, whites are *the part of the world that cares the most about the whole*. If you want to save all those endangered species, save whites first.

To boil our project down to a bumper sticker, we stand for "Truth, Justice, and a Nice White Country"—actually, a lot of nice white countries. The political mainstream, by contrast, stands for lies, injustice, and mixing up every white nation into a multicultural, multiracial mess, destroying distinct identities and making hatred and violence inevitable.

1. TRUTH

In what sense do we stand for truth? White Nationalists tell the truth about the differences between the races, the sexes, and national identities. We tell the truth about the differences between the normal and the abnormal, the healthy and the sick, the good and the evil, the just and the unjust. The rest of the political spectrum, however, is premised on telling lies about these distinctions or ignoring them completely. Political correctness is just a species of lying: lying about fundamental human differences.

2. JUSTICE

In what sense do we stand for justice? And in what sense is the rest of the political spectrum opposed to justice?

Mainstream politics today, Left and Right, is ruled by political correctness, which boils down to making false excuses for privileged groups, who aren't responsible for their failures, and leveling false accusations against whites, who are presented as a virtually omnipotent and uniquely malevolent race that is responsible for the failings of everyone else.

So what would justice look like, if we stopped lying about human differences?

Aristotle distinguishes between retributive and distributive justice. Retributive justice deals with punishment. Distributive justice deals with rewards. Retributive justice requires making the punishment fit the crime. Under the reign of political correctness, however, criminals are falsely excused and innocent whites are falsely accused of their crimes. Distributive justice requires that rewards be proportionate to merits: equal people should be treated equally. Unequal people should be treated unequally. But Aristotle also pointed out that justice requires that unequal rewards be *proportionate* to unequal merit. There is no justice if a man who is 10 times better has 100 times more.

Justice in an unequal world means rewarding unequal people unequally. And that means that there will be hierarchies in society: some people will have more power, more responsibility, more wealth, and more honor than others. Justice means that in every field of endeavor, there will be elites: the best singers, the best athletes, the best civic leaders, etc.

3. ELITISM & HIERARCHY?

I think it is a mistake for people on the Right to reject equality *as such* and to endorse "hierarchy" and "elitism" *as such*.

Treating unequal people equally is injustice. As William Blake says, "One law for the lion and ox is oppression." But it is also unjust to treat equal people unequally. (Two laws for two lions is oppression as well.) In short:

- ❖ We are not opposed to equality as such, but only to *unjust* equality.
- ❖ We are not for hierarchy as such, but only *just* hierarchies.
- ❖ We are not for elitism as such, but only for *just and deserving* elites, elites based on *merit* rather than money or birth or political corruption.

When White Nationalists praise hierarchy and elitism as such, it is natural for people to wonder, "What's in their elitism for me?" After all, there can be corrupt and evil elites. There can be arbitrary and unjust hierarchies. *Thus White Nationalists should stand first and foremost for justice*. With the understanding that distributive justice in an unequal world will lead inevitably to just hierarchies and merit-based elites.

4. THE COMMON GOOD

White Nationalism, as I have argued, should be both populist and elitist.[1]

White Nationalism is populist, because a social system is just *only if it pursues the common good* — the good of the whole people. An unjust social system is ruled for the benefit of *factional interests*, whether of one man, a small elite, or the majority.

White Nationalism is elitist, because the common good is best pursued in a society ruled by the best — meaning the most intelligent, idealistic, and public spirited, not merely the rich — and the best people are always a minority, an elite.

But to make sure that such an elite does not become corrupt and start to rule in its own interests at the expense of the common good, there should also be a popular, "democratic" element of government as well, to counter-balance the factional interests of the ruling elite.

---

[1] See my "Notes on Populism, Elitism, and Democracy," in *New Right vs. Old Right* (San Francisco: Counter-Currents, 2013).

5. AN ELITIST STRATEGY FOR A POPULIST MOVEMENT

The white race is currently leaderless. We have no group looking out for white interests in the political realm. If a White Nationalist society is to come into existence, it will need a leadership caste. To *bring* a White Nationalist society into existence, we need to start creating that leadership caste today. That means that our movement must aim at creating a racially-conscious, racially-responsible elite. We must search for whites of higher than average intelligence, morality, and taste—whites who are above average in courage and public spiritedness. But as a populist movement, we believe that this new elite can and must be recruited from all social classes within the existing society.

6. A NICE WHITE COUNTRY

Margot Metroland uses an apt phrase to describe what we want: a nice white country. Terms like the ethnostate are, of course, useful because they are precise: what we want is to create sovereign nations for all distinct white ethnic groups. But it is much easier for people, particularly Americans, to relate to the idea of a nice white country.

After all, Americans are constantly searching for nice white schools, nice white suburbs, nice white churches, nice white restaurants and parks and playgrounds. Many may not be willing to own up to their racial motives. Not yet, anyway. But the desire to feel comfortable among our own kind, particularly when we have children, is what has been driving half a century of suburbanization and exurbanization.

When whites finally wake up to the fact that the system will no longer let us have a separate peace—that we can no longer *run away* to find nice white schools and nice white communities—but that we have to finally stand and fight for a nice white country—then White Nationalism will be a political possibility.

Until then, we need to keep laying the metapolitical groundwork for that moment: we need to spread our ideas and build our community. We need to aim for the day when every American finds the idea of a nice white country at least morally and politically conceivable. We need to aim for the day when every American, if he does not know an actual White Nationalist, at least knows someone who does—preferably someone who does not correspond to negative stereotypes of our kind. Hastening that day is what Counter-Currents and the North American New Right are all about.

❖ ❖ ❖

The present volume collects—by popular demand—some of my best recent essays from the Counter-Currents/*North American New Right* webzine. They primarily offer metapolitical commentary on political issues and events. Thus this collection most resembles my *Confessions of a Reluctant Hater* (San Francisco: Counter-Currents, 2010). For more "foundational" essays, see my *New Right vs. Old Right* (San Francisco: Counter-Currents, 2013).

I wish to thank Colin Liddell for his blurb and advice about the contents and ordering, Matthew Peters for his meticulous proofreading, James J. O'Meara for his thorough index, Kevin Slaughter for his always superlative design work, Michael Polignano for creating the Kindle edition and for technical help throughout the creation of this book, and Kevin MacDonald, Tito Perdue, Charles Krafft, Tom Goodrich, Leo Yankevich, Jez Turner, Margot Metroland, Kerry Bolton, Guillaume Durocher, Lana Lokteff, Buttercup Dew, Irmin Vinson, and Ted Sallis for their blurbs for the jacket, cover, and website. I also want to thank the readers, writers, commenters, and donors who make Counter-Currents Publishing and the North American New Right possible.

This book is dedicated to the memory of my friend Beryl Cheetham, for her personal kindness to me and her selfless dedication to the White Nationalist cause.

New York City
December 1, 2015

White Extinction*

White Nationalists frequently claim that the current social and political system has put our race on the road to biological extinction. If present trends are not reversed, whites will disappear as a distinct race.

To many whites, this sounds like an absurd and alarmist claim, given that there are anywhere from 700 million to one billion of us on the planet today. Part of that skepticism is, I believe, simply psychological denial in the face of an unpleasant prospect. Non-whites seldom show skepticism about white extinction. Indeed, our enemies take our eventual disappearance for granted and openly gloat about our decline.

I wish to argue, however, that white extinction is not an alarmist fantasy, but an alarming fact, the inevitable conclusion of sober, informed analysis. Since my eyes glaze over when anyone resorts to mathematical models, charts, graphs, and technical jargon, I will construct my argument in the simplest possible terms. First, I will merely argue that white extinction is a *plausible* idea, not a far-fetched and fanciful one. Then I will argue that, given present trends, white extinction is not just possible, but *inevitable*.

Biologists claim that up to 99.9% of species that have existed on this planet are now extinct. Furthermore, many extinct species enjoyed dramatic advantages over whites. For instance, most extinct species existed far longer than our race before facing extinction. The average lifespan of a species is 10 million years, whereas whites have been around for only about 40,000 years. Some extinct species also existed in far greater numbers than whites today. For instance, in 1866, a single flock of passenger pigeons was observed in southern Ontario. The flock was

---

* This essay is based on a talk that I gave in Seattle on January 26, 2014 at Charles Krafft's Douglas L. Reed Oyster Feed. I want to thank Charles Krafft and everyone present for their warm welcome and stimulating discussion.

one mile wide, 300 miles long, and took 14 hours to pass. It is estimated to have contained 3.5 billion birds, which is 3-and-a-half to 4 times the entire white population of the world today. Less than 50 years later, however, the entire species was extinct due to hunting and habitat loss. In 1914, Martha, the world's last passenger pigeon, died in the Cincinnati Zoo.

Some living species have existed for a very long time. The horseshoe crab has been around 450 million years. The coelacanth fish has existed for 400 million years. The lamprey has been around for 350 million years. The New Zealand Tuatara lizard has been around for 200 million years. But based on natural history, we can say that *simply by virtue of existing*, there is a 99.9% chance that our race will become extinct. If we want to be among the long-term survivors, we certainly can't just depend upon luck.

Human beings—whites especially—do have an advantage over other species: our intelligence and creativity can allow us to discover and defeat the causes of extinction. Unfortunately, that same intelligence is now being used to create artificial conditions that promote white extinction. Extinctions are divided into natural (like the dinosaurs) and man-made (like the dodo and the passenger pigeon). White extinction is not natural but man-made. Thus, if our race is to survive, the first thing we must do is not defeat nature, but other men.

Extinction is not merely the death of all members of a race. After all, every living thing dies. But if all the members of a race die *without replacing themselves*, then the race becomes extinct. Thus extinction is not merely death—which comes to us all—but *failure to reproduce*. Extinction is inevitable if a race fails to reproduce itself. Extinction *just is* failure to reproduce.

For the existing white population to reproduce itself, each couple must average 2.1 children—2 children to replace themselves, and .1 to replace the race by taking up the slack of those who fail to reproduce at all. The image of a "normal" family—father, mother, and two children—is actually the happy, smiling face of racial annihilation, for if sub-replacement fertility persists long enough—if more people die than are born—our race will eventually cease to exist. If you subtract units from a finite set long enough, you will reach zero. If you take more money out of your account than you put in, you will reach zero. It is simple, mathematical necessity, first-order arithmetic.

Having a third child is the difference between contributing to the death or the growth of our race. Thus White Nationalists need to do everything in our power to create a new "normal" image of the three child white family, as opposed to the one or two child family.

Unfortunately, white birth rates as a whole and in every white country are below replacement. This means that white extinction is inevitable if current trends are not reversed.

What are the causes of reproductive failure, i.e., extinction? Biologists give four basic causes:

1. *Loss of habitat*, meaning the environment necessary for sustaining and reproducing the species. Loss of habitat can take place through sudden or slow geological or climate change, the loss of food sources, etc.
2. *Invasive species*, meaning competition for resources by another species in the same ecological niche.
3. *Hybridization*, meaning reproduction, but not reproduction of one's distinct biological type. Hybridization is only possible if a sufficiently similar species invades one's ecological niche.
4. *Excessive predation*, meaning that a species is killed by predators faster than it can reproduce itself. Predation includes epidemics. Excessive predation is, in effect, genocide: the killing off of an entire group. Genocide can, however, be divided into hot and cold varieties. Hot genocide is the quick and violent extermination of a group. Cold genocide is the slow destruction of a group simply by establishing conditions that make its long-term survival impossible. Cold genocide could, therefore, also include the other causes of extinction: habitat loss, invasive species, and hybridization.

All of these causes of extinction can be natural or man-made. Now let's examine our ongoing extinction in terms of these four biological causes.

Habitat loss: the ongoing conquest of nature through white science and technology would seem to be expanding white habitats. Man can live at the north and south poles, the bottom of the oceans, and even in space. It is conceivable that someday we will be able to transform other planets into human habitats. But there is a sense in which white reproduction is suffering due to habitat loss: whites do not reproduce in unsafe environments, and one of the greatest causes of unsafe breeding environments is the presence of non-whites.

Now, in the past, whites had high birth-rates while surrounded by non-whites. But these non-whites were enslaved or otherwise subordinate and forced to emulate white standards of behavior. So whites specifically feel unsafe around free and feral non-white populations. The search for safe white breeding spaces is one of the driving forces behind suburbanization and exurbanization since the collapse of white supremacy, the emancipation of indigenous non-white populations, and the flooding of white lands by non-white immigrants.

One could argue that the mere *presence* of non-whites in white breeding spaces is not sufficient to suppress white fertility, since non-whites are feared specifically as potential sources of resource competition, hybridization, and predation, which brings us to the other causes of white extinction.

Invasive species: whites in virtually every white nation are now facing demographic competition from non-white immigrants. Even if non-white immigration is cut off, whites will still face demographic competition from existing non-white populations which are usually more fertile than whites.

Hybridization: race-mixing or miscegenation is a form of reproduction, in the sense that both parties pass their genes on to the next generation. But it is simultaneously a cause of racial extinction, since it fails to reproduce the racial type. Miscegenation is inevitable if different human races are allowed to associate freely in the same environment. Thus in the past, when racial integrity was valued, there were social and legal barriers to miscegenation in multiracial societies. Those barriers have been swept away.

But people are not merely "free" to miscegenate. Miscegenation is actively encouraged by the media and educational system.

Miscegenation is also being forced upon whites by inter-racial rape, which is almost always perpetrated by non-white men on white women. This form of rape is also being actively promoted by cultural phenomena such as pornography and non-white resentment mongering, and by social policies that encourage non-white immigration, the integration of white and non-white populations, and failure to adequately police and punish non-white criminals. Fortunately, most white rape victims have access to abortion.

Predation: whites are not currently being subjected to fast, hot, across-the-board genocide, but the presence of large, hostile, violent, unsegregated, and poorly-policed non-white populations contributes to white extinction by causing the murder of white children and fertile adults and causing other whites to restrict their fertility because of unsafe reproductive environments.

In the case of white extinction, all of these causes are man-made. Whites suffer habitat loss, invasion, hybridization, and predation from non-whites because of social policies that have dismantled white supremacy and segregation in multiracial societies, promoted non-white immigration into formerly white societies, dismantled barriers to miscegenation and actively promoted it, and promoted non-white predation by importing and/or emancipating and integrating non-white populations and failing to adequately police and punish them.

In addition to purely *biological* causes of white extinction, we are also facing distinctly *cultural* causes. These fall into two basic categories: *ideological* and *technological*. Ideological causes of white extinction include individualism, celibacy, feminism and other forms of sex-role confusion, misplaced environmentalism, and white demonization and guilt, all of which promote reproductive failure. Such ideologies were, of course, little threat to white survival until the invention of cheap and reliable birth control technologies.

In a way, it is fortunate that the causes of white extinction are man-made, because all of them are within our power to correct.

There are two things that we must do.

In the short run, we need to raise white birthrates. This is not a long-run solution, because the problem is not that there are too few whites but too many non-whites. From an ecological point of view, a stable population of a billion or even half-a-billion whites is not necessarily a good thing. We cannot define victory as a population race with fast-breeding non-whites until the globe is laid waste.

But in the short term, we need to halt the decline of our race until we can put long term solutions into place. When my ancestors first arrived in Virginia in the second decade of the 17th century, we belonged to a tiny minority on this continent. But we conquered it, in part because behind us was the demographic momentum of burgeoning populations in the homeland. It would be an enormous help if whites had that kind of demographic wind in our sails again.

In the long run, however, White Nationalism is the only real solution for the problem of white extinction.

The biological causes of white extinction can be addressed by the creation of homogeneously white homelands, either through racial partition and secession schemes or the removal of non-white populations. Homogeneously white homelands would secure white habitats and simply eliminate competition, hybridization, and predation from other races.

The cultural causes of white extinction can be addressed through education and social incentives: individualism can be replaced with an ethic of racial responsibility; sex-role confusion can be eliminated by the reassertion of traditional and biological sex roles: women as mothers and nurturers, men as protectors and providers; white guilt and self-reproach can be replaced by white pride and self-assertion; affordable family formation can be a cornerstone of social policy, with special incentives for greater reproduction from highly genetically valuable individuals; the option of celibacy, as well as non-reproductive sex, could also be preserved and promoted for some as part of an overall eugenic policy, to discourage breeding by individuals with genetic problems.

Some people regard the creation of homogeneously white

homelands as unnecessary. I will consider four such arguments.

First, some might argue that it is possible for whites to survive without homelands or political power as small relict populations within larger non-white populations. Unfortunately, historical evidence does not support this. Andrew Hamilton's review of Riccardo Orizio's *Lost White Tribes* indicates that such populations are eventually lost to hybridization.[1]

Second, one might argue that white relict populations can resist hybridization by adopting highly ethnocentric attitudes and marrying only among one's group, like Jews and Hindus. The problem with this suggestion is that such policies have not worked for Jews or Hindus. Jews are a highly miscegenated population. But Jewish identity can survive miscegenation, since one is a Jew not through pure Jewish descent but merely through a taint of the blood of Abraham. In the case of the Hindus, the caste system was adopted only after a great deal of mixing had already taken place.

Of course, as a White Nationalist, I think it is a good thing for whites to adopt ethnocentric attitudes and eschew all race-mixing. But those attitudes will not save us if we are reduced to small, politically powerless relict populations in a sea of non-whites. But if we adopted such ideas today, the best way of implementing them would be through the creation of homogeneously white homelands.

Third, one might argue that white extinction will not occur because our very decline might include self-correcting mechanisms which will eventually cause our population to stabilize or rise again. Now that family formation is difficult and unnecessary, divorce is easy, and birth control and abortion are widely available, individuals who are inclined by genes and culture not to reproduce—or not to reproduce with their own kind—simply aren't. That means that the next few generations of whites will be smaller, but they will be increasingly composed of people who are predisposed to reproduce with their own kind. If that is true, then after a while, white birthrates will rise again. Thus

---

[1] http://www.counter-currents.com/2013/08/journeys-among-the-forgotten-riccardo-orizios-lost-white-tribes/

whites are not going extinct. We are merely going through an evolutionary bottleneck that will ultimately render us immune to the forces that are arrayed against us.

I believe that this argument is quite plausible, but it is not a case against pursuing White Nationalist policies. First, it may never happen, thus we would be fools to abandon the struggle to white homelands on the chance that evolution will do our work for us. Second, the selection pressures it posits will not make us immune to outright genocide, so it is not an alternative to creating sovereign, homogeneously white homelands. Finally, if these selection pressures do exist, it means that people will become increasingly receptive to White Nationalist policies, and once implemented, such policies will support such selection pressures. In short, White Nationalism and the population bottleneck theory are complementary and mutually-reinforcing.

Fourth, one might argue that cutting off immigration and returning to white supremacy, segregation, and legal and cultural barriers to miscegenation would be sufficient. I grant that such policies would be improvements, but not long-term solutions. First, if nothing is done to address below replacement white fertility and higher non-white fertility, whites will eventually be reduced to tiny relict populations, as in scenario one. Then we will become extinct. Second, these policies were tried and failed. The conservative fixation on doing the same thing over and over and expecting a different result is a definition of lunacy. If these policies are tried and fail again, our race may never recover.

The hour is too late for such foolishness. When our existence as a people is at stake, we can no longer afford conservative half-measures and wishful thinking. Only White Nationalism can prevent white extinction.

Counter-Currents/*North American New Right*
February 14, 2014

WHITE GENOCIDE

White Nationalists are united in the belief that our race is threatened with simple biological extinction. This is often dismissed as alarmism, but, as I have shown, one can make a very simple and compelling argument that whites will go extinct if present trends continue. The purpose of White Nationalism is to interrupt those trends.

Some White Nationalists go one step further, arguing that our race is being *intentionally* driven to extinction, i.e., that whites are the targets of *genocide*. This claim too is dismissed as not just alarmist but crazy. Nevertheless, I shall argue that white genocide is actually happening. There are people in positions of power who are promoting policies that they know will lead to the extinction of the white race. Unless, of course, we stop them.

To establish the white genocide thesis, we must do three things. First, we need to define genocide in a way that is consistent with a slow process leading ultimately to extinction. Second, we need to show that white extinction is not a mysterious force of nature but the result of human choices and actions. Third, we need to show that white extinction is not just an unforeseen, unintended consequence of these policies, but rather their deliberate, intentional effect.

It seems counter-intuitive to claim that whites are the victims of genocide. Whites are not being slaughtered by the millions, which is the image that most people have of genocide. To all appearances, our race is powerful, prosperous, and populous. But defenders of the White Genocide thesis point to the 1948 United Nations Convention on Prevention and Punishment of the Crime of Genocide, which in Article II defines genocide as

> . . . any of the following acts committed with intent to destroy, in whole or in part, a national, ethnical, racial or religious group, as such:

(a) Killing members of the group;
(b) Causing serious bodily or mental harm to members of the group;
(c) Deliberately inflicting on the group conditions of life calculated to bring about its physical destruction in whole or in part;
(d) Imposing measures intended to prevent births within the group; . . .[1]

This definition of genocide is much broader than outright mass murder. In particular, points (c) and (d) are consistent with characterizing policies that destroy a group slowly, over long periods of time, as genocidal as well. So genocide comes in two forms, which we can call fast, hot genocide and slow, cold genocide. White extinction falls into the latter category.

White extinction means that in every white nation, reproduction rates have fallen below replacement, which means that more whites will die than are being born, until whites cease to exist as a distinct race.

There are five principal causes of white extinction. I am sure that other factors could be added to this list, but if just these five problems were addressed, I would no longer fear for the future of our race.

- ❖ An ethic of hedonism, individualism, and selfishness that denigrates reproduction and family life;
- ❖ Feminism, which encourages women to pursue careers instead of making family life their primary occupation;
- ❖ The widespread use of birth control and abortion to decouple sex from pregnancy and pregnancy from child-rearing;
- ❖ The rising costs of family formation, chiefly caused by racial integration—which is the driving force behind suburbanization and ex-urbanization in order to find safe spaces for whites to raise families—and by non-

---

[1] https://treaties.un.org/doc/Publication/UNTS/Volume%2078/volume-78-I-1021-English.pdf

white immigration and offshoring industry, which lower wages for whites;
❖ Miscegenation, in which individuals reproduce their own genes but not their race by mixing with another race.

These factors are not blind forces of nature, like an asteroid colliding with earth. They were all created by human beings. Some of them, like feminism, birth control pills, legalized abortion, and overturning racial segregation, immigration restrictions, and bans on miscegenation are quite recent. They were hatched in the minds of intellectuals, artists, scientists, politicians, educators, and advertisers. They were made real by changing people's beliefs and values, and by altering the laws and institutions that govern us.

But all of these things could be changed. People could be taught to value family life over selfishness, hedonism, and careerism; feminism could be discouraged; access to birth control and abortion could be restricted; laws could be changed to make family formation affordable; racial separation, immigration restriction, and economic nationalism could become policy again; miscegenation could be outlawed. Indeed, White Nationalists support just such policies to halt white extinction.

But to establish the white genocide thesis, we must show that white extinction is the *intended* result of the policies we oppose. The first three causes of white extinction are simply products of the pursuit of individual freedom. The last two are products of individual freedom and racial egalitarianism. So isn't it possible that white extinction is just the *unintended* consequence of individualism and racial egalitarianism?

Of course it is possible, and in many cases, it is true. The majority of people who advocate individualism and racial egalitarianism are simply unaware that these values are promoting the ongoing extinction of the white race. Our job is to inform them.

But when such people are informed, their reactions fall into several categories. Some will simply refuse to accept that white extinction is taking place. Of those who accept that white extinction is actually happening, some will wish to stop it, and others will not. Of the latter, some will simply not care, and others will actually cheer the process on.

There is, however, a difference between people who might sign on to policies promoting white genocide *after the fact* and those who might conceive and execute such policies before the fact and with full awareness of their consequences. What evidence is there that such people exist?

First, the burden of proof needs to be shifted. For is it really plausible that the leaders of dozens of white nations have adopted similar policies antithetical to the long-term survival of their own peoples, yet *none of them knew what they are doing*?

Yes, it is fashionable to deride politicians for thinking only in terms of the next election. But that is not really true. Politicians are, for instance, rather far-sighted when it comes to their personal career ambitions and plans. Beyond that, our ruling elites do not consist simply of democratic politicians. Moreover, the ruling elites in every form of society are noted for thinking and planning ahead. Both government intelligence agencies and private think tanks are in the business of generating long-term predictions based on current trends, and planning accordingly. Thus it is just not plausible that our leaders are unaware of white extinction. They either don't care about it, or they want it to happen.

Second, it is no longer controversial that Jews are massively overrepresented among Western elites in politics,[2] the media,[3] business,[4] academia,[5] and the professions.[6] Jews are, moreover, among the principal promoters of trends conducive to white genocide, for example: non-white immigration, racial integra-

---

[2] https://en.wikipedia.org/wiki/List_of_Jewish_American_politicians

[3] http://www.kevinmacdonald.net/PrefacePPB.pdf

[4] http://www.theoccidentalobserver.net/category/jews-and-the-financial-collapse/

[5] http://www.kevinmacdonald.net/Professors.pdf

[6] Carmel U. Chiswick, "Occupation and Gender: American Jews at the Millennium," Department of Economics, University of Illinois at Chicago, April 2009.

tion, miscegenation, feminism, and sexual liberation.

Of course any attempt to blame Jews for white genocide can be hijacked into hairsplitting about historical causation. From a practical point of view, however, it is more important—and less controversial—to note that the organized Jewish community is the linchpin of opposition to nationalist, especially racial nationalist, attempts to rectify these problems going forward. How we got here is ultimately less important than how we can save ourselves. And Jews are blocking the exit.

Now, is it really plausible that the leaders of the Jewish community "know not what they do"? *Jews, after all, are the people most aware of the conditions that promote or prevent genocide.* Thus Jews support the existence of a Jewish state, Israel, as a refuge from genocide. Yet they oppose any attempt to preserve white homelands for white peoples. Israel is for Jews, but Poland, Sweden, Germany, France, and so forth are for everyone. Jews see intermarriage as a threat to Jewish survival, but they promote miscegenation for other groups and oppose anyone who would ban it. Jews recognize that a strong sense of Jewish identity, including pride in their history and achievements, is necessary for Jewish survival, but they promote multiculturalism and white guilt for the rest of us.

Now, not all Jews promote destructive ideas merely for the *goyim* while exempting themselves. Jews may promote intermarriage for others, but they practice it as well and at higher rates than other groups.[7] Jews promote feminism to others, but the primary victims of Jewish feminism are the Jewish men who marry these harridans, while other Jewish men opt to marry out to avoid them. Jews promote an ethos of selfishness, individualism, and materialism to others. But they practice it as well, which is one reason why secular Jews have very low reproduction rates.[8]

In short, many Jews don't just preach nihilism, they practice

[7] http://www.jta.org/2013/10/01/news-opinion/united-states/pew-survey-u-s-jewish-intermarriage-rate-rises-to-58-percent

[8] http://www.jewishpolicycenter.org/4058/israel-demographic-miracle

it as well. Unfortunately, because Jews are so influential, they have the power to drag us along in their wake. They are the vanguard of nihilism. They are not hypocrites, preaching nihilism for thee but not for me. But that makes them even more evil, because hypocrisy is the tribute that vice pays to virtue, and they don't care enough to even offer lip service.

But while some Jews are leading us into extinction, others are goading us from behind but have no intention of sharing in our fate. These are the Jews who praise multiculturalism, open borders, and miscegenation for us, but prefer to opt out because they know that such policies would lead to their extinction.

They aren't just being "inconsistent" about principles. They are being perfectly consistent with their real principle of collective self-interest. They are not upholding "double standards," because their single standard is collective self-interest. These Jews have a live and let die philosophy. They seek to profit from our destruction as a people, and they not only promote our decline but actively suppress our resistance to it.

Aside from Jews that are actively pushing and pulling us toward our destruction, there are surely some who are doing neither. Some simply lack the power to do us harm, even if they might want to. Others are entirely ignorant of what their leaders are doing. But one category is conspicuous by its near absence: righteous Jews, i.e., Jews who know white genocide is taking place, who understand their people's role in it, and who have warned whites and worked to stop it. That relative silence is actually more damning than the never-ending din of anti-white hatred emanating from the Jewish community.

In short, we know that white genocide is happening, because Jews in high places, with the power to promote or prevent white genocide, cannot be unaware of what is happening, yet they do nothing to stop it and everything to stop us from stopping it.

The third and most compelling piece of evidence for white genocide is that people actually *say* that they support it. The only people who say outright that whites should be exterminated are marginal cranks, like Dr. Kamau Kambon, a sometime Black Studies professor and the owner of Blacknificent Books, who declared, "We have to exterminate white people off the face of the planet."[9]

The subtler advocates of white genocide, like Noel Ignatiev, a Jewish Harvard Ph.D. and the editor of the journal *Race Traitor* (subtitled *Treason to Whiteness is Loyalty to Humanity*), speak of "deconstructing" the "concept" of whiteness,[10] which sounds like a harmless language game until you grasp that they think that race *just is* a social construct.[11]

But the most common advocates of white genocide simply promote race-mixing as a solution to racism. They tacitly agree with White Nationalists that racial diversity within the same system leads to strife, so to eliminate strife, they promote miscegenation to create a homogeneous mongrel race. The most influential advocate of what I call "miscegenationalism" was European unity pioneer Count Richard Coudenhove-Kalergi, who was himself of mixed race (his father was white, his mother Japanese). In his book *Practical Idealism*, he declared:

> The man of the future will be of mixed race. Today's races and classes will gradually disappear owing to the vanishing of space, time, and prejudice. The Eurasian-Negroid race of the future, similar in its appearance to the Ancient Egyptians, will replace the diversity of peoples with a diversity of individuals.[12]

Interestingly enough, Coudenhove-Kalergi did not envision the disappearance of the Jewish people but instead expected them to be the ruling elite of a miscegenated world. (He himself was not Jewish.)

---

[9] http://www.carolinajournal.com/exclusives/display_exclusive.html?id=2869

[10] http://harvardmagazine.com/2002/09/abolish-the-white-race.html

[11] http://www.counter-currents.com/2015/07/why-race-is-not-a-social-construct/

[12] https://en.wikipedia.org/wiki/Richard_Nikolaus_von_Coudenhove-Kalergi

Why is it important to establish that white extinction is actually white genocide? It is easy to understand why people might shy away from such a truth, for it implies that whites are not just the victims of a ghastly mistake, or an impersonal system, or an inhuman cosmic or historical destiny, but of knowing malice — of principled enmity — of diabolical evil. It is hard to accept that such evil exists, much less that it wills our annihilation. But if we are to save ourselves, we have to understand the forces that are arrayed against us. We need to know that our attempts to raise people's consciousness and win their allegiances will eventually come up against not just ignorance and indifference but diamond hard malice. Eventually we will make all the friends that we can make, persuade all the people we can persuade, and only enemies will remain — enemies that cannot be converted but must simply be defeated.

Counter-Currents/ *North American New Right*
September 15, 2015

HE TOLD US SO:
PATRICK BUCHANAN'S *SUICIDE*
OF A SUPERPOWER

Patrick J. Buchanan
Suicide of a Superpower: Will America Survive to 2025?
New York: Thomas Dunne Books, 2011

As a White Nationalist, my darkest political fear (for the short run, anyway) is that the United States might retain sufficient vestiges of political realism to pull itself together for an Indian Summer of Caesarism before the big cold sets in. Specifically, I fear that someone could put our present Jewish-dominated, multiracial system on firmer economic and political footing. All the instincts of our best conservative thinkers and politicians, like Patrick Buchanan, strain in this direction.

I speak of "Caesarism" because the existing democratic system produces politicians too beholden to special interest groups to serve the common good, thus it has become increasingly necessary to repose important political decisions in the hands of non-elected bodies, such as the commission that oversaw the closing of military bases. The logical extension of this trend is the emergence of a dictatorship, which at least would have a *chance* of saving America.

But a period of conservative Caesarism would be the worst possible outcome for our race, for no conservative would address Jewish power or the danger of whites being demographically swamped by non-whites who are *already here legally*. Thus a benevolent conservative dictator just might prolong the system's life long enough for the forces of anti-white racial degradation and replacement to drive our people past the point of no return.

I agree that we need a time-out from immigration to give White Nationalists some extra time to get our act together. I wish all immigration restrictionists well. But the last thing I want is the present system to stabilize itself, for realistically the system's collapse is our only hope for the creation of a White Republic — provided, of course, that White Nationalists develop into a viable political movement that can offer a credible alternative once the present system collapses.

Patrick Buchanan's *Suicide of a Superpower* argues, with crushing persuasiveness, that the United States is headed toward a collapse. He is so convinced of this that he is even willing to venture an end date in his subtitle, albeit in the form of a question: Will America Survive to 2025? I found this striking, because when I first conceived of Counter-Currents in the Spring of 2010, I found myself thinking in terms of a 15 year make-or-break period for a North American New Right. At the very least, such a date focuses the mind wonderfully.

In Chapter 11, "The Last Chance," Buchanan offers a slate of reforms that might actually prolong the life of the republic (if implemented by a dictator). But I see no reason to think that any of his proposals will be implemented given the generally low levels of intellect and courage among American conservatives. But ultimately, that is a good thing for whites.

Chapter 1, "The Passing of a Superpower," summarizes America's economic decline particularly *vis-à-vis* China. This chapter, like the rest of the book, is extremely well-documented. I will be returning to this book again and again for data, and for that reason alone, I recommend it to all white advocates.

Chapter 4, "The End of White America," chronicles our race's demographic and cultural decline in America because of low white fertility, high non-white fertility, and torrents of non-white immigration.

Chapter 5, "Demographic Winter," puts the American experience in global perspective. It seems that below replacement fertility is a characteristic of every First World society, including practically every white nation plus Japan, China, Singapore, Korea, and Jews in Israel.

The common denominator is not modernity, or mere secularism, as Buchanan argues, because the Soviet bloc countries were modernist, materialist, and secularist yet had growing populations. Nor is it a Jewish conspiracy to suppress fertility, which could not explain the trends in Israel and the Far East.

Rather, the problem seems to be a form of modernity that stresses individualism and consumerism. We have created societies in which the people who should be having families instead restrict their fertility to pursue higher education, careers, hobbies, or ecological responsibility, allowing the stupid and ugly people to inherit the earth.

In the white nations, this problem is compounded with Jewish-engineered race replacement policies, primarily non-white immigration. Jews do not have the power to impose these handicaps on Asian nations, and they have no interest in imposing them on themselves.

Chapter 6, "Equality or Freedom?," is a surprisingly frank and utterly devastating critique of egalitarianism. Chapter 7, "The Diversity Cult" and Chapter 8, "The Triumph of Tribalism" are similarly frank and crushing critiques of the idea that diversity is a strength. Tribalism, not globalism and universalism, are deeply rooted in human nature. Buchanan shows that despite economic globalization, political nationalism has been the dominant trend in the 20th and 21st centuries. Thus, by pursuing diversity, America and other white nations are betting against history and human nature.

Chapter 9, "'The White Party,'" explains why the Republicans are the *de facto* party of white America, arguing that the party has no future if it refuses to represent the interests of the white majority. Beyond that, the party must work to preserve the white majority. Again, Buchanan presents a devastating case. But is there one Republican in a thousand with the moral courage necessary to explicitly represent white interests, much less act to preserve a white majority?

Chapter 10, "The Long Retreat," is a critique of US foreign policy, arguing that the United States needs to downsize its international commitments and expenditures. Currently we maintain more than 1,000 military installations around the world. US troops are present in 148 countries and 11 territories. The United States is committed to intervene on behalf countries around the world, and to maintain our massive budget deficits, we are borrowing from our allies and their enemies alike.

Again, Buchanan's argument is carefully documented and quite compelling.

I saved the bad chapters for last. In Chapter 2, "The Death of Christian America," Buchanan has the brazen effrontery to assert that Europe civilization is identical to Christianity, such that the decline of Christianity entails the decline of European civilization. Historically, this is of course false. European man existed before Christianity and will persist after Christianity disappears. Christianity, like Marxism, may be just a phase our people are going through, one of many in our long history since the Ice Ages.

Yes, religious people are currently more fertile than non-religious people, but religion is not the only factor that encourages fertility. During the baby boom of the Third Reich, Germans did not suddenly become more religious. Nor did Americans during the post-WW II baby boom. The common denominator was high national optimism. And even if people need an Imaginary Friend to tell them to have babies, Christianity is not the only pro-natal religion.

A White Republic should at least *try* to preserve freedom of religion (or irreligion) and work to create secular incentives for the best people to reproduce early and often. For example, why not encourage bright young women to have families *before* going to college by offering a free college undergraduate degree to every mother of three children who stays home with them to the age of six?

Buchanan also asserts that America is a Christian nation. This is false on the face of it, as the United States has never had an established church, and the inhabitants of America have never been entirely Christian. That did not, of course, prevent Christians from thrusting their religion into the public square anyway. Over the last hundred years, there has been an attempt to push Christianity back out of the public square by atheists, agnostics, liberals, and members of other religious groups, including Jews. Buchanan sees this as a terrible decline. I am not entirely comfortable with the process, but overall, I consider it progress toward religious tolerance, which is a worthy ideal.

In Chapter 3, "The Crisis of Catholicism," Buchanan discusses his own church's decline from its post-WW II heyday due to Vatican II. He says nothing about how the Catholic Church became so large and influential in America before it committed suicide. He does, however, mention that there were only a few thousand Catholics in America at the time of the Founding. Given the strength of anti-Catholic sentiment in America, the rise of Catholicism was made possible only by the so-called separation of church and state, i.e., the refusal to allow an established church and the embrace of religious toleration, which is a product of the Enlightenment liberals, Freemasons, and deists whom Buchanan despises. It is a heritage worth defending from Muslims—and Christians—who would turn back the clock.

Now, some might be tempted to think that Buchanan is engaged in a cynical bait and switch routine: "Now that I have gotten your attention with the impending doom of the white race, can I interest you in a time-share . . . ?" But Buchanan sincerely believes the package deal of Christianity, the white race, and European civilization. (Let's hope they hurry up and elect a black pope.) He puts his chapters on Christianity right near the beginning, where the foundations of an argument go. But Buchanan's in-your-face Christian apologetics are quite unfortunate, for if our race is going to have a future on this continent, it is by uniting on the basis of deep roots of common identity, not by emphasizing highly divisive religious differences.

There are many ways in which it is true that America is committing suicide. But there is also a sense in which America is being murdered. Kevin MacDonald, among others, has chronicled how America is ruled by a hostile Jewish elite that has instituted many of the ideologies and trends decried by Buchanan as suicidal, including multiculturalism and massive non-white immigration. Jews, of course, more than any other people, are aware of the necessary conditions of collective survival. They are concerned to secure these conditions for their own people even as they deny them to us. The obvious conclusion is that they mean for us not to survive as a people. America is being corrupted, exploited, degraded, and murdered by the organized Jewish community.

Buchanan, of course, knows all this. But he has avoided saying so because it is not politic. He wishes to maintain his access to television and publishers. He wishes to maintain his credibility and connections. His friend Sam Francis felt the same way. He wanted to bide his time, preserve and augment his capital, keep his powder dry. But he fantasized about the day when he would finally whip it out, when he would drop the J-bomb. Unfortunately, Sam died with his credibility intact. And you can't take it with you. You can only spend it while you are here. Patrick Buchanan is now 73 years old, 16 years older than Sam was when he died. What is he saving himself for? There is so much more he could do for our people.

Suicide of a Superpower is a useful and important book. I recommend it to all White Nationalists. It is not a White Nationalist book, but it gets the reader almost all the way there. If we can't close the deal with this kind of set-up, we aren't worth our salt.

Suicide of a Superpower could save America, although it will not be heeded. And when America goes down, people will say that Patrick Buchanan told us so. That will be a nice epitaph for America — and for Buchanan.

But saving America is not the same thing as saving the white race. If our people have a future on this continent, it will only be by freeing ourselves of the wreckage of America and American conservatism. Conservatism is all well and good if one has something worth conserving. Once we have the White Republic, then we can dust off Buchanan's proposals and put them to work conserving our system, not the enemy's.

Counter-Currents/*North American New Right*
November 28, 2011

JARED TAYLOR'S *WHITE IDENTITY*

Reading through Jared Taylor's splendid new book *White Identity*, I found myself thinking again and again of Allan Bloom's 1987 book *The Closing of the American Mind: How Higher Education has Failed Democracy and Impoverished the Souls of Today's Students*. In content, the books could hardly be more different, even though both take aim at reigning liberal illusions. But *The Closing of the American Mind* surprised everyone by becoming a best-seller, in spite of its intellectually challenging style and serious, politically incorrect message. *White Identity* is a similarly weighty and sobering book, and if America has any hope of survival, it should enjoy a similar popularity.

The aim of *White Identity* is to convince intelligent whites that racial "integration" and "diversity" are not sources of strength and enrichment but of inevitable conflict and suffering, because racial consciousness and preferring one's own race over others are rooted in human nature. Thus they cannot be eradicated, and they can be ignored only at one's own risk. Whites, however, have made a cult of ignoring and suppressing their racial consciousness, based on the belief that white "racism" (and only white racism) is the source of racial conflict and the suffering and backwardness of other races. Thus the eradication of white racism (and only white racism) will be sufficient to create a society in which all the different races and cultures can mingle in an atmosphere of tolerance and harmony.

Taylor's audience and source materials are primarily American, but his lessons apply to all white nations where such notions have become prevalent since the Second World War.

The first three chapters of *White Identity*, "The Failure of Integration," "The Myth of Diversity — Institutions," and "The Myth of Diversity — Daily Life" offer an overwhelming factual and logical refutation of the ideas that racial integration, diversity, and multiculturalism are possible to achieve, or good for society even if they could be achieved.

The fourth chapter, "The Science of Human Nature," offers

a masterfully clear and concise summary of the scientific explanation for why racial integration and diversity will inevitably fail. I think that Taylor is wise to focus here entirely on "Genetic Similarity Theory," which explains the universality of consciousness of genetic similarity and difference (race being one such difference) and preference for those who are genetically similar over those who are genetically different.

In short, Taylor deals with the science of racial *difference*, not the science of racial *inequality*. Even if the races were all equal in their genetic capacities, they would still be different, aware of those differences, and inclined to prefer their own over strangers. Taylor thereby sidesteps making invidious comparisons among the races, as well as the dead end of cognitive elitism, which is different from and incompatible with racial nationalism. (Cognitive elitists love intelligence, not their race, which contains dumb as well as smart people.)

Chapters five, six, and seven—"Black Racial Consciousness," "Hispanic Consciousness," and "Asian Consciousness"—deal with the robust racial consciousness of America's three principal non-white groups. Reading these chapters will be a very depressing experience for white liberals, because the inevitable conclusion is that no matter how hard they strive to see the world from a race-blind, universal perspective, *non-whites will simply not reciprocate*. Thus the white liberal dream of a post-racial world will founder on the rock of non-white racial consciousness, which if anything is only growing stronger as American society becomes more diverse (something that would be predicted by Genetic Similarity Theory). It is another masterstroke to construct an argument for the suicidal futility of multiculturalism on the foundation of reciprocity, a value that deeply resonates with all whites.

Chapter eight, "White Racial Consciousness," deals with the downfall of white racial consciousness in America. Throughout most of American history, up until the 1950s and 1960s, white racial consciousness was perfectly healthy, meaning that it was in keeping with human nature and the requirements for long-term racial and cultural survival and flourishing. Taylor sums up this consciousness as follows:

White Americans believed race was a fundamental aspect of individual and group identity. They believed people of different races differed in temperament, ability, and the kind of societies they built. They wanted America to be peopled by Europeans, and thought only people of European stock could maintain the civilization they valued. They therefore considered immigration of non-whites a threat to whites and to their civilization. It was common to regard the presence of non-whites as a burden, and to argue that if they could not be removed from the country they should be separated from whites socially and politically. Whites were strongly opposed to miscegenation, which they called "amalgamation."

Taylor summarizes the post-World War II consensus about race as follows:

Race is an insignificant matter and not a valid criterion for any purpose—except perhaps for redressing wrongs done to non-whites. The races are equal in every respect and are therefore interchangeable. It thus makes no difference if a neighborhood or nation becomes non-white or if white children marry outside their race. Whites have no valid group interests, so it is illegitimate for them to attempt to organize as whites. Given the past crimes of whites, any expression of racial pride is wrong. The displacement of whites by non-whites through immigration will strengthen the United States. These are matters on which there is little ground for disagreement; anyone who holds differing views is not merely mistaken but morally suspect.

The fatal flaw of the present consensus is that only white people have become so deracinated, and if abandoning racial consciousness is not reciprocated by other races, then it is akin to unilateral disarmament in the face of hostile, armed enemies. That will not lead to a tolerant, multicultural utopia, but to civil war—hot or cold—in which selfish, race-wise groups out to serve their own interests at the expense of one another and America as a whole will strip whites to the bone. If whites refuse to take our own side in this struggle, we will lose our wealth, our power, our culture, our country, and ultimately our future as we deliver our destiny into the hands of people who hate us for our strengths and despise us for our weakness. It is a path to white dispossession and, ultimately, to white extinction. It is a process that is already well underway, as Taylor demonstrates in his long and depressing final chapter, "The Crisis We Face."

I have two main criticisms of *White Identity*.

First and foremost, although *White Identity* is beautifully written and constructs a crushing case for its theses through ingenious arguments and a vast array of carefully chosen facts, its conclusions are ultimately rather unambitious. In Taylor's words:

> This book will have been a success if at least a few readers have become open to the possibility that the following statements are true: People of all races generally prefer the company of people like themselves. Racial diversity is a source of conflict, not strength. Non-whites, especially blacks and Hispanics, nurture a strong sense of racial pride and solidarity. Whites have little sense of racial solidarity, and most whites strongly condemn any signs of it. Immigration from non-European countries is changing the United States in profound ways, many of which whites find disagreeable. To the extent that these statements are true, they have serious implications both for the country as a whole and for whites as a group.

Taylor succeeds in these aims, but I suspect that for most readers, the overall effect of this book will be despair and inaction. For Taylor offers only the most tepid of practical recommendations: "Clearly our immigration policies should be reexamined." Or the book's final words: "Only whites have no racial identity, are constantly on the defensive, and constantly in retreat. They have a choice: regain a sense of identity and the resolve to maintain their numbers, their traditions, and their way of life—or face oblivion."

The trouble is that Taylor gives no indication of what, precisely, whites need to do to save ourselves, or any indication that it is even possible at this stage. And without a specific and appealing vision of an alternative and some indication of how we might get from here to there, most readers will sensibly conclude that the white race is doomed.

Of course, Taylor may be betting that leaving these matters open will be less discouraging than leveling with people about the harsh and terrible measures necessary to save us. For instance, halting all non-white immigration will slow but not halt our demographic eclipse, since the non-whites who are already here are outbreeding us handily. And do we really want to live in a constant breeding race until the natural world is completely despoiled? The white race has a future in North America only if we can separate ourselves from more than 100 million non-whites, for example through expulsion or territorial partition.

Yes, the book is long enough already, but even a few historical examples of conquered and colonized white peoples who have regained control of their destinies—the Irish, the Spanish, the Russians—would be enough to convince people that all is not lost.

Second, Taylor's chapter on "White Racial Consciousness" offers nary a clue as to how in the last 50 years or so, healthy white racial consciousness around the globe has become almost completely perverted, setting our race on the path to extinction. But if racial consciousness is so soundly rooted in nature, how can something so contrary to nature even take place? The explanation is to be found in the work of Kevin MacDonald, particularly *The Culture of Critique* and *Cultural Insurrections*: white ethnocentrism, and only white ethnocentrism, has been pathologized by the organized Jewish community as a tool of ethnic warfare against whites. Without the perspective afforded by MacDonald's work, the shift Taylor chronicles is ultimately mysterious and may give rise to the mistaken view that the white race has essentially been seized by a suicidal impulse.

Still, even with these caveats, *White Identity* is an important contribution to white survival. It will be particularly effective as a tool for opening the eyes of white liberals and skittish conservatives who can't yet handle too much truth in one book. But ultimately *White Identity* is a propaedeutic or introductory book to White Nationalism, which avoids the most uncomfortable yet necessary topics.

Now that *White Identity* has been launched, I hope Jared Taylor will consider turning his attention to the harder questions, discomfiting though they may be. We certainly need his talents. Jared Taylor turns 60 this year, so surely he has the time. But consider this: Sam Francis was only 57 when he died in 2005. We are in a race against time, all of us.

Sam Francis' untimely death contains a lesson for us all. Sam knew far more than would say, because he wished to conserve his credibility and audience in anticipation of the day when he would write his *magnum opus*. But he died before he could spend any of that credibility he saved so carefully.

At a certain point, one has to ask: What are we saving ourselves for? Our race is dying, and those few of us who know this need to stop saving ourselves and start spending ourselves, secure in the knowledge that anything we save will be taken from us by death in the end.

Counter-Currents/ *North American New Right*
May 13, 2011

KONY 2012 & JASON RUSSELL

Kony 2012 director Jason Russell's 15 minutes are almost up, so I thought I would get my thoughts on record before he is hopelessly *passé*.

Most commentary has focused on Joseph Kony and Jason Russell themselves. This is understandable, since Kony is a vibrant cannibal statesman and Russell is an obvious magnet for bullying. But I want to begin with some comments on the movie. *Kony 2012*, which was uploaded to YouTube on March 5th,[1] is excellent propaganda—albeit in service of a stupid aim—and Jason Russell, aged 33, is a highly talented filmmaker. (*Kony 2012* is the tenth video he has made about Kony.)

Now before you object, we have to remember that this documentary is directed at Americans—at American 'tards to be precise. Thus everything smarmy, annoying, and pretentious in the video is not just Jason Russell being Jason Russell. It is there because it is carefully calculated to appeal to 'tards. And it does. Over 84 million of them, and counting—nipping at the heels of that talking dog video.[2]

On Russell's posters, Kony's face appears alongside the faces of Osama Bin Laden and Hitler. Why not Stalin and Mao? Because the average American would not recognize either of them. Beyond that, the purpose of the video is, in effect, to start a war with Kony and his Lord's Resistance Army, and the United States has fought wars against Bin Laden and Hitler. So it makes perfect sense.

Everything about this video is calculated to appeal to the idealism of whites. Undergirding white idealism is an element of grandiosity. The old version of white idealism—the imperialistic, crusading "white man's burden" version—was based on frank expressions of white pride and supremacism. Whites felt entitled to improve non-whites because we looked down on them and wanted to raise them up to our level, and if that meant

---

[1] http://www.youtube.com/watch?v=Y4MnpzG5Sqc
[2] http://youtu.be/nGeKSiCQkPw

invading and colonizing their lands and supplanting their religions and cultures, then so be it.

The modern version of white idealism on display in *Kony 2012* is premised on white guilt and self-hatred, but it is equally supremacist and grandiose, for if one is *guilty* of everything, then one is *responsible* for everything, i.e., one can *do* anything. Every time one pities another, one secretly congratulates oneself for being superior. Every time one blames one's race for the world's woes, one slyly congratulates oneself as being part of the only people who really matter, the only real agents of history. Everybody else is just along for the ride.

If whites are responsible for black crime, wars, cannibalism, corruption, and chaos, that means that blacks are *not* responsible. They are not agents. The all-powerful white man has somehow turned them into zombies hell-bent on self-destruction. Proclaiming oneself a Christ figure and offering to suffer for the sins of others is obviously pretentious. But declaring oneself a race of devils and doing penance for the sins one has caused others to commit is equally pretentious. And the whole game is given away when the white devils' penance consists of invading Africa all over again.

Kony 2012 appeals to white grandiosity on all sorts of levels, not just the explicit message. Three of the more subtle ways of inflating the ego of the viewer are the ideas of exceptionalism, of being on the "cutting edge" of progress, and of "thinking globally."

The exceptionalism of this video is ludicrous, but nothing flatters the American 'tard more deeply than the idea that he is engaged in something utterly unique and unprecedented. We are told, for instance, that today, unlike every previous generation, our actions will shape the course of history for subsequent generations. (That's the difference between us and them.) We are told that if Americans commit troops to finding Joseph Kony, this will be the first time in American history that we have sent troops abroad on a moral crusade unrelated to calculations of national and economic interests. I kid you not.

The idea of progress is enormously flattering to the ego, for it basically offers us the opportunity to look down upon Plato and

Aristotle, Dante and Goethe, Kepler and Newton, Bach and Wagner simply because we were born after them and have been raised to a higher level of civilization by the work of all our forebears. And of course, we can always raise ourselves to an even higher level than "those people" (our knuckle-dragging peers) by integrating our lives with the "cutting edge" of technology, like Facebook and Twitter. Early on in the film, Russell informs us portentously that there are more people on Facebook than there were alive on the planet 200 years ago. Later, we are also informed that Facebook and Twitter have "changed everything" by allowing "the people" to shape policy directly, bypassing the moneyed interests and establishment media. Moral superiority is only a free Facebook and Twitter account away.

The idea of "thinking globally" is underscored from the very beginning. This movie does not begin with the Big Bang, but it does start out in the solar system. Then we see our planet, a blue oasis of life in the black desert of space. We see a baby being born. All of us begin this way, Russell informs us. And all of us *matter*. Throughout the movie, Russell moves masterfully from the global to the particular. One graphic shows the faces, in color, of two people who know about Kony's crimes against the backdrop of thousands of black and white images of the ignorant. As the images recede, they form a globe. Later, we see a vast sea of faces in color. That's progress! Another graphic illustrates the thousands of victims of Joseph Kony. Then it zooms in on the face of one child, whom we have already met. It is seductive. We *see* the big picture. We see ourselves as *the kind of people* who see the big picture. Yet we never lose sight of each precious individual. That's just the kind of people we are. We see the universe in every grain of sand.

And now that we have achieved enlightenment, we are told what to do. We need to "Tweet" Oprah, Ryan Seacrest, and other members of the Hollywood Brain Trust to support sending US troops to Uganda. We need to donate a few dollars to Invisible Children ($10 million were donated last year), for which we will receive an Action Kit: a box including two Kony 2012 bracelets, as well as posters, stickers, yard signs, and flyers designed to raise awareness of Kony.

The bracelets have serial numbers. Enter your number into a website, and one has an account. One can geo-tag one's posters and flyers with one's phone and track one's impact in real time. The goal of the campaign is to change the conversation of the culture by making Jospeh Kony famous. This campaign will culminate on April 20th, with the Cover the Night initiative, in which Russell's followers will blanket the world with Kony propaganda. (I hope the kit contains information on how the get bailed out of jail on the morning of April 21st.) The video ends with three things the viewer can do right away, from the comfort of his own keyboard.

The reactionary in me wants to sneer and poke fun at all this, but the revolutionary in me is taking notes. Because this is the kind of work that White Nationalists should be doing. Imagine if the South Africa Project,[3] which has done excellent work raising awareness of anti-white genocide in South Africa, were to grow into something like Russell's Invisible Children charity, which spent nearly $9 million last year on its projects, including the *Kony 2012* video. And Invisible Children is just one of many charities funneling aid into the black hole of Africa.

Now, there's nothing wrong with thinking globally, if one really is thinking. And there's nothing wrong with idealism, provided one has the right ideas. The problem with Invisible Children and every other pro-black charity is that they are premised on massive moral, political, and demographic delusions. Listening to Jason Russell, you would think that whites run the world and are essentially invulnerable, while Africans are an endangered species.

But the truth is that whites do not run the world. We do not even run our own countries. We are ruled by Jews who are promoting low white fertility, racial miscegenation, and race-replacement immigration by fast-breeding non-whites as a deliberate policy of anti-white genocide. As the global white population is in demographic decline, Africans cannot slaughter and eat one another fast enough to prevent their populations from doubling every few decades.

---

[3] http://www.southafricaproject.info/wordpress1/

Jews, moreover, are masters at manipulating the altruism and idealism of people like Jason Russell into sacrificing white genetic interests to non-whites, although such behavior also has rather deep roots in white history and psychology. In the United States, for instance, Jews had little or no role in the abolition of slavery, but they played a large role in the Civil Rights movement, which was grafted onto the indigenous stock of abolitionism even as it was used to further Jewish ethnic interests.

As for taking sides in African civil wars: Africa is filled with savage warlords who commit horrifying atrocities. It is only natural to feel sympathy for the victims of such atrocities. But is it really logical to conclude that the victims are fundamentally morally different from their persecutors? If they were stronger, would the victims treat their persecutors with any more humanity? Would they not also rape, torture, mutilate, slaughter, and cannibalize their enemies in the grand African fashion? If this is the case, then why take sides in their conflicts? And why, of all things, bring them here and resettle them as refugees? That's just asking for trouble.

In the specific case of Joseph Kony, sending US military advisers to Uganda *de facto* strengthens the existing Ugandan government of Yoweri Museveni, who also uses child soldiers and has been guilty of torture and repression since assuming office in 1986. Joseph Kony, moreover, has not been seen in Uganda since 2006, which raises the question of whether Invisible Children, like so many other charities, has long outlived its usefulness.

On March 15th, Jason Russell was picked up by police in Southern California and taken to a psychiatric ward for observation. As Jim Goad put it so cattily:

> several witnesses reported seeing a naked man mincing and flitting around the street while waggling his finger like a disapproving Mick Jagger. He was reportedly screaming at passersby, pounding his fists on the pavement, interfering with traffic, and vandalizing cars. According to at least one witness, Russell was openly masturbating in the warm California sun. At press time, it remains unclear whether

the alleged masturbation and car-vandalizing were separate incidents or were instead fused into one very weird act of vehicular sexual assault.[4]

But why take Goad's word for it? See for yourself on YouTube.[5] (The naughty bits are tastefully blurred.)

Apparently, the claim of masturbation was unfounded. In the clip, Russell can be heard ranting about the devil. His wife Danica and a spokesman for Invisible Children claim that he suffered a psychotic break induced by stress, as well as malnutrition and dehydration. Russell does not live in an African refugee camp, so why was he starving and dehydrated? He does say in his Invisible Children bio that he is in training for an "Iron Man" competition, so perhaps that explains it.

Russell's ego, however, seems to be made of weaker stuff. Apparently, he had been upset by criticism directed at his film and at him personally. Danica Russell claims that "because of how personal the film is, many of the attacks against it were also very personal, and Jason took them very hard." He is expected to remain hospitalized for a while. I wish him well and implore his doctors not to let him read Jim Goad's piece, or he might never recover.

Everything about Jason Russell's persona makes men want to corner him in the locker room and give him a wedgie. This is how Russell answered the question "Who am I?"

I am a rebel soul: dream evangelist. I am obsessed with people. I tell stories by making inspiring movies that move people's emotions, and then I take those emotions and transform them into action. My middle name is Radical. I married my best friend. We have known each other since we were six and seven. I have a three-year-old boy named Gavin Danger & a one-year-old girl named Everley Dar-

---

[4] http://takimag.com/article/touching_yourself_for_charity_jim_goad#axzz3hpBTSMcr

[5] http://www.tmz.com/2012/03/18/jason-russell-video-naked-meltdown-kony/

ling. I truly believe I am the luckiest person on earth because of my family, friends and the ability to go to a dream factory every day for work.

He also says, "If Oprah, Steven Spielberg and Bono had a baby, I would be that baby." Naturally, his favorite superhero is Peter Pan.

Russell certainly gives off a narcissistic vibe, as do most theater people. He gives himself and his son Gavin a lot of screen time in *Kony 2012*, which I think is effective — if a bit cloying. But I can see how people interpret it as a giant ego trip, which fits in with the underlying grandiosity of his message.

Russell is also good-looking, and he knows it, judging from his constantly changing hair styles and colors. He dresses like a metrosexual hipster. His speech is fey and sibilant, and he *loves* musicals. Naturally, he's being teased as a fag, but he's probably not gay. He's just "modern." Yes, he minces and prances and wags his finger like Mick Jagger. But Mick isn't gay either. He's just English.

Russell seems congenitally liberal and PC, but he is actually an Evangelical Christian, which produces the same ethomasochistic behavior as secular liberalism, although the operating system is slightly different. The two most un-PC — and thus probably the most honest — statements he has made is that he finds pregnant women sexy and wants to have nine more kids with his wife.

What, then, could explain Russell's breakdown? I have a theory that actually explains his effeminate behavior as well as a lot of other things, such as his interest in Africa, his talent at making propaganda films, the choreographed crowd scenes from *Kony 2012*, and even his choice of April 20th (Hitler's birthday) for the Cover the Night vandalism spree: there really is a woman trapped in Jason Russell's body and struggling to get out, and her name is Leni Riefenstahl.

Counter-Currents/*North American New Right*
March 21, 2012

THE REPUBLICAN PARTY
MUST PERISH

The North American New Right does not take sides in elections, because no system candidates are on our side. Thus we do not endorse candidates, legislation, ballot initiatives, etc. We do not think of ourselves as citizens of the United States or Canada or any existing white regime. We think of ourselves as exiles from the White Republic to come.

Our aim is to create a new school of thought and social movement that will lay the metapolitical foundations of the White Republic—not to waste time participating in the existing system, which is rigged against us. The present system is not a vehicle that can take us to the White Republic. So we must emotionally and intellectually let it go, so we can focus on building a vehicle that can move us forward.

But it does advance our metapolitical goals to comment on contemporary politics in the United States and other white nations from a White Nationalist point of view. It is in that spirit that we offer our commentary on the 2012 US presidential election.

I have already argued that it would be better for White Nationalists for Barack Obama to win.[1] Gregory Hood has also argued that it would be better for White Nationalists for Mitt Romney to lose.[2] One of the benefits of a Romney defeat is that it will hasten the day when the Republican Party perishes as an institution, and the destruction of the Republican Party is a good thing for whites in America.

The outcome of the 2012 US presidential election is now in the hands of white working-class voters in the state of Ohio. This is ironic, since this constituency is disdained, exploited,

---

[1] http://www.counter-currents.com/2012/09/the-2012-us-presidential-election/

[2] http://www.counter-currents.com/2012/11/why-romney-must-lose/

and betrayed by both parties.

Mitt Romney, the candidate for Capital, regards them as uppity, ungrateful peasants whose unions must be broken and who must be replaced by cheaper, more grateful peasants from the Third World, either though importing immigrants or exporting jobs. And Barack Obama, of course, regards them as just a bunch of Archie Bunkers.

Either party, of course, could have locked these voters in by now, if they had merely promised plausibly to represent white working class interests. Both parties, of course, have no problem promising to look after the interests of Jews, Wall Street, and the big corporations. The Democrats also have no problem promising free stuff to non-whites.

But when it comes to the white working and middle classes, it almost seems like both parties have a fit of conscience. It almost seems that they are hesitant even to *lie* to them about representing their interests. Instead, they promise nothing and simply try to scare voters into voting *against* the other party rather than *for* anything they stand for.

So it all comes down to whether white working class people in Ohio are more afraid of Mitt Romney of Bain Capital and Paul "Privatize It" Ryan—or that creepy mulatto/Muslim/socialist Barack Obama.

The Democratic Party is a coalition of a shrinking population of Jews, a ballooning population of other non-whites, and a shrinking population of alienated and deracinated white liberals. The Republican Party is the *de facto* party of the shrinking population of normal white Americans.

The Democrats are the party of net tax consumers, of the people who take more than they give. But the Democrats are more insidious than that, for they are also consuming the moral capital of America as well. The Republicans are the party of the people who produce more than they consume and maintain the nation's moral capital (such as it is).

There is no question that if everybody who votes for Mitt Romney in today's election dropped dead, America would be finished as a nation. You can't have a working society when the parasites far outnumber the hosts. But if everybody who votes for Barack Obama dropped dead, most of my family would perish, but America would still survive. America without the Left would be somewhat more prosperous, and there would be far less crime, ugliness, and degeneracy. Unfortunately, it would also be a duller country, culturally-speaking; town and country alike would be befouled by development and pollution; there would also be more wars for Israel; but the country would at least exist.

The Democrats have no problem making explicit appeals to the identity and interests of their constituencies: Jews, non-whites, environmentalists, gays, feminists, etc. But Republicans refuse to make explicit appeals to the identity and interests of whites, even while they pander to Jews and other groups that overwhelmingly vote against them. Nor will Republicans take the necessary steps to preserve the white majority—stopping non-white immigration, addressing higher non-white birth-rates—even under the guise of race-neutral programs.

But in a game in which the race or identity card trumps all, the party that refuses to play that card is doomed, and with it their constituency, white America, i.e., America. So why do Republicans persist in playing by rules that doom America and their party?

There are external and internal pressures that maintain this course. The main external pressure is the cultural hegemony of (1) moral universalism and (2) anti-white racism, which most Republicans refuse to challenge. But some Republicans realize that they cannot preserve their party or their nation without rejecting the current rules. This is where the internal pressures come in.

Republicans police their ranks to ensure ideological conformity. To mollify the demographic concerns that might lead Republicans to challenge the current rules, they promote transparently dishonest talking points about replacing their shrinking white electorate with non-whites. Those who are not fooled are simply driven out.

To determine who maintains this suicidal ideological consensus and why, follow the money trail. Half the money raised by Republicans comes from Jews (75% for Democrats), and a large percentage of the rest comes from wealthy non-Jews (an even higher percentage for the Democrats).

Capitalist elites, however, do not care about nationalism. They profit from importing non-whites and shipping American jobs to non-white nations.

Jews, of course, care about nationalism: their own nationalism, not American nationalism, which is merely a tool to be used or discarded whenever it serves Jewish interests. As for America, Jews support the same policies as capitalists: easy entry, easy exit.

Both Jews and the plutocracy are threatened by American nationalism and seek to suppress it. Both groups are well aware that that present demographic trends doom the white race in North America and the Republican Party. But both groups do not care.

Indeed, since Jews are more aware than any people of the conditions that promote or prevent genocide, one has to conclude that their promotion of policies conducive to the destruction of the white race is no accident but rather their conscious preference and aim.

In fact, I am convinced that at the core of the Republican Party are people who *actively wish to promote the destruction of the white race and the Republican Party*. Why am I convinced that the Republicans are being subjected to a controlled demolition from the inside? Because if I were the enemy, that is exactly what I would do.

The enemy fears that the Republicans could, eventually, become desperate enough to actually try to represent and preserve the white majority. They know that if the Republicans simply followed the Sailer Strategy[3] of explicitly appealing to white voters, they could maintain power and would set themselves on the path of actually preserving and enhancing the white majority.

Thus the enemy suppresses dissent and promotes the delusion that the Republicans will be saved by non-whites, know-

[3] http://www.vdare.com/articles/the-sailer-strategy-updated-three-steps-to-save-america

ing that they don't have to keep up the act much longer, since demographic trends will finish off the Republican Party soon enough. Indeed, the Left is already gloating about it in public. It is now openly acknowledged that this is the last election in which the Republicans can hope to win without appealing explicitly to white racial interests.

That simply means that in the next election cycle, the controllers will redouble their efforts to keep the party on its downward course. Naturally, this means that they will also redouble their efforts to purge dissenters, and there will be more dissenters to purge as individual Republicans realize that they will have to break the party rules to hold onto their power and perks.

Like the *Titanic*, will the Republican Party go down in one piece or split in two, giving rise to a more racially populist party? Of course, we should be wary of the human jetsam of the Republican Party. Just because a politician is too "dirty" for the Republicans does not mean he is clean enough to represent white interests.

What do you do when you discover that your house is thoroughly riddled with termites? Do you strip the paint and plaster and try to replace each rotted board one at a time? Do you seek to tweeze out the vermin, hoping that you have gotten them all and that the colony will not flare up again? What happens when you discover that the termites managed to put their name on the deed and are evicting you?

Obviously, you just walk away and let them carry on their work of destruction while you build a new house with better materials, which you have termite-proofed from the start. But, in political terms, what would that mean?

Right-wing populism is the sweet spot in American politics, which is why the establishment fears, loathes, and co-opts it (when forced to). What would a pro-white Right-wing populism look like?

First and foremost, it would have to declare itself *explicitly* as a vehicle for promoting white interests, including working to preserve and enhance the white majority.

Second, although populism makes the common good the

standard of justice, the rich and powerful have the whole system looking out for them, so a Right-wing populist movement would focus on protecting the interests of the white working and middle classes. It would be pro-private property, widely distributed, but against the concentration of wealth. It would promote the creation of small and medium-sized businesses to broaden the middle class. It would promote economic protectionism to restore American manufacturing jobs.

How would such a party be termite-proofed? Not only should it exclude Jews, plutocrats, and free market ideologues from the start, it should also promote policies that would send them packing.

For instance, why not propose radically egalitarian tax policies? Since the Federal government could go back to funding itself with tariffs, how about zero income or capital gains taxes on the first $1 million/year—and 100% confiscation of all income, including capital gains, above $1 million/year? But since we want to encourage artists and inventors who actually create new things (not *performing artists*), why not exempt them? Why not adopt a Social Credit economy and simply abolish usury? Why not run on a platform of complete debt repudiation?

But wouldn't America's richest people, 35% of them Jewish, just up stakes and leave the country? Wouldn't they renounce their citizenship and move to places with less burdensome taxes? Yes, of course they would. *But we want them to leave.* We want anybody who can't make ends meet on $1 million/year, and who is rootless enough to renounce his citizenship over money, to leave. We don't want people like that having any say over our politics. If we are going to regain control over our destiny, *they have to go.*

But wouldn't the economy collapse just like in *Atlas Shugged*? Yes and no. First of all, we *want* certain segments of the economy to collapse. No more banks. No more hedge funds. No more day traders, speculators, flippers, and the like. The goal of our system is to have a large, prosperous middle class secure against inflation and deflation, boom and bust, with socialized medicine, short work weeks, generous retirement benefits, "5 to 9" conservative policies, and a green, ecologically sustainable economy. Our people will have generous incomes, and if somebody wants to sell products to them, we don't care where they live or what race they are, so long as the products are manufactured by our people, within our borders.

A Right-wing populist movement within the present system is not the same thing as White Nationalism. It might not be a suitable vehicle to bring about White Nationalism, although we are watching the Golden Dawn carefully. But such a movement would go a long way toward breaking up the current power structure, radicalizing and racializing the white population in the process. And that would definitely be good for White Nationalism.

The defeat of Mitt Romney will hasten the day that the Republican Party perishes and the White Republic emerges.

Counter-Currents/*North American New Right*
November 6, 2012

THE CONSCIENCE OF A CUCKSERVATIVE

In the United States, the center-Left Democratic Party is a coalition of white liberals, non-whites, sexual minorities, religious dissenters, and environmentalists, in which the organized Jewish community is the senior partner.

All of these groups want a larger, more intrusive, more profligate government to ensure the inclusion and upward mobility of previously marginalized groups: women, non-whites, homosexuals, trannies, snail darters, etc.

The center-Right Republican Party is far less diverse: 90% of its votes come from white people—disproportionately male, conservative, straight, family-oriented, and Christian white people. The Democrats are increasingly the party of the underclass and the super-rich. The Republicans are increasingly the party of the middle class. Republican voters typically want a smaller, less-intrusive, fiscally responsible government that leaves them the freedom to raise their families, produce wealth, and carry forward a nation and way of life that their ancestors created and that suits them just fine.

The Republicans are the party of the people who built and sustain America. If every Democratic voter dropped dead, we would lose 10% of our most creative people and 90% of our craziest, crookedest, and most destructive. The result would be a slightly boring but highly productive, orderly, and happy society—Switzerland on a continental scale.

If every Republican voter dropped dead, however, the country would be finished in short order, for the dirty secret of the Left is that they are parasitic on the Right. Consumption is parasitic on production; vice is parasitic on virtue; the sick are parasitic on the healthy; evil is parasitic on good. We can live without them, but they cannot live without us.

However, if you look at Republican politicians and pundits, you would think that the exact opposite is true, for they completely accept and cringingly fear the moral authority of the

Left. If the Left calls Republicans "racists," they obsequiously choose a black running mate, adopt a black child, or avow their belief in color-blind individualism. Only a few Republicans actually talk back to the Left, but most spirited response you'll find is "*You're* the real racists," which of course does not challenge the underlying premise that racism is evil—or the deeper assumption that the psychotic parasites of the Left have any moral authority whatsoever.

The Democratic Party has no qualms about representing the interests of its constituencies. It offers upward mobility to the marginalized, and to its white constituents, especially the refractory straight male ones (especially those who happen to marry white women and reproduce themselves), it offers the promise of absolution from collective guilt for an ever-growing litany of isms and phobias by taking active part in their political dispossession and cultural degradation.

The rules of Democratic politics are simple: every group can appeal to its particular interests except whites, particularly straight white males. Whites have no collective interests, only collective guilt for the sufferings of the rest of humanity. Any hint of positive white self-awareness, much less organized white-interest politics, is stigmatized as racism, nativism, even National Socialism—and we know where *that* leads.

To exist, the Republican Party needs to get middle class white people's votes. Astonishingly, though, Republicans will not appeal to the ethnic interests of white voters. But they will appeal nakedly to the crassest ethnic interests of blacks, mestizos (including outright invaders), and Jews—groups that persist in giving most of their votes to Democrats.

Republicans will occasionally "dog whistle"—i.e., make vague, coded references—to the racial interests and anxieties of whites, albeit merely to fleece them of votes, without any intention of lowering themselves by actually doing anything. The best that white Republicans can hope for is to be the indirect beneficiaries of "implicitly" white policies framed in universalist terms.

By treating appeals to white ethnic interests as simply immoral, Republicans are, in short, playing by rules dictated by the Democrats. And of course the Democrats have rigged the rules in their favor.

Imagine American politics as a poker game. Each ethnic group has a place at the table and a certain number of chips, representing its collective wealth and power. Whites have the largest stack. But every group gets to play a wild card, "the race card," *except* for whites. No matter how big our initial advantage might be, if we play by those rules, we will lose hand after hand, until we have surrendered our wealth, our power, our country, and any control we might have over our destiny — or we kick over the table and refuse to play a game rigged against us.

Because Republicans insist on playing a game that they, and white Americans, can only lose, the alt-Right slur "cuckservative" has struck a chord and gone viral. "Cuckservative" is a combination of "cuckold" and "conservative."

Republicans and the Left are decrying the term for being inherently "racist" and sexual, and they are right. It is also inherently anti-Semitic.

The core of cuckoldry is a violation of one's genetic interests. When the cuckoo lays its eggs in another bird's nest, tricking them into incubating and feeding its young, it is advancing its genetic interests at the expense of the cuckolded birds. (The first act of a cuckoo chick is to murder the birds' real offspring.) When a man is cuckolded, he is tricked into caring for another man's children instead of his own. The male horror of cuckoldry is older than the human race itself. If a widowed lioness has small cubs, a male lion will kill her cubs before he mates with her, rather than provide resources for another lion's offspring.

Republicans are cuckservatives, because they are more interested in pursuing the interests of non-whites than of their own white constituents. This implies that only *white* Republicans are cuckservatives. Jewish Republicans are quite successful at pursuing their own ethnic interests, as are other non-white Republicans.

There are three main reasons why Republicans have consented to playing by the Left's rules.

The most superficial reason is that they fear bad press, social shunning, or a face-to-face encounter with a foul-mouthed, finger-jabbing, hyper-aggressive Jew. (For instance, the infamous Michael Hart incident at the 2006 American Renaissance Conference.)

Another superficial reason is simple corruption. Republicans have been bought by Jewish donors who wish to secure Israeli interests at American expense. Republicans have been bought by agribusiness lobbies to keep the borders open to Mexican invaders. This is just outright betrayal of white interests, nothing more.

A third and deeper reason that Republicans refuse to play the white race card is they think that their ideals of liberty and limited government are *universal rather than tribal anyway*. So there's just no upside to tribal appeals (beyond a little dog-whistling in a tight race). Yes, Republicans are aware that forswearing white identity politics puts them at a disadvantage, at least in the short run. But since they believe in the universality of their principles, they believe that non-whites can eventually come to embrace them too. Republicans think they just need to show sufficient openness — and suppress all manifestations of white ethnocentrism — to bring them around. Until then, they are willing to pander to non-white ethnic interests, but merely as a means of converting them, not as an admission that ethnic politics and unassimilable minorities are here to stay.

But liberty, capitalism, and constitutional government are not universal. They are tribal values of whites. If they were valued in Asia, surely they would have been practiced there. If they were valued in Latin America, they would have been practiced there. If they were valued in the Middle East, they would have been practiced there. If they were valued in Africa, they would have been practiced there. And white countries would not then be swamped by immigrants from these countries.

The rest of the human race does not aspire to be like white people. The immigrants coming here do not wish to assimilate our values and contribute to our civilization. We are not even *trying* to assimilate them anyway. Instead, they are just coming here to take the fruits of our civilization. They don't want to be us, or be part of us. They just want to dispossess us.

For nearly 1,000 years, the Chinese practiced a horrific form of torture called *lingchi*, the death of a thousand cuts, in which a victim was tied to a wooden frame and then slowly cut to pieces. The full torture took three days and involved 3,600 cuts. (*Lingchi* was abolished only in 1905. The Chinese skin animals alive to this day.) To prolong the agony, the victims were given opium so the pain did not cause them to lose consciousness or die too quickly.

The grandiose notion that white tribal values are actually universal, and that the rest of the world will become part of our community — without them or us even trying — is nothing but an intellectual opiate that numbs white Americans as we lose our wealth, our power, our homelands, and our futures to non-whites, slice by bloody slice.

The cuckservatism controversy is an important opportunity for White Nationalists. The concept has caught the eyes of the mainstream. It perfectly encapsulates our critique of the Republican Party. Wherever the term is being discussed, we need to be there, and we need to follow the lead of Michael Enoch and Hateful Heretic of The Right Stuff, who are stating our case in simple, sincere, moderate language.

This is an opportunity to awaken white Americans to four facts.

First, whites are being demographically displaced because of political policies, but this can be reversed with different policies.

Second, white political values are tribal, not universal. Thus they will perish if our tribe perishes.

Third, the Republican Party is playing by rules that are designed to destroy the white electorate and the party itself. Thus we need an alternative.

Fourth, no matter how much Republicans try to placate the Left, they will still be called racists. They are already doing the time, so they might as well do the crime.

So far, the Republican response has been standard stupid party. The true believers are reiterating their faith in universalism and stigmatizing the term as racist. The prigs are also claiming it is anti-Christian and pornographic, so don't go there. The tinfoil hat crowd are accusing us of being Democratic infiltrators.

Still, it is slowly dawning on Republicans that they are in a deep hole. We are leading the best of them toward the light. But some of them will die in that hole. Let's make sure our race does not die with them.

Counter-Currents/*North American New Right*
July 29, 2015

FERGUSON, GARNER, & THE
END OF GENTRIFICATION

"One law for the lion and the ox is oppression."
— William Blake

I recently picked up *Face to Face with Race*,[1] Jared Taylor's anthology of first-person accounts of race relations in America from various contributors to *American Renaissance*. Interestingly, the harrowing stories of racial animosity in New York City struck me as exaggerated, based on my own experiences in New York.

I do not question the accuracy and honesty of these reports, some of which go back to the 1990s, so I have to ask: Has non-white behavior actually improved in the United States, despite continued multiculturalism, non-white immigration, and erosion of white norms? Crime statistics certainly bear out this impression, particularly for New York City.[2]

But what has caused it? Are the races finally learning to live together peacefully in a multiracial, multicultural society? Is all the multicultural propaganda finally paying off? I doubt this for two main reasons.

First, racial and ethnic consciousness are hard-wired into the brain.[3] It is natural for us to feel greater trust for people who are like us, greater fear of those who are unlike us. The human forebrain might be taught to disdain and ignore these feelings, but they never go away, and in some circumstances — like emergencies — they will trump our multicultural programming. This means that any multicultural amity that might exist is psychologically superficial. Thus multiracial institutions are weak and prone to break down under pressure.

---

[1] Jared Taylor, ed., *Face to Face with Race* (Oakton, Virginia: New Century Foundation, 2014).

[2] http://en.wikipedia.org/wiki/Crime_in_New_York_City

[3] http://www.kevinmacdonald.net/whiteethnocentrism.pdf

Second, whites seem to be the only people who widely accept multiculturalism as an ideal. Whites think that if they only set aside everything about their interests, tastes, and expectations that might clash with those of other races, they can demonstrate sufficient openness and good will that non-whites will drop their resentment, hike up their pants, join hands, and help them usher in a new age of post-racial harmony. Non-whites, however, are encouraged to be as ethnocentric, aggressive, and accusatory as possible in their dealings with whites. Thus present-day multiculturalism is a formula for the exploitation and victimization of whites, which can only increase racial tensions.

Although I am sure there is a host of reasons why non-white crime is down in many urban areas, two stand out: aggressive policing and "gentrification."

In New York, crime fell during the Giuliani and Bloomberg years because the NYPD was aggressive and efficient in locking up criminals.

During the same period, whites began to "gentrify" racially-mixed neighborhoods. Gentrification begins with gays, straight singles, and childless young couples attracted by low prices, interesting architecture, walkable neighborhoods, and shorter commutes to work and cultural attractions.

When whites create and attract new businesses, property values and rents rise, and non-whites find themselves priced out of the neighborhood. Many non-whites, aided by Section 8 housing money, end up in "slumburbs" like Ferguson, Missouri, where they ruin the lives and property values of "white bread" suburbanites disdained by hip urban "gentry." Simply by decreasing the non-white percentage of the population, gentrification decreases crime—partly by relocating it to the suburbs.

Gentrification and aggressive policing are mutually reinforcing phenomena: lower crime encourages gentrification, and once whites move into racially-mixed neighborhoods, they demand even more aggressive policing to bring the neighborhood up to their standards.

When I lived in Atlanta, I spent a lot of time reading at a

particular coffee house. One afternoon, I listened in on a conversation between a young gay couple (one white, the other black) and a few of their friends. All of them were starry-eyed liberal utopians. A few months before, the couple had purchased a great old house for practically nothing because it was in a black neighborhood. As soon as they moved in, they were horrified by the loud noise, littering, loitering, and street crime. Nothing in their presumably suburban and middle-class upbringings had prepared them for feral inner city blacks. And with perfectly clean consciences, they set to work cleaning up their neighborhood, which entailed frequent calls to the police, who obligingly locked up some of their neighbors. The shiftless and criminal element that remained free started looking for more comfortable environments.

If this couple had been straight, white, and conservative, their behavior would have immediately been decried as racist. And it *is* racist. For, in effect, what they were demanding is that the police enforce *white* standards of behavior on a black neighborhood. But because they were a liberal, gay, interracial couple, they got a pass on what is essentially racist oppression. Indeed, in places like Atlanta, Washington, D.C., and New York City, white liberal gentrifiers have been getting a pass on this kind of racist oppression for more than 20 years now.

But the death of Michael Brown in Ferguson, Missouri, and Eric Garner in Staten Island, New York City spell the end of gentrification, for both deaths came about because the police were simply routinely enforcing white behavior standards, and aggressive enforcement of white standards is what makes gentrification possible in the first place.

The altercation in Ferguson began when Officer Darren Wilson told Michael Brown and his friend to walk on the sidewalk rather than in the middle of the street. Blacks typically have less intelligence, less empathy for others, and less impulse control than whites. Thus they simply can't be bothered with the white man's rules. When I lived in Atlanta, I would see blacks dart into 4 lanes of moving traffic rather than go to a crosswalk and wait for the signal. It was like those wildlife parks, where zebras and antelope dash in front of your Range Rover. "Urban wildlife" was my term for such behavior.

The altercation in Staten Island began when police apprehended Eric Garner for selling single cigarettes. Typical black impulsiveness and high time preferences mean that they will gladly pay more per unit for a single cigarette now rather than walk ten feet or wait ten minutes to buy a whole pack. Forcing blacks to buy cigarettes by the pack is just more arbitrary white man's law, which gets in the way of hustlers like Eric Garner (who had 30 previous arrests[4]) making a living gratifying the impulsiveness of his kind.

I think that in both cases, the police acted rightly to enforce the existing laws and broader white standards of behavior. Whites built this country, after all. I also think that Officer Wilson was right to kill Michael Brown. It was a clear case of self-defense.

Eric Garner did not deserve to die. But he did deserve to be arrested, and his death was simply an accidental effect of his arrest.

The police were right to subdue this large, agitated, black street criminal by force. Softer measures would have endangered the police themselves, and we cannot expect the police to defend our safety if they cannot defend their own.

The police were right to ignore Garner's protests that he could not breathe, because if you can talk, you can breathe. Garner also claimed he "dindu nuffin" before his arrest, an all-too-typical lie that the police have heard a thousand times before. (Blacks have a very weak sense of moral responsibility and shame.) If the cops thought that Garner's claim that he could not breathe was also false, whose fault is that, exactly?

Garner did not die from being roughly subdued by the police. He died of cardiac arrest in the ambulance because he was obese and in poor health. He just wasn't up to the rigors of being arrested. But *he* chose his life of crime. And the police can't give a free pass to fat criminals because they might find arrest too strenuous.

---

[4] http://www.inquisitr.com/1659026/eric-garner-criminal-past-emerges-30-arrests-in-34-years-including-assault/

Frankly, neither life is much of a loss, and I resent being told that "Black Lives Matter," when it is all too obvious from black behavior that they regard both their lives and ours as quite cheap.

So the angry black mobs protesting both deaths are wrong on all the facts. But they are still fundamentally justified in their anger.

American blacks have a huge chip on their shoulder. Let us call it the chocolate chip. A chip on one's shoulder means a set of preexisting grievances that are merely triggered by current events. Such behavior is essentially neurotic, because the reaction is seldom appropriate, either in kind or intensity, to what triggers it.

Sensible blacks should feel ashamed of Michael Brown's behavior. Frankly, they should also feel somewhat safer because of his death, for if his criminal career had not been cut short, his own community would have been his most likely victims. Eric Garner did not deserve to die, but neither was he a credit to his race.

Still, the deaths of Michael Brown and Eric Garner, regardless of the facts, have tapped into a vast reservoir of bitterness about "racism."

It is easy to be dismissive of black complaints about racism. Legal racial discrimination and segregation have been dismantled decades ago. Blacks today are objectively a privileged group in America, the beneficiaries of immense unearned wealth and prestige. But even with all their privileges, blacks are the sorriest racial group in America. Yet that is largely due to their own biological nature, not white ill-will. Blacks are arrested for more crimes because they commit more crimes. Blacks are poorer than whites because they work less, are less intelligent, and lack self-control.

But there is an underlying truth to the black charge that their unhappiness is largely due to deep, systemic American racism. America is essentially a white society. It is the kind of society that first arose in Europe and never arose in Africa. Europeans and Africans have dramatically different biological natures. (The best account of the biological differences between whites and blacks is Michael Levin's *Why Race Matters*.[5] Levin does not just focus on intelligence, but also on a whole array of moral and psychological differences.)

Our differing natures give rise to different kinds of societies, societies that conform to our natures, that fit them as comfortably as properly-sized shoes. European societies are just not a good fit for Africans, just as African societies are not a good fit for Europeans. And when we force Africans to live in European societies, it is like forcing them to wear tight shoes. When we impose white norms on blacks, we resent them for not meeting our expectations, and they resent us for setting expectations they cannot meet.

One law for the white man and the black man is oppression. But America was created by whites, so naturally it is run by the white man's law.

Routine liberal oppression of blacks has been the fuel of gentrification for more than two decades. But the Obama administration will no longer tolerate it. In a country of more than 300 million people, it is inevitable that the enforcement of even the most minor laws will sometimes escalate into accidental or justifiable deaths. If the administration does not back the police in such cases when they are merely enforcing white community standards, then those standards will no longer be enforced. That is the death knell of gentrification and the false impression of workable multiculturalism that it fosters.

Moving whites into the inner cities and non-whites into the suburbs has massively increased interactions between the races. Racial diversity inevitably leads to tensions, hatred, and violence. Aggressive policing has kept a lid on the violence. But Barack Obama and Eric Holder have removed the lid, which can only increase polarization between the races. The collapse of gentrification could even increase solidarity between whites as well. Besieged urban liberals may come to sympathize with suburban whites who are fighting the same battle against the same enemy. They may even come to understand why earlier

---

[5] Michael Levin, *Why Race Matters* (Oakton, Virginia: New Century Foundation, 2005).

generations fled to the suburbs. But now that the enemy is in the suburbs as well, the hipsters might as well stand and fight.

From a White Nationalist perspective, anything that increases non-white lawlessness, racial polarization, and white solidarity are good things. The worst possible outcome is a police state that keeps the lid on racial violence and polarization for a few more decades, allowing miscegenation, collapsing white birthrates, and surging non-white populations to drive our race on this continent beyond recall. Thus White Nationalists must resist the conservative tendency to side with the police and demand increasingly aggressive enforcement of white standards. Why try to preserve a society in which everything white is slated for destruction? Don't we want to "burn this bitch down" too?

The races really are different. Thus to maintain white standards, we must oppress blacks. But I don't wish to oppress blacks, and neither do most decent, fair-minded whites. But that leaves us only two options. First, we can surrender our standards and let blacks rule us, which is a non-starter, given the history of post-colonial Africa, post-white Detroit, and the widely televised chimp-out in Ferguson. Second, we can maintain our standards and go our separate ways by creating separate, racially homogeneous homelands for whites and blacks in North America. That is the ethnonationalist solution. It is the only solution that takes the well-being of both races into account.

Counter-Currents/*North American New Right*
December 17, 2014

IRRECONCILABLE DIFFERENCES:
THE CASE FOR RACIAL DIVORCE

White Nationalists believe that our race is on the road to simple biological extinction, and that the only real solution is to create homogeneously white homelands with pro-natal, pro-family institutions.

To make White Nationalism a reality, however, we have to convince our people that such policies are necessary, that they are moral, and that they are possible.

Political separation along ethnic lines does not happen every day, and it usually involves hatred, violence, and bloodshed. So most whites simply do not wish to contemplate it. But all-too-many whites are quite willing contemplate a smaller-scale form of separation, namely divorce. And indeed, the model we recommend for peaceful and humane racial separation is the so-called "velvet divorce" between the Czechs and the Slovaks.

If the relationship between whites and blacks in America today were a marriage, we would have divorced long ago. The same is true of whites and Jews, and any other non-white group. White Nationalists are simply proposing a policy of racial divorce.

Legally, there are two kinds of divorce: fault and no fault. In a fault divorce, at least one party is held responsible for the breakdown of the marriage. Causes include:

- ❖ spousal abuse
- ❖ substance abuse
- ❖ incarceration
- ❖ adultery
- ❖ infecting one's spouse with a sexually-transmitted disease
- ❖ insanity
- ❖ abandonment

In no fault divorces, neither party is held to be singly responsible. The main causes are separation and irreconcilable differences. Irreconcilable differences include:

- ❖ Strong personality differences
- ❖ Strong lifestyle differences
- ❖ Strong differences between work and spending patterns
- ❖ Lack of trust
- ❖ Lack of reciprocity
- ❖ Constant bickering
- ❖ Long-simmering resentment
- ❖ Contempt
- ❖ Inability of the relationship to meet the emotional needs of one or both partners

It is interesting that even something as seemingly trivial as different work and spending habits can be a cause for divorce. But earning and spending are a large part of life, and mismatches there can easily spill over into and upset the rest of one's life.

In the case of blacks and whites in America, there is plenty of fault on both sides. But focusing on historical grievances is actually a trap, simply because groups may be victims, but they are not perpetrators. Collective guilt is meaningless. And many *individual* whites and blacks today have not harmed or been harmed by one another, so collective historical grievances are not sufficient cause for many to contemplate racial divorce.

For instance, I think it was a terrible crime to introduce black slaves to the New World. But I do not feel a shred of guilt for it. And although my life has been negatively impacted by the presence of blacks in America, most black individuals have done me no harm, and some have actually benefited me. Thus my desire for racial divorce has nothing to do with guilt or innocence or moral judgments of any kind.

Racial divorce is not really about individuals at all. It is about the incompatibility of groups. There are above average blacks who are credits to white society, and there are below average whites who drag our race down. But the character of a society is determined by the average, not the outliers. Thus my desire for racial divorce is based simply on the recognition that whites and blacks *as groups* have irreconcilable differences that make it impossible for them to be fully happy when forced to live in the same system.

All the common causes of no fault divorce apply to the relationship of blacks and whites in America: on the whole, the races have different personalities, different lifestyles, different work and spending habits, etc. When forced to live in the same system, these differences create tensions. To use a trivial example, blacks have a very different sense of the passage of time, and when a long line of white people forms while a black Post Office clerk inanely chats away with the customer at the window, the result is resentment. We resent blacks for failing to live up to our standards, and blacks resent us for imposing white standards in the first place.

These problems are not based on history but on nature. Even without black slavery and black crime—even if the past could be completely wiped away and blacks and whites could start fresh on a desert island—these differences would give rise to new frictions and new resentments.

Given these differences, it should come as no surprise that relations between whites and blacks are poisoned with endless bickering, distrust, contempt, and long-simmering resentment and bitterness. Reciprocity is central to our idea of moral conduct, and unequal peoples cannot practice real reciprocity.

Again, if this were a marriage, it would have ended in divorce a long time ago. Any responsible marriage counselor would recommend a no fault divorce as quickly as possible, because such a relationship is on the road to a fault divorce, when bitterness becomes hatred and hatred becomes violence.

It is false to claim that White Nationalism is based simply on racial hatred. As the author of *Confessions of a Reluctant Hater*, I do not deny that hatred plays a role. But I believe that hatred must be seen primarily as the *product*, rather than the *cause*, of bad racial relationships. I hate other groups *because* of multiculturalism. I believe in racial divorce because I *don't want* to hate other groups.

Most people who divorce do not simply hate one another. Presumably, they originally married out of affection. So usually there is a love-hate relationship. And although blacks and whites in America were forced together — the equivalent of a shotgun marriage — elements of genuine affection have still managed to grow up between the races. So there is a love-hate relationship here as well.

But in some cases, there is no hatred in divorce at all. Both parties simply recognize that they would be happier on their own, and they cordially separate. Furthermore, once people divorce, it is not uncommon for them to like one another *more*. It is easier to admire some people at a distance. Some people remember why they got married in the first place. Some even make the same mistake twice.

The main reason why individuals are willing to stay in un-happy and even abusive marriages is the conviction that their own happiness does not matter. They believe that duties to God or community or family are more important. Or they be-lieve that they deserve to be unhappy because of feelings of guilt and worthlessness. Divorce is legitimate only if individual happiness is legitimate.

The same is true of bad racial relationships as well. Whites will never be free until we recover the conviction that we have the right to be happy, to flourish as a race rather than just fill the stomachs and empty the bedpans of the Third World.

When Barack Obama prissily reminds whites of the alleged horrors of the Crusades a millennium ago, lest headlines about ISIS give us any ideas about separation from the Muslim world today, or when Jews traumatize our children with Holocaust "education," we have to see them for what they are: abusive spouses telling us that we are worthless, that we do not de-serve to be happy, to keep us in subordinate, exploitative, par-asitic relationships.

There is nothing more obscene than being exploited because of one's conscience, by means of one's conscience, by those who lack conscience altogether.

White Nationalists tend to be uncomfortable with divorce. We think that divorce rates are too high, because people are too individualistic and unwilling to compromise or to grow as in-dividuals to make marriages and families work. But for all that, we recognize that individual happiness still matters, and that, try as we must, some marriages cannot work and should be dissolved for the good of all.

Our reluctance to condone divorce and our willingness to work to save even doomed marriages should give us insight into the minds of white liberals, many of whom are trying to make multiculturalism work out of the same essentially decent motives.

Yet white liberals are also willing — perhaps too willing — to condone divorce on the grounds of individual happiness. We need to make this tendency work for us. White Nationalism will seem much more appealing if our people come to see that multiculturalism is a marriage made in hell.

Counter-Currents/ *North American New Right*
March 13, 2015

WHY I SUPPORT SCOTTISH INDEPENDENCE

I support Scottish independence because I am a nationalist, specifically I am an *ethnonationalist*. Ethnonationalism is the view that different peoples, nations, ethnic groups, etc. should have politically autonomous homelands.

The ethnonationalist argument is simple: *identity matters*. Different peoples are different because they have different histories, different cultures, different conception of the good life. These differences can be glorious. We would not want there to be a world without a France or an Italy or an England. But when different peoples have to share the same political system, such differences lead to conflicts, resentment, even violence.

Ethnic and racial diversity *always* lead to conflict, resentment, and violence. Diversity is not a strength, but a weakness. Therefore, the best way to ensure peace and progress is to break up diverse societies into ethnically and racially homogeneous ones.

England and Scotland have many deep cultural and historical differences, but the main political issues that separate them are rather simple. Scotland is overwhelmingly in favor of the Labour Party, while England is not. Scotland is progressive, England conservative. Politically speaking, both countries would better get what they want by going their separate ways. White Nationalists needn't worry too much about either outcome. Neither a socialist Scotland nor a capitalist England would have any problems that cannot be fixed by racial nationalism.

As an aside, I am rather dismayed at the discussion of this issue at American Renaissance. Jared Taylor is opposed to Scottish independence[1] because the Scots want to create another Nordic welfare state (complete with suicidal immigration policies). Many of his commentators seem to be free-market zombies, intoning dire predictions that socialism leads to poverty and op-

---

[1] http://www.amren.com/news/2014/09/scotland-should-stay-in-the-union/

pression. (Like Norway, Sweden, Finland, and Denmark, for instance?) Further proof that White Nationalism desperately needs to free itself from free market dogmas. Too many White Nationalists still think that capitalism or conservatism or Christianity are more important than the national self-determination of white peoples. Our people will never be safe until white racial preservation—that is to say, white ethnonationalism—matters to us more than capitalism or socialism or conservatism.

As an ethnonationalist, I support Scottish secession on principle, meaning that I think that national self-determination produces the best outcomes for all peoples. Thus I also support independence for Wales, Cornwall, Ulster, the Isle of Man, . . . even England! I dream of the day when tiny Sark can return to its feudal system, overturned by English plutocrats and E.U. bureaucrats.

But I also think that there are more specific good outcomes promised by Scottish independence. Without Scotland, the evil Labour Party, which has been caught red-handed "electing a new people" by flooding the UK with non-white immigrants, will never again rule over England. And since Labour has a solid lock on Scotland, they will not *need* to replace the Scots with non-whites (although they will probably try it on other grounds). Of course the Tories are just a different kind of evil, but the UK without Scotland has a real chance of moving to the Right on immigration, and that is a good thing. A UK without Scotland also has a better chance of leaving the European Union, which would severely weaken one of the most insidious anti-European forces.

Scottish independence also undermines multiculturalism across the board. Because if people as similar as the English and Scots cannot share the same political system, how are the English going to fare with Pakistanis and Sikhs and Africans, who are far more different? These are questions that the multicultural establishment does not want people asking.

I find the arguments for Scottish independence to be compelling, except for one: their opposition to nuclear weapons. An independent Scotland should keep any English nukes within its borders. They should not make the same mistake as the Ukrainians, who traded the third largest nuclear arsenal on the planet for American and Russian *promises* to respect their territorial integrity. Ukraine would be intact today, not dismembered and bleeding, if they had relied on their own arms, not the promises of others. Never throw away a nuclear deterrent.

Of course both an independent Scotland and a slightly reduced UK still face common problems, the greatest of which is European man's march to extinction due to low birth-rates and race-replacement through immigration. Neither country will be saved by politics as usual. Racially conscious Scots and Englishmen—and Welsh, and Cornish, and the other white peoples of the British Isles—need to replace the ethnocidal system that is destroying us. But the more independent European nations that exist, the greater the chance of a White Nationalist party coming to power in one of them.

Furthermore, independence does not preclude international cooperation. And ethnonationalism does not preclude pan-European consciousness. Indeed, independence actually promotes such values. Before whites can face our common enemies—and perhaps even cooperate in fighting them—we need to stop fighting one another over lesser issues. Because whether Scotland is socialist and England conservative is far less important than whether there will be white people on this planet in 200 years. Once the Scots and English stop fighting about those matters, perhaps both peoples can turn their attention to the question of common racial survival.

But the first step is national self-determination. England and Scotland need a divorce. It is painful to leave even a bad relationship. But once the pain is past, both parties will find renewed vitality, new energies that can be put to constructive uses, because they will no longer be wasted on frustrating and fighting and resenting one another.

I hope that Scottish independence is just the first step in the dissolution of the United Kingdom and the birth of new possibilities for the Scots and all European peoples.

Counter-Currents/ *North American New Right*
September 17, 2014

"LET'S CALL THE WHOLE THING OFF"
IN DEFENSE OF "PETTY"
NATIONALISM

As I write, the Scottish independence referendum remains undecided, but the "No" camp is in the lead. Regardless of the outcome, though, Scotland will have more independence, either leaving the UK altogether or enjoying greater autonomy within it.

I was, frankly, surprised that many White Nationalists and Alternative Rightists oppose Scottish independence, which strikes me as a rather simple application of the ethnonationalist principle that different peoples need independent homelands to express their distinct identities and pursue their unique destinies, as free as possible from the meddling of others.

When different peoples are forced to share the same system of government, it breeds conflict, resentment, even violence. Thus to preserve peace and promote the well-being of all peoples, multicultural states should be replaced with ethnically homogeneous ethnostates.

In the case of England and Scotland, the Scots support a more generous welfare state than the English will allow. England pulls Scotland to the Right, and Scotland pulls England to the Left. Both countries will better satisfy their political preferences by peacefully going their separate ways.

If the white race is going to be saved, we must have homogeneously white homelands. That means bidding farewell to tens of millions of non-whites. The best way to persuade people of the fundamental justice and humanity of these seemingly drastic measures is to promote ethnonationalism for all peoples.

Thus when we see any instance of a distinct people splitting off from a multiethnic nation—particularly in a peaceful and humane manner—we should applaud it.

Because if peoples as similar as the Czechs and the Slovaks or the Scots and the English can't live together, this makes it much easier for us to argue that whites should separate from non-whites, who are far more different. And examples of peaceful and humane ethnic separation allay fears of race war and violent ethnic cleansing.

Beyond that, secession upsets the existing anti-white establishment, and that is a good thing. The more mischief, the merrier.

Scottish independence would be good for Scotland, good for England, and good for the ethnonationalist cause world-wide. And that is good for white survival.

If Scotland votes "No," it may slow down secessionism in Scotland and across Europe, but it will not stop it. Indeed, secessionists might learn valuable lessons which will make let them succeed next time around. If at first you don't secede . . .

Some White Nationalists, like Jared Taylor, don't support Scottish independence because they disapprove of what the Scots might do with it: they want a Scandinavian-style welfare state. I would understand this position from a Scot, but from a foreigner it surprises me, since the whole point of Scottish independence is that foreigners *don't have to like how the Scots govern themselves*. Because that would be Scotland's business — finally. (Taylor does have a Scottish common law wife, so Scotland is not entirely foreign to him.)

As for the complaint that the Scottish National Party wants to join the EU and import trouble from the Third World: aside from the fact that it is Scotland's business, (1) the referendum is on Scottish independence, not the policies of the Scottish National Party, which might not get its way, and (2) the UK (and thus Scotland) already belongs to the EU and is already importing Third Worlders, so voting "No" guarantees that such policies will continue anyway, whereas voting "Yes" carries no such guarantee.

But again, if you don't like Scottish policies, you don't have to live there. That's the beauty of having many different nations.

Others don't support Scottish nationalism because they disapprove of their motives. They think the Scots are being "petty": too influenced by bread and butter issues and negative feelings toward the English.

But there is nothing wrong with voting about bread and butter issues. No state is legitimate if it does not represent the interests of the body politic, and democratic voting is a good way to make sure the interests of the masses are heard, not ignored.

As for pursuing practical necessities: there is a hierarchy of needs. A society solely devoted to basic biological needs is what Socrates called a "city of pigs." But every nation needs prosperity, security, and peace before it can turn its attention to higher values and remoter aims. So in a healthy society, there is no necessary conflict between material and spiritual values. High culture requires a solid material foundation.

Every nation first needs to secure its sovereignty before it can worry about other issues. Thus there is no necessary conflict between small state nationalism and broader racial and global concerns. Indeed, both England and Scotland would have more time and energy to ponder and pursue higher goals if they were not pulling in different directions while yoked to the same political system.

Many Englishmen take the idea of an independent Scotland personally. "Do these Scots think they are too good to be ruled by the English?" One surprisingly common claim is that there is nothing to Scottish nationalism but petty resentment of the superior English. The Scots, naturally, find such posturing intolerable. It is rather unseemly for a dominant people to simultaneously play the victim and act condescending.

Many comment threads on Scottish independence have descended into vicious, juvenile ethnic baiting. But the slurs and bile displayed by both sides of the debate just reinforce the desirability of separation. When my brother and I would fight, my mother would break it up by sending us to our separate rooms to simmer down. Let's send the English and Scots to separate countries. They might even learn to better appreciate one another.

Another tendency on the Right that is dismissive of "petty" nationalism are those who dream about a new European imperium. I agree that Europeans need to develop a pan-European consciousness as well as some sort of loose political federation. These would have two aims: preventing fratricidal wars between white nations and protecting our race from other racial and civilizational blocs like Africa, the Muslim world, India, and China.

But a pan-European consciousness need not and should not conflict with distinct national groups. It certainly should not promote and depend upon the creation of a "homogeneous" European type, which is emerging in colonial societies like the United States. It should be a priority of all European peoples to maintain their cultural and subracial differences, thus ideologies and institutions that dissolve distinct European identities should be rejected.

It is worth pondering whether such a European federation need be anything more than a military alliance akin to NATO, which would include all of Europe but exclude the US and Russia, since both nations may have European roots but are multiracial continental empires with universalistic, messianic, imperial ideologies.

The defense of the race in Europe requires a common military, a common emigration policy, and common environmental regulations. But does a European federation really require a central parliament and bureaucracy to define the Euro-sausage, the Euro-Santa, and the Euro-currency? Couldn't currency, industrial policy, and trade barriers be determined by the constituent states? We should be guided here by the principle of subsidiarity, meaning that decisions should be decentralized as much as possible.

However, *before* we can create forms of white political unity that do not undermine the sovereignty and identity of our various peoples, we need to break down all illegitimate, homogenizing multiethnic societies. Just because some sort of loose federation is desirable in a racially awakened and cleansed Europe, that does not imply that today's European Union, or United Kingdom, or France, or Spain, or Russia are good things—such that we should oppose Catalan or Basque or Breton or Corsican independence as "moving in the wrong direction." Because by breaking up multiethnic empires into ethnically distinct and homogeneous states, they are moving in *the right direction*.

Wherever there are distinct peoples longing to control their own destinies, I want there to be distinct homelands. Pan-secession against all empires must come *before* the emergence of our kind of pan-European consciousness and federation—for our approach does not undermine the distinct identities and sovereignty of European peoples. And such secessionism is a growing phenomenon, which we should applaud and encourage, for with each success, our dreams come nearer to realization, including our dream of loose federal unity.

No ethnonationalist can seriously argue that today's United States or EU or UK or Russia should be preserved against secessionist tendencies because someday whites might need a very different kind of federation. Thus it is quite natural to suspect such individuals of simply shilling for the existing powers—all of which oppose the legitimate national self-determination of some European peoples. "In the name of European peace and security, you should submit to the rule of the Germans" is simply a non-starter. That is not the end of "brother wars" but the beginning of the next one.

When a Pole or a Czech or a Hungarian reads Guillaume Faye extolling the idea of a "Eurosiberia" stretching from Greenland to Vladivostok, he naturally wonders how it will differ from the Russian-dominated prison house of nations from which these countries recently escaped. The only way to allay such fears is to submit any federation to the veto power of the "petty nations," which means that sovereignty would ultimately remain in the hands of distinct European peoples.

That veto power effectively exists today. For it is natural, normal, and right for every people to first secure its own sovereignty before it can worry about racial and global issues. This means that European unity will never be peacefully achieved by extending existing illegitimate imperial institutions. That is simply a dead end. Which means that a petty nationalist veto will be baked into any legitimate form of federal European unity that will emerge.

Concessions to *Realpolitik* or Geopolitics can only be made through the temporary or permanent renunciation of ethnona-tionalist principles. But nobody hears and nobody cares when White Nationalists decide to throw our lot in with one of the existing powers. Our voices are simply drowned out by the babble of the mainstream.

We lack money, numbers, power, and prestige. Our only strength is the truth of the ethnonationalist idea. Thus we need to support ethnonationalism on principle wherever it emerges: Scotland today, tomorrow the world.

Counter-Currents/*North American New Right*
September 19, 2014

GRANDIOSE NATIONALISM

Racial Nationalists all know the dangers of "petty" nationalism. It seems silly for genetically and culturally very similar peoples, like the Scots and the English, to seek political separation while both countries are being colonized by Africans and Asians. It is shameful when whites ally themselves with non-whites to gain advantages over other whites in economic and political rivalries. And it is tragic when these differences lead to bloodshed.

White Nationalism is all about halting our race's programmed march to extinction, whereas petty nationalism, by stirring up discord and strife, seems merely to be hastening our race to its doom.

But the solution to "petty" nationalism is not what I shall call "grandiose" nationalism, namely, the idea of *the political unification of whites* — whether of Europe (the "Imperium" of Francis Parker Yockey), or of Europe and Russia (the "Eurosiberia" of Jean Thiriart and Guillaume Faye), or of the whole Northern Hemisphere (the "Borean alliance" or "Septentrion" of Jean Mabire and Volchock). And if political unification is such a great thing, why leave out Australia, New Zealand, and the Southern Cone?

The essential feature of any scheme of political unification is the *transfer of sovereignty* from the constituent parts to the new whole. If sovereignty remains with individual states, then one does not have political unification. Instead, one has an "alliance" between states, or a "treaty organization" like NATO, or an "intergovernmental organization" like the United Nations, or an economic "customs union" like the European Common Market, or a hybrid customs union and intergovernmental organization like the European Union.

The principal benefits attributed to political unification are (1) preventing whites from fighting one another, and (2) protecting whites from other racial and civilizational power blocs like China, India, and the Muslim world. These are noble and necessary aims, but I think that grandiose nationalism is not the way to attain them.

1. GRANDIOSE NATIONALISM IS NOT NECESSARY

Political unification is not necessary either to prevent whites from fighting one another or to secure whites from external threats. These aims can be attained through alliances and treaties between sovereign states. A European equivalent of NATO, which provides Europe with a common defense and immigration/emigration policy and mediates conflicts between sovereign member states would be sufficient, and it would have the added value of preserving the cultural and subracial distinctness of different European groups.

The threat of non-white blocs should not be exaggerated. France, the UK, or Russia alone are militarily strong enough to prevail against anything that Africa, India, or the Muslim world can throw at us—provided, of course, that whites are again *morally* strong enough to take their own side in a fight. A simple alliance of European states would be able to deter any Chinese aggression. Thus a defensive alliance between European states would be sufficient to preserve Europe from all outside forces, whether they be armed powers or stateless masses of refugees and immigrants.

As for white fratricide: the best way to defuse white ethnic conflicts is not to combat "petty" nationalism but to take it to its logical conclusion. If different ethnic groups yoked to the same system are growing restive, then they should be allowed to go their own ways. Through moving borders and moving peoples, homogeneous ethnostates can be created, in which each self-conscious people can speak its own language and practice its own customs free from outside interference. Such a process could be mediated by a European treaty organization, which could insure that the process is peaceful, orderly, humane, and as fair as possible to all parties.

2. GRANDIOSE NATIONALISM WOULD BE COUNTER-PRODUCTIVE

Whenever White Nationalists speak of multiracial societies, we stress that forcing different races to live in the same political system is a recipe for tension, hatred, and conflict. But this truth applies to different European peoples as well. All forms of ethnic diversity within the same political system cause weakness and conflict. Thus political unification would actually heighten rather than ease tensions between European peoples.

Since the fall of the Soviet Empire, the tendency in Europe has been toward ethnonationalism, either by the Czech and Slovak road of peaceful partition or Yugoslav road of war and ethnic cleansing. What is a more realistic path to peace: putting Yugoslavia back together, then Czechoslovakia back together, then unifying them both in a single state, with all the rest of Europe— or allowing peoples with long historical grudges to completely disentangle their affairs and lead their own lives? What is more likely to produce European amity: a shotgun wedding or an equitable divorce?

A unified Europe would have many different peoples and languages in the same political system. But these peoples would not have equal influence on policy. The strongest and most populous nations would dominate. Thus a unified Europe would take on the quality of an empire, in which the most powerful nation would impose its standards and way of life on the rest.

NATO is dominated by the United States. The European Union is dominated by Germany. If NATO were to collapse and Russia were to enter the EU, the result would be pretty much what Hitler envisioned: a German-dominated Europe rendered autarkic and invincible by Russian natural resources. Germans and Germanophiles would rejoice at that outcome, but the French, English, and Russians would beg to differ.

The EU today is well short of real political unification, but it is already a source of tensions and discontent—between individual nations and Brussels, and between North and South Europe, which are finding a single currency and monetary policy to be a bad fit. If the EU tried to impose real political unity on Europe, its members would bolt, and it would face the choice of accepting dissolution or preserving itself through coercion.

If petty states can veto European unification, it will not happen voluntarily. Thus they must be deprived of their veto. Europe will only be politically unified by force, and that inevitably means one nation imposing empire on all the rest. European unity will, in short, be the cause, not the cure, of the next "brothers' war."

Some proponents of a politically unified Europe actually admit that their vision is incompatible with European subracial and cultural diversity. Thus Constantin von Hoffmeister and more recently Richard Spencer (both of them married to Russians) have extolled the emergence of a "homogeneous European man." In Hoffmeister's words:

> The mixing of different European nationalities should therefore be encouraged. We must support sexual unions between Russian women and German men, Spanish men and Swedish women. Only by radically breaking down the artificial barriers dividing Europe can we create the new breed of man . . .[1]

While acquiescing to this sort of deracination and pan-mixia makes sense in European colonial societies, which were settled by Europe's most rootless and restless, it makes no sense to promote this as a *policy* for the European motherland, which is populated by those who stayed behind. The New Right is about preserving differences, including the subracial and cultural differences between Europeans. Grandiose nationalism, however, would lead to the destruction of these differences in order to create a smoothly functioning white empire, whether its proponents recognize this outcome or not.

Thus grandiose nationalism is just a racialist, loosely Right-wing version of homogenizing modernity. But ethnonationalists beg to differ. In fact, we insist on it. We will even fight for it. Thus Europe will not be politically unified.

Fortunately, European amity and security can be reconciled with European political and cultural diversity simply through a defensive federation of sovereign European ethnostates—the more such states, and the more they reflect the underlying ethnic

---

[1] Constantin von Hoffmeister, "Our Motherland: Imperium Europa," in Norman Lowell, *Imperium Europa: The Book that Changed the World* (Imperium Publishing, 2008), 24.

diversity of Europe, the better.

3. Dreaming about Grandiose Nationalism Undermines Real Nationalism

In Europe today, all the energy is in "petty" nationalism. Most nationalists, for example, are opposed to NATO and the EU. Thus when grandiose nationalists stand on the sidelines and cluck about "petty" nationalism, at best they are irrelevant, and at worst—if anyone takes them seriously—they might undermine the energy and commitment of nationalists who actually have a chance of accomplishing something.

If grandiose nationalists weaken real nationalism, they also strengthen the existing powers. Some significant grandiose nationalists oppose anti-EU sentiment because they dream that nationalists might actually "take over" the EU someday. But of course that will never happen unless "petty" nationalists make progress in EU member states. Thus the net result of grandiose nationalism—again, if anyone took it seriously—would be to strengthen the existing ethnocidal EU.

Of course, if political unification is really a good thing, then grandiose nationalists should also be pro-NATO as well, since maybe "we" can mount a "take over" there as well. Yet I know of no grandiose nationalists who are pro-NATO, perhaps because such a position would be mocked as transparent shilling for the existing anti-white global hegemon.

But many grandiose nationalists are pro-Russia. In fact, they are for NATO getting out of wherever Russia wants to get into. Again, it is easy to see how this serves the interests of existing anti-white powers, but harder to see how it promotes the long-term survival of the white race.

Petty nationalism energizes but divides people. How, then, should White Nationalists preserve the energy of petty nationalism while mitigating its dangers? The answer is to build upon the pan-European consciousness that already exists in the leadership cadres of "petty" nationalist groups across Europe.

THE UKRAINE CRISIS

White Nationalists believe that multiculturalism—i.e., racial and ethnic diversity within the same state—leads inevitably to conflict and bloodshed. Therefore, the best way to ensure peace and harmony is to replace multiculturalism with ethnonationalism, which is the principle that each distinct people should have its own homeland.

The strife in the Ukraine is not, at root, caused by Russian or "Western" intervention, for these would find no purchase if Ukraine were not already an ethnically divided nation. Although Ukraine is overwhelmingly ethnically Ukrainian, like Yugoslavia and Czechoslovakia, it is still an artificial state containing a number of distinct national groups: Ukrainians, Russians, Tatars, Poles, Bulgarians, Hungarians, Romanians, Moldovans, Armenians, Jews, etc.

Moreover, the Ukrainian majority is divided between Eastern Ukrainians, who tend to speak Russian and see Russia as a natural ally and trading partner, and Western Ukrainians, who tend to speak Ukrainian and wish to maintain their independence from Russia. Some Western Ukrainians wish to cozy up with NATO and the EU. Others want to maintain independence from both Russia and the West.

The Crimean peninsula was part of Russia from when it was wrested from the Turks until Nikita Khrushchev attached it to Ukraine in the 1950s. The Crimea contains a large ethnic Russian population and Russia's Black Sea naval base.

Even in the absence of outside intervention, the ethnic and linguistic diversity of Ukraine is a recipe for conflict. Such conflicts can be mitigated or postponed by such policies as federalism, decentralization, assimilationism, or granting quasi-autonomy to restive minorities. Such half-measures are perennial temptations, based on the hope that one can hold onto territory and resources by placating or corrupting or co-opting the leaders of other ethnic groups.

But the problem of ethnic or racial diversity can only be settled, once and for all, in two ways.

First, there is the Czechoslovakian model: like the Czechs and the Slovaks, the different peoples of the Ukraine could simply "divorce" and go their separate ways, partitioning the country between them. Once the country is partitioned, people would be free to move at their leisure to whichever nation they prefer. Crimea and other parts of Eastern Ukraine could, if they wished, join Russia.

Second, there is the Yugoslav model: through civil war and military intervention, Ukraine could be partitioned along ethnic lines, although at the cost of great suffering and bloodshed. Instead of peaceful, voluntary population transfers, there would be forced ethnic cleansing.

And, since neither Russia nor the United States can resist meddling in such conflicts, the stage would be set for a much wider conflict, even a Third World War. The First and Second World Wars started with small, regional disputes too.

Furthermore, even in the absence of outside influence, Ukrainian President Viktor Yanukovych had to go. Yanukovych is a crook who plundered his country and was essentially selling its geopolitical alignment to the highest bidder in order to retain his grip on power. Yanukovych was from Eastern Ukraine. He is of Russian, Polish, and Belarussian descent. His regime and his power base already leaned toward Russia. But what decided the matter is simply that Russia was the highest bidder. Thus, from an ethnonationalist point of view, Yanukovych had to go, not because he chose Russia over the West, but because no self-respecting people can tolerate its destiny being sold to the highest bidder merely to keep a criminal in office a little longer.

It does not matter if such a criminal regime was democratically elected. Legitimacy derives from serving the common good, not getting the most votes in an election. It does not, moreover, matter if such a regime is deposed by violence and lawlessness, since the good of the people is the supreme law, and Yanukovych left no other options.

One of the most remarkable features of the Ukrainian revolution is the open participation of far Right groups, most prominently Svoboda (Freedom) and Right Sector, which is a more radical, activist-oriented group that split off of Svoboda. These groups are being smeared as "neo-Nazis" by both the anti-American Left, which is always eager to paint US interventions in the worst possible light, and by the Russian regime, including its apostle and apologist to the Far Right, Alexander Dugin, whose credibility with ethnonationalists should be reduced to zero by now. Some Leftists are even deeming Yanukovych's overthrow the "Brown Revolution."

It is a lie, however, to label the Ukrainian revolution "neo-Nazi," for two reasons. First, Right Sector and Svoboda were only part of the coalition that brought down Yanukovych, which also included centrists, Leftists, feminists, gay rights advocates, and ethnic minority agitators, including Jews, Tatars, and Armenians.

Svoboda was founded in 1991 and is one of the five leading parties in Ukraine. Its strength is based in Western Ukraine. Svoboda regards Russia as the chief enemy of Ukrainian sovereignty, which is obviously true, but Svoboda is not pro-EU or NATO. Svoboda is a nationalist populist party, which quite clearly draws inspiration from German National Socialism, but with a post-War, pan-European sensibility. Ukrainians are also well-aware that Hitler wanted to make Ukraine a German colony, not an independent nation. Svoboda leader Oleh Tyahnybok has been widely criticized for his anti-Semitic statements, but he has never backed down. The World Jewish Congress has called for Svoboda to be banned. Svoboda members and sympathizers also draw inspiration from Traditionalism, the European New Right, and the writings of Kevin MacDonald. Svoboda members and sympathizers are, moreover, among Counter-Currents' healthy Ukrainian readership.

Of all European nationalist parties, Svoboda is probably the most radical and consistent, yet it is also one of the most successful. It deserves to be studied and emulated. Unfortunately, despite an admirable political platform, Svoboda is at present committed to maintaining the artificial Ukrainian state.

That stance could change, however. Indeed, Svoboda is the only Ukrainian party that could appeal to its fundamental principles to ratify the loss of the Crimea and Eastern Ukraine, should the widening Russian intervention make that a *fait ac-compli*. Furthermore, since Svoboda's power base lies in Western Ukraine, the loss of the East would increase its percentage of the overall electorate.

The new interim government in Kiev appears to be as corrupt as the old one. Ukraine's political culture as a whole is one of the most corrupt in Europe, which is the cause of widespread cynicism. As long as Svoboda represents the interests of the people and stays relatively aloof from corruption-as-usual, they will only gain in future elections.

Like many White Nationalists, I admire Vladimir Putin because he is an important geopolitical counterweight to the United States and Israel (blocking the road to war in Iran and Syria), he has sought to address Russia's demographic crisis, and he looks and acts like a real-life James Bond. But Putin is not an ethnonationalist. Indeed, he imprisons Russian nationalists and is committed to maintaining Russia's current borders, which include millions of restive Muslims in the Caucasus.

Putin's interest in the Ukraine is purely geopolitical. He is playing chess with NATO. His only concern with Russians in the Crimea or pro-Russian Ukrainians in the East is the pretext they provide for interventions that might strengthen Russia's geopolitical standing at the expense of NATO.

From a global White Nationalist perspective, anything that weakens NATO and the US is a good thing, but I cannot approve if it conflicts with the ultimate principle of ethnonationalism. If, however, Putin were to take back the Crimea, virtually ridding Ukraine of its Russian and Tatar minorities and leaving Ukraine smaller but more racially and culturally homogeneous, it might be a case of doing the right thing for the wrong reason.

The one power that has absolutely no business in the Ukraine is the United States. The US has been pursuing a recklessly anti-Russian foreign policy since the collapse of the USSR, egged on largely by Jews consumed by a neurotic hatred of Russia. Americans need to wake up and speak out before the same people who sold us the ruinous Iraq and Afghan wars light the fuse of World War III.

Counter-Currents will continue to follow the Ukraine crisis.

We will publish articles by and interviews with Ukrainian nationalists and others who are there on the ground. As a White Nationalist, I believe in nationalism for every nation, and I hope that the Ukrainian revolution leads, eventually, to national autonomy for all peoples within the current Ukrainian borders. I also wish the best for Svoboda and other Ukrainian racial nationalists, who might well bring about such a bright future and serve as models for other European nationalist movements. White Nationalists in North America will do whatever we can to lend moral support and fight against US intervention.

Counter-Currents/*North American New Right*
March 3, 2014

THE UKRAINE CRISIS:
TAKING OUR OWN SIDE

My attempt to set out a consistent ethnonationalist position on the Ukraine crisis has provoked a good deal of debate.

The situation in Ukraine clearly illustrates that even very closely related peoples—Russians and Ukrainians—can be so divided by language and history that they are willing to shed one another's blood. When such conditions arise, the most pragmatic and humane solution is the Czech and Slovak model of amicable divorce and partition, as opposed to the Yugoslav model of arriving at the same result through bloody warfare and ethnic cleansing.

Thus, I am all for Ukrainian nationalists who seek to chart an independent course for their nation. I understand their distrust of Russia and their desire to rid themselves of Viktor Yanukovych, and I hope they will also reject the US, EU, and NATO as a false alternative. Ukrainian White Nationalists understand this already, and I hope they will convince more of their compatriots.

But according to the same ethnonationalist principles, I also think that it makes sense for the Crimea to leave Ukraine and re-join Russia. I think that it might make sense for the Eastern part of Ukraine to move in that direction as well. It makes far more sense for Russia to rule Crimea (in spite of its Ukrainian and Tatar minorities) than Chechnya and Dagestan.

I also made it clear that, although Vladimir Putin is my sentimental favorite in any clash between Russia and the US, he is no friend of ethnonationalism in Russia or anywhere else. Furthermore, the Ukraine crisis does not present an either/or choice between Russia and the West, because there are actual ethnonationalists in Ukraine—namely Svoboda and Right Sector—who seek a nationalist third way between American and Russian domination. White Nationalists should be on the side of Svoboda, Right Sector, and an independent Ukraine. Because national self-determination is what we want for all peoples.

Neither Right Sector nor Svoboda is perfect, but if Western White Nationalists are willing to overlook the fact that Putin jails Russian White Nationalists for "hate" and claims to be fighting against "fascism" and anti-Semitism in Ukraine, then I feel entitled to be somewhat indulgent of the comparatively minor gaffes of Ukrainian White Nationalists.

Both Svoboda and Right Sector, for instance, support maintaining Ukraine's current borders. Both oppose making Russian an official language of Ukraine. This seems rather "petty nationalistic" to me. But the rank and file supporters of even the most enlightened European nationalist parties include many individuals wedded to the worst petty nationalist outlooks. However, if I wanted to promote the partition of Ukraine on ethnic and linguistic lines, *but could not say so, for fear of losing the support of petty nationalists*, I might support similar measures—which do no real harm, but are highly symbolically potent—to heighten tensions, polarize the population, and hasten ethnic separation. And these entirely predictable consequences seem to be playing themselves out.

The principal disagreements with my position are the following.

First, it is claimed that Svoboda and Right Sector are in bed with, or even controlled by, "the Jews." Astonishingly, the very same people who raise this objection have "no comment" about the fact the Putin enjoys cordial relations with Russia's Jewish community, has prominently placed Jews in his government, and claims to be fighting against Ukrainian anti-Semitism. Why, then, is Putin not controlled by "the Jews" as well?

In fact, there are Jews on both sides of this conflict, as there are in every conflict, which is really what Jewish hegemony means: no matter what the outcome, they are always poised to profit. This does not mean that Jewish influence is benign, that we should ignore it, or that we should not be suspicious of politicians who associate with Jews. But it does mean that, by itself, the involvement of Jews proves nothing about the other agents in play or the likely outcome.

The news is not that a Jew heads the interim government in Kiev. (Which turns out to be untrue, in any case.) The news is

not that a Jewish oligarch has been appointed a governor in
Ukraine. The news that that Svoboda — one of the most radical
nationalist parties in Europe, which includes National Socialist,
New Right, Traditionalist, and Jew-wise elements — is also in
the new government. The news is that Svoboda and Right Sector members took to the streets, risked life and limb, and were
instrumental to bringing down the Yanukovych government.
Western White Nationalists should be applauding our Ukrainian cousins for their courage and commitment — and asking
ourselves what we can learn from them — not picking nits,
straining gnats, and swallowing Putin.

Second, it is objected that Russia is the only power capable
of countering US-dominated globalization, thus we *must* support Russia in this crisis, lest she fail and with her the last best
hope for European man. Where to begin?

1. Russia is not the only power capable of countering the
American drive to unipolar hegemony. Don't count out China
and India.

2. Russia will not disappear if she loses this round. Besides,
Russia may have lost Yanukovych, but she looks like she is
winning in Crimea, and Eastern Ukraine may also join her.

3. White Nationalists are the most disdained and powerless
people on the planet (except in Ukraine, where they have ministers in the interim government). Our sympathies toward Russia, good or ill, have no power to affect the outcome of this crisis.

My eyes glaze over at sports analogies, but the psychologies
of political partisanship and sports fandom are very similar.
Both involve individuals imaginatively identifying themselves
with a team. Once this identification is established, fans believe
that simply by rooting for their team — even in their own living
rooms — they can influence the outcome of the game. It is an essentially magical form of causality. Fans also feel the pride of
victory and the dejection of defeat as if they were members of
the team, rather than just passive spectators. Too much political
commentary fits this description. Ardent partisans feel that the
fate of nations hinges on the opinions of powerless people on the
other side of the planet. So you'd *better* hold the right opinion.

But, given that White Nationalists are pretty much power-less (outside Ukraine, that is), what is the purpose of political commentary at all? I am not writing this because I think I can affect the outcome of the Ukraine crisis. I am writing this be-cause, although White Nationalists do not have the advantage of money or political power, we do have the power of the eth-nonationalist idea, an idea whose truth and relevance is demonstrated by the Ukraine crisis.

If White Nationalists can offer more credible analyses and solutions to political crises than the powers that be, that may well change the world. In any case, *better ideas are the only ad-vantage we have today*, and it seems silly to throw that advantage away in favor of the swooning, delusional sycophancy of those who treat Vladimir Putin as the Second Coming of Jesus, Hit-ler, or the Beatles.

4. The more I know about Russia, the more I think that she is not an alternative to globalization, but just another form of globalization.

The United States is a menace to the world because it has become an imperialistic proposition nation with a messianic mission to impose the universal good of liberal democracy and decadent crap culture on the rest of the world. Of course, these ideals are only trotted out when they serve the interests of our ruling Jewish and plutocratic elite.

Both inside and outside Russia, there are ideologues who wish to cast her as a socially conservative version of the impe-rialistic proposition nation, whose messianic mission entitles her to meddle with her neighbors whenever it serves the inter-ests of her ruling elite. This concept of Russian identity has deep historical roots, and it is just as menacing to genuine eth-nic self-determination as Americanism.

For a White Nationalist, ethnic identity and ethnic self-determination trump social conservatism. We prefer liberal Sweden to "conservative" Uganda. We prefer that sovereign peoples work out their own problems rather than have solu-tions imposed upon them. We want nothing of universal prop-osition empires, liberal or conservative. We want the ethnic core populations of both the United States and Russia to free themselves of these self-conceptions, which are a menace to their own ethnic interests as well as those of their neighbors.

Third, it is claimed that Svoboda and Right Sector should be discounted—that in the end the only real choice is between the US and Russia—and that, in effect, all efforts to build a nationalist alternative are wasted. Indeed, even sympathy with attempts to build a nationalist alternative is wasted.

Such views from White Nationalists are, frankly, surprising. Do they think that all attempts to create a nationalist alternative are futile? Or is the futility confined just to Ukraine? If it is the former, then why not just pack it in? If the latter, then what are we to make of the fact that nationalists are significantly more successful in Ukraine than in any other white countries?

There is a false certitude in these dismissals of Ukrainian nationalists. Some people just *know* that Ukraine will fall into the clutches of the EU and NATO. Some people are *certain* that Putin is unfolding some grand master plan. Such views underestimate the role of contingency and the unexpected in history. A lot can happen in Ukraine between now and the May 25th elections. And haven't we learned that the outcomes of presidential elections can easily be reversed in Ukraine? As for Putin, he is just gambling, but he has a good poker face and knows how to project certitude and momentum. Given his opponents, he will probably win in Crimea.

The idea that we have to choose between Russia and the US, lest our "vote" be wasted, is the same argument that maintains the Democrat vs. Republican hegemony in the United States. And since there are no fundamental differences between the parties, that means that the same establishment holds on to power no matter which party wins election.

The ultimate political power is not the ability to win elections. It is the ability to frame every election so that, no matter what the outcome, the same people remain on top. Which means, for one thing, that *everybody's* vote is wasted, because voting changes nothing. I call this kind of power "hegemony."[1]

The only way to break hegemonic power is to refuse to play

---

[1] See my essay "Hegemony" in *New Right vs. Old Right*.

a rigged game and seek instead to create alternative institutions.

From the Ukrainian nationalist point of view, both the US and Russia are threats to national sovereignty. Instead of taking one side or the other, Ukrainians need to take their own side and build a genuine alternative. That is what Svoboda and Right Sector are doing in Ukraine. It is what White Nationalists should be doing everywhere.

Counter-Currents/*North American New Right*
March 17, 2014

KEVIN STROM ON
RUSSIA & UKRAINE

Kevin Strom is one of White Nationalism's best writers. I seldom disagree with his work, and even when I do, I find it highly valuable as a clear synthesis and statement of beliefs I oppose. A case in point is his August 16, 2014 American Dissident Voices podcast "Jewish Aggression," Part 2, on the conflict between Ukraine and Russia.[1]

Strom seeks to reduce the Ukraine crisis to a conflict between international Jewry and a Jew-wise Russia. To argue this thesis, Strom dismisses other actors and motives on the Ukrainian side and offers a false picture of the relationship between Russia and Jewry.

Strom begins, "In order to weaken Russia, and eventually install a pro-Jewish government there, the Jewish/US axis has engineered a *coup d'etat* in Ukraine." This is wrong on three counts.

First, the United States and Jewry did not "engineer" the Maidan protests that led to the fall of Viktor Yanukovych's government. The initial small protests on the Maidan against Yanukovych's policies attracted little attention. But when they were brutally dispersed by police, Ukrainians of all political convictions, from far Left to far Right, gathered to protest police brutality and generalized corruption, and the protests grew into a revolution. The Maidan protests were not initially or primarily pro-EU or anti-Russian. They were against Yanukovych's corruption and lawlessness and for honest government.

Second, once the Maidan protests were underway, the US government and other Jewish-dominated organizations tried to shape the outcome. But it is simply untrue to say that they "engineered" them.

Third, beyond that, it is false to claim that Yanukovych was

---

[1] http://nationalvanguard.org/2014/08/jewish-aggression-part-2/

ousted by a *coup d'etat*. In truth, as the death tolls mounted, he lost his nerve and fled the capital. Describing Yankovych's fall as a "coup" and the interim government that followed him as a "junta" is just lying Russian propaganda that should not be used by discerning individuals.

Strom continues:

> Russians have historically been among the most Jew-aware people on Earth. A century ago the Imperial Russian government set many restrictions on Jewish activity there to prevent the exploitation of its citizens. When that government was overthrown and Russia was converted into the Soviet Union by the Jewish-dominated Bolsheviks in 1917, a period of overt Jewish rule took place in which millions of the best men and women in Russia were killed, imprisoned, and had their property stolen. Under Communism, "anti-Semitism" was a capital offense.
>
> When a non-Jew, Stalin, evidently an even more vicious player of power politics than his Jewish "comrades," took control, he distrusted the tribally-focused Jews and proceeded to systematically reduce their power, killing quite a few of them in the process. When faced with the German invasion in 1942, and realizing that more than a few Russians and Ukrainians (Ukraine was then a part of the Soviet Union) were welcoming the Germans as liberators, Stalin ditched much of the Communist party line and embraced Russian nationalism. As a result the post-war Soviet Union became less and less Jewish-controlled and more and more under the control of Russian nationalists. Despite still paying lip service to Marxism, by the 1960s Russian leaders were openly opposed to Zionism, and Jews, no longer favored, were queuing up by the thousands to leave the country. . . .

This is a very misleading picture which conceals the fact that Jews have *always* been a privileged people in Russia. They were privileged under the Tsars. They were privileged under Stalin

and the post-Stalin Soviet regime. And they are privileged under Putin. One has to treat Jewish claims of Russian anti-
Semitism very skeptically, since Jews are hardly scrupulous in
throwing that epithet around.

According to Aleksandr Solzhenitsyn's *Two Hundred Years
Together*—ably and extensively reviewed by F. Roger Devlin[2]—
there were practically no Jews in Russia until the partitions of
Poland in 1772, 1793, and 1795, which brought Russia vast territories overlapping today's Poland, Ukraine, Lithuania, and
Belarus. The partitions took place during the reign of Catherine
the Great, who set the foundations of subsequent imperial Jewish policies.

From the start, Jews were free subjects of an empire in
which most whites were serfs. (Serfdom was only abolished in
1861.) In 1785, Jewish communities were granted self-govern-
ment. In 1786, public offices were opened to Jews.

In 1790, merchants in Moscow petitioned the Empress for
relief from Jewish competition, which was granted in Russia
proper, laying the foundations of the Pale of Settlement, which
encompassed the former Polish-Lithuanian territories, plus
"New Russia," i.e., Ukrainian territories conquered by Catherine the Great from the Turks.

Although Russians were protected from Jewish competition
by the Pale, the relationship was reciprocal: Jews within the
Pale were protected from Russian economic competition. In
short, the Pale of Settlement was a vast area given to Jews for
unlimited and ruthless economic exploitation of whites, leading to massive poverty and misery.

If Jews were a privileged people in Imperial Russia, whence
the perennial *kvetching* about Russian anti-Semitism? Simple:
Jews did not think they were *privileged enough*. They wanted to
exploit the whole of the Russian Empire, which they duly
seized during the Bolshevik revolution.

Given the overwhelmingly Jewish nature of Bolshevism,

2 http://www.counter-currents.com/2015/07/solzhenitsyn-on-the-
jews-and-tsarist-russia/, http://www.counter-currents.com/2015/07/
solzhenitsyn-on-the-jews-and-soviet-russia/

when Stalin purged the party, he of necessity purged many Jews who opposed him. After the foundation of Israel, Stalin purged Jews for Zionist tendencies. But Jews who did not oppose Stalin were not purged and indeed enjoyed positions of power and trust throughout his regime.

For example, the Ukrainian-born Jew Lazar Kaganovich, one of history's great butchers, was the architect of the Ukrainian famine and the Gulag. He enjoyed Stalin's confidence to the very end. He may have had a hand in Stalin's death. It is even claimed that Stalin married a shadowy Kaganovich sister named Rosa. After Stalin's death, Kaganovich remained on the Politburo until 1957, when he tried to engineer a party coup against Khrushchev. In 1961, he entered an evidently comfortable and secure retirement and died at the age of 97, just after the fall of Communism.

If Jews were a privileged people under Stalin, what is the basis of claims of Stalinist anti-Semitism? Again, Jews simply felt that they were not privileged enough. Also, Jews propagate the idea of Soviet anti-Semitism to obfuscate the overwhelming Jewish culpability in the crimes of communism. Finally, Stalin may not have hated Jews as such, but many Jews hated Stalin, and that is sufficient ground to be called an anti-Semite

After Stalin, Jews remained a privileged people as well. After all, what other group could emigrate *en masse* from Russia?

Under Putin today, Jews remain a privileged group. Yes, when Putin came to power, he redistributed some of the ill-gotten wealth of largely Jewish oligarchs, and some of the oligarchs have predictably squealed about anti-Semitism. But Putin's policies were certainly not anti-Semitic *per se*, as a new crop of Jewish oligarchs has emerged under Putin's tenure.[3]

Even Strom admits that "Putin speaks highly of Jews and disparagingly of anti-Semitism, though he keeps some pet Jews (with no trace of real power) in his circles [Who are these Jews, and how does Strom know they have no real power? Does one appease people who have no "real power"?], and though he

---

[3] http://www.jpost.com/Jewish-World/Jewish-Features/At-Putins-side-an-army-of-Jewish-billionaires

has outlawed 'extremism' as a versatile way of cementing his rule . . ." But Strom has convinced himself that Putin doesn't really mean it. Because Putin acted against some Jews, Strom is convinced that he really opposes all Jews as Jews.

Strom claims that the aim of the "Jewish/US axis" is "to weaken Russia, and eventually install a pro-Jewish government there" and "the Jewish power structure is most anxious that Russia be surrounded, its government overthrown, and a new 'democracy' installed there." But this does not hold water, since there is already a pro-Jewish government in Moscow. As far as Russian Jews are concerned, Putin is quite pro-Jewish. There are Jews on the American side, Jews on the Russian side, and Jews on the Ukrainian side of this conflict. No matter what the outcome, Jews are positioned to benefit. This is one meaning of Jewish hegemony. But it also means that the events in Ukraine cannot be reduced to a simple "Jews versus Russia" opposition.

Strom has also convinced himself that Putin's foreign policy is based not on calculations of Russia's national interests, but on a desire to combat international Jewry:

> . . . in the last few years, every time the US/Israeli war-mongers were attempting to start another war in the Middle East—first in Iran and then in Syria—Vladimir Putin checkmated them. For these things, the Jews cannot forgive him. They are very worried about a resurgent, nuclear-armed, and Jew-aware Russia—and any alliances she may build in an increasingly Jew-aware world.

Putin's policies certainly irritate the Israelis. They irritate American neoconservatives. And they irritate the broader American Jewish community, which harbors extremely irrational anti-Russian hatreds going back to the 19th century. But Putin's policies are not directed at Jews as such. Instead, Putin regards the United States as his primary adversary, Israel as a US client, and international Jewry as a divided community whose favors he ardently seeks to woo.

Strom has even convinced himself that Putin might not really mean it when he says he is fighting against "fascism" in Ukraine, or that by being a good nationalist, he is effectively a fascist, even if he denies it:

> Vladimir Putin, whatever he may believe personally, is forced by political necessity to praise the "heroic Soviet soldiers" who "saved the Motherland from Hitler." Russia has quite as many "my country is always right" patriots as does America, where the fighters in the "good war" (which wasn't good at all) must be praised in Politically Correct terms by all politicians or those politicians will face political suicide. Putin therefore presents himself as (and may even believe himself to be) an "anti-Fascist" even while he pursues essentially nationalist policies, simply because those are the policies that are objectively good for Russia, even going so far as to decry the low White birthrate and implement laws designed to increase it.

Putin has adopted a range of sensible policies, but the fact that he is committed to maintaining Russia as a multiracial, multicultural empire means that all these sound policies actually work against the racial interests of Russian whites, who suffer from catastrophically low fertility and are being outbred by Muslims from the Caucasus and Orientals in the East. (Incentives to raise birthrates will not help if they are applied equally to more fertile non-Russians as well.)

Putin's form of conservative, race-blind, Jew-friendly civic nationalism is actually the worst case scenario for whites, since it places an essentially anti-white system on firmer political and economic foundations, which will allow its anti-white, ethnocidal trends to proceed more efficiently until Russia's white population is biologically beyond recall. But Putin doesn't think this way, because he is not a "fascist," i.e., a racial nationalist—not even an "implicit" one.

Thus when Putin claims that he is battling against fascism and anti-Semitism in Ukraine, he really means it. And, as a "fascist" and anti-Semite, Strom needs to take him at his word.

Vladimir Putin is not our "secret friend."

What does Strom have to say about the real "fascists" and anti-Semites in the Ukraine crisis, namely the political party Svoboda (Freedom) and its radical break-away group Right Sector?

> Since late last year, the Jewish power structure, through its puppet, the United States, was trying to overthrow the legitimate elected government of Ukraine [This reads like Russian boilerplate. Since when does the National Alliance recognize elections as legitimating anything?], which had taken a position of moderate and positive engagement with Russia [a rather delicate description of Yanukovych selling his country's alignment to the highest bidder]. Hundreds of millions of US taxpayer dollars were expended to recruit a group of supposedly "right wing fascist" mercenaries [Is Strom asserting that the US created and/or pays and/or controls Right Sector? What is the proof?], who were carefully watched at all times by Jewish and US intelligence operatives [Sounds like a likely deduction being passed off as fact], since they were not entirely trusted. These groups were politically and philosophically descended from the Ukrainians who joined the German forces in World War 2 to liberate their country from Communism. [And should thus have Strom's default sympathy.] The understanding of the members of these groups ranged from full awareness that the Jews were responsible for the historical starvation and enslavement of Ukrainians — to jingoistic petty nationalists who blamed everything on "Russians." Frustrated by political impotence [Svoboda has actual elected officials] and long-fooled by American anti-Communist rhetoric [or perhaps merely alarmed by Russia's paeans to the glories of Stalininsm], they were ripe for exploitation. These mercenaries were provided with weapons and other military hardware. They provided much of the "muscle" for the overthrow of Ukraine's president Viktor Yanukovych last February.

. . . The naive nationalists in Ukraine were fooled.
They were tricked into fighting the wrong enemy. They
were fooled by promises of support from their *real* enemy—the regime in Washington. They were fooled because they were petty nationalists, not racial-nationalists.
I pray that some of them are racial-nationalists now. They
were fooled—not unlike the way their grandfathers were
fooled into thinking that the Russian foot soldiers who
enforced the Jews' orders to starve Ukraine were the real
enemy. They didn't see the big picture.

Strom wishes to argue that Jews, not Russians, are responsible for all the evils of Communism, thus Ukrainians who dislike and distrust Russians are being "petty" and deluded.

This is contradicted by Strom's own claim that during
World War II "Stalin ditched much of the Communist party
line and embraced Russian nationalism" in order to beat the
Axis and regain control over Ukraine. If there really was a
point that the USSR ceased being a recognizably Jewish regime
and became a Russian nationalist regime instead, then why is it
not reasonable for Ukrainians to resent specifically Russian
domination?

Moreover, Russian domination over Ukraine goes back to
the 18th century, and Ukrainians remember that it was the
Russians who created the Pale of Settlement, confirming and
expanding Jewish exploitation in Ukrainian lands.

Finally, Ukrainians have every reason to dislike and distrust
Russians for their actions today. It is Russians who seized control of Crimea (a real *coup*), sending in Russian troops operating as partisans (without uniforms), and legitimating it with a
farcical referendum which only offered two choices—Crimean
independence or being absorbed by Russia—and then probably
rigging the whole thing anyway, just to be sure. It is Russians
who have incited unrest in Eastern Ukraine, providing troops
and weapons to separatists (and lying about it all the while),
leading to the needless deaths of thousands.

As for Svoboda and Right Sector, they are not perfect, but in
terms of their ideological roots, principles, and goals, they are

Jew-wise racial nationalists. Yet Strom is willing to make excuses for what he assures us are Putin's merely strategic nods
to Jewish power and Russian petty nationalism, but he is unwilling to accord Svoboda and Right Sector similar courtesies.

It means nothing to Strom that Putin puts a beanie on and
prayerfully presses his hand to the Wailing Wall like every
other white leader. "We can trust Vlad," Strom whispers assur-
ingly, "because he's just lying to the Jews and the Russians."
But if the leader of Svoboda—an actual member of the interim
government—meets with John McCain, or if the leader of Right
Sector engages in some wink-wink, nudge-nudge to calm the
local Jews, Strom intuits treason in their hearts.

Why the double standard? Why the indulgence for Putin
and jaundice toward Ukrainian White Nationalists?

Even as Russia claims to be fighting against anti-Semitism in
Ukraine, pro-Russian propagandists seem anxious to sway foreign anti-Semites to their side by making a great deal of the
Jews involved in the Ukrainian interim government, the subse-
quently elected government, and the outside parties that have
tried to shape the Ukrainian Revolution.

For instance, Volodymyr Groysman is a deputy prime minister, and Ihor Kolomoisky is governor of the Dnipropetrovsk
region. Both of them are Jews. Unfortunately, there is a great
deal of casual dishonesty among anti-Semites, which leads to
many false accusations. For instance, Prime Minister Arseniy
Yatsenyuk, President Petro Poroshenko, and Kiev Mayor Vitaly
Klitschko have all been called Jews, but no firm evidence has
been offered for these claims. (If Klitschko is a Jew, it is rather
odd he named one of his sons after Max Schmeling.) American
Jewish neocon Victoria Nuland—whom anti-Semites tiresome-
ly refer to by her family's original German name Nudelman, as
if it were somehow more "Jewish" than Nuland—was on the
scene and certainly up to no good during the Maidan protests.

But what does this all mean? The Maidan Revolution was
made by a wide coalition of groups, including Ukrainian White
Nationalists, and the subsequent governments have reflected
the different strands of this coalition. Yet pro-Russian/anti-
Ukraine propaganda treats the involvement of Jews as reveal-

ing the *essence* of the Ukrainian regime. They refer to the government as "Jewish," *tout court*, and shamelessly slander Ukrainian White Nationalists as Jewish puppets, stooges, and collaborators.

But the involvement of Jews in the Putin regime is treated as accidental and negligible. Strom assures us that they are mere "pets" with "no trace of real power." It is hard to judge such claims, of course, because Strom does not name names. Using English, French, and German sources, it is actually quite difficult to discover the ethnicity of many of Putin's ministers, which itself is suspicious. But two are explicitly identified as Jews even by Wikipedia: Igor Levitin (Transportation Minister, 2004–2012) and Mikhail Fradkov (Director of Foreign Intelligence from 2007 on). Director of Foreign Intelligence is certainly not a position with "no trace of real power." You can be assured if Ukraine had a Jewish Director of Foreign Intelligence or Transportation Minister, we would never hear the end of it.

Again, why the double standard? If there are Jews on both sides of the Russia-Ukraine conflict, why does the presence of Jews in the Ukrainian government prove that it is "Jewish" while the presence of Jews in the Russian government apparently means nothing at all (lest it undermine the false narrative that Russia is "Jew-wise" and working to counter international Jewry)?

The fact-fudging rush to brand the Ukrainian government "Jewish" aims to obscure the true nature of the Ukrainian situation, namely, that Ukraine has a parliamentary system with a number of different parties, in which common aims and enemies can lead to unlikely coalitions. Most importantly, it seeks to obscure the fact that the Ukrainian Revolution is by no means over. The situation in Ukraine is fluid and developing. It is too soon to say that Ukraine will be sucked into NATO and the EU, that it will lose its independence to the West, that it will be flooded with non-white immigrants and asylum seekers, etc. Certainly not if Ukrainian nationalists have anything to say about it.

Unfortunately, ongoing Russian intervention has pushed Ukraine closer to the West, caused the various parties to set

aside their differences to pose a united front, and disproportionately absorbed the energies of the nationalists. But when
the insurgency in the East is over, then the nationalist struggle
for an independent Ukrainian third way will resume. In the
meantime, it is simply intellectually dishonest to pretend that
one already knows the outcome.

But let's grant, for the sake of argument, that in the end, the
nationalists will lose and Ukraine will become absorbed by the
West. Is it really the position of Strom and other Russia apologists that Svoboda and Right Sector *should have never even tried*?
The Putin apologists claim that it is futile for Ukraine to ever
seek national self-determination, that Ukraine is doomed either
to be a Russian satellite or an American one. My question is: Do
they think that nationalism is futile in *all* cases? Is it futile in
France? Is it futile in Germany? In Denmark? In Sweden? Do
they think that it is futile for Americans to try to build an alternative to the Democrat vs. Republican hegemony?

What kind of White Nationalists believe that White Nationalism is
futile everywhere it is tried? Such people obviously are in no position to lead, so they should step down. Or, since they presumably believe that *Russian* nationalism, at least, is not futile, perhaps they should simply become full-time apologists for Russia. Unfortunately, some websites are already drifting in that
direction.

Or do these White Nationalists believe that our cause is futile *only* in Ukraine? If so, why? The answer is obvious: because
they are engaged in special-pleading for Russia. (Presumably
they would say the same thing about Belarus, too, should that
nation grow restive in Moscow's shadow.)

So both options really reduce to the same shameful toadying
for Russian petty imperialism under the delusional conviction
that it is really a battle for all whites against America and international Jewry.

This delusion is the "big picture" that Strom thinks the
Ukrainian nationalists have missed and that the whole world
should see:

The big picture of Jewish power ranged against the freedom and self-determination of all peoples—and against the very survival of our race itself. That's the reality of what's happening in Ukraine—that's the reality of what's happening all around the world today, from Cleveland to Gaza to Stockholm to Vladivostok: the Jewish war against our freedom, against our future, and against our very existence. And showing our people that reality is our highest duty.

I agree fully with Strom's general point that Jewish power is arrayed against the freedom and self-determination of all peoples, and this is the chief impediment to white survival. But that is not the battle in Ukraine today. Russia is not fighting against international Jewry. Putin is engaged in petty imperialist aggression against a former vassal state that wishes to assert its legitimate rights to freedom and self-determination.

Being an independent nation means being able to make decisions your neighbors dislike. Respecting the independence of other nations is easy when they only make decisions that please you. The hard part is accepting decisions that displease you. And Russia consistently fails this test with the former Soviet Republics and Warsaw Pact nations. Even though around a quarter century has passed since communism in Europe began its implosion, the Russians have not mentally adjusted to the fact that they cannot boss their neighbors around.

Even more alarmingly, the Russians continue to identify themselves with the Soviet Union—even the regime of Stalin, one of the evilest men in human history—and this identification has been growing stronger, not weaker, with time. For instance, Russia angrily protests—and local Russians have actually rioted—whenever its former imperial subjects move, destroy, or deface Soviet-era monuments to the Red Army that brought slavery, torture, deportations, and death to their countrymen—or when they try to honor their countrymen who joined the Axis crusade against communism. Thus it is somewhat beside the point to blame Jews for the crimes of communism when today's Russians are happy to claim them. In truth, all the efforts of George Soros and the US government pale by comparison to Russia's ongoing NATO recruitment drive.

Thus I completely sympathize with the desire of Russia's neighbors to enter NATO. They would be fools not to. Every nation must worry about securing its basic sovereignty before it can turn its attention to remoter dangers and larger civilizational issues, and Russia's former dominions are right to see her as the primary threat.

If Russia did not want NATO extended to her borders, she should have been a better neighbor. But it is never too late to start.

Moreover, NATO expansion is not a threat to Russia's sovereignty and legitimate interests. It is arrant nonsense for Strom to claim—and here he is just following standard Russian propaganda—that the purpose of the "coup" in Ukraine is "to encircle and conquer Russia." Russia has the second largest nuclear arsenal on the planet, which is enough to deter any conquest. The claim that Russia is in danger of conquest is no more credible than the Jewish claim that "another holocaust" is around the corner if Jews do not get their way—as if Israel's mountain of nuclear, biological, and chemical weapons were not a sufficient deterrent either.

It would be wonderful if a powerful nation like Russia really were fighting international Jewry and its minions in the name of the self-determination of all peoples. But that is not the case. Strom's account of the Ukraine-Russia crisis is a tissue of delusions and distortions. But I do not wish to pick on Kevin Strom, who is merely expressing views that are widely held in the White Nationalist community due to intense Russian propaganda efforts. (We should be flattered, I guess, that they think us worthy of deceiving.) I have chosen to respond to Strom in particular simply because of the virtues of his argument: as always, he states his views clearly and compellingly. But in this case, he fails to convince.

Counter-Currents/ *North American New Right*
September 2, 2014

"NORTH AMERICANISM":
A CAUTIONARY TALE*

Imagine that in 2025, the United States as we know it disappeared. Internal corruption and imperial overreach made the regime incapable of dealing with a number of crises: spiraling government growth; continued economic stagnation; droughts, floods, and earthquakes; racial conflict exacerbated by massive non-white immigration, blatant anti-white discrimination, and desperate economic scarcity; and, of course, the ruinous costs of a new series of wars and interventions in the neighborhood of Israel.

The federal paychecks and handouts stopped. Blacks and browns ran amok, and the federal government could do nothing to stop them. By default, sovereign functions devolved to states, counties, cities, even warlords—anyone who could provide law and order. The official secessions began at the periphery: Alaska and Hawaii went first. But eventually the United States was reduced to the thirteen states: New England, plus New York, New Jersey, Pennsylvania, Ohio, Maryland, West Virginia, and Delaware. The capital was moved to New York City.

Among the newly freed states, many of those with overwhelming white majorities reorganized themselves as white ethnostates, adopting humane and pragmatic policies of separating from non-whites and resettling them outside their borders. Some of these states—Washington, Oregon, Idaho, Montana, and Wyoming—joined into a Northwest Republic. In the South, the Confederacy was reborn and began resettling blacks in New England, where they were still well-loved. Most of the Midwestern states remained independent republics. A Mormon theocracy popped up in Utah, and God decided that Mormons were to be a white people after all. Those portions of

---

* A satire of Alexander Dugin's *The Fourth Political Theory* (London: Arktos, 2012) and related writings.

California, Texas, and the other Southwestern states with large Mexican populations dissolved into chaos, but white control was slowly reestablished through bitter ethnic warfare against savage gangs and drug cartels.

By 2035, the free states were mostly at peace, and the rump of the United States had survived its crisis and reached an equilibrium of sorts through the emergence of a political strongman who managed to clamp down on ethnic and ideological conflict and lash his sullen subjects—the vast majority of them non-white—into rowing in unison again.

As for the rest of the world: the collapse of American power was a blessing overall. The disappearance of NATO and the European Union led to the resurgence of nationalism across Europe. Jews and European Leftists tried to resist this by stoking petty nationalistic resentments between Europeans and by organizing non-white insurrections under the banner of Islam. Although there was a great deal of bloodshed and destruction, ultimately the violence worked in Europe's favor, since it unified Europeans behind a swift and decisive program of ethnic cleansing of both Jews and Muslims. Europe was no longer unified, but it was entirely European.

In the Near East, Israel made an abrupt about face in its foreign policy. Without the United States to subsidize its economy and fight its wars, Israel was forced to launch a "Good Neighbor Policy." The globe laughed. Then, one by one, countries started making "such deals."

In the Far East, China emerged as the world's only superpower. Consequently, the Japanese re-armed overnight, complete with a nuclear deterrent, and the Koreas reunified with a South Korean economy under a North Korean nuclear umbrella.

At New York University, a professor with ties to the US government and intelligence apparatus, began dreaming of how to restore the glory of the empire. His strategy was quite clever.

First, because his goal was to restore something old and terrible, he had to sell it as something entirely new and wonderful, a completely new paradigm of political theory. Since it was anything but new, it had to define its newness in non-essential terms. To protect itself from criticism, it had to present and fuzzy and moving target, cloaking itself in obscure jargon and constantly redefining itself in the face of resistance.

Second, because the politics of identity now ruled the world, and the people of the former US states thought and spoke entirely in identitarian terms, he had to cast the restoration of the American Empire as a new form of identity politics. Since America had split apart on racial grounds, it could not be unified in terms of racial identity. Besides, his goal was not racial integrity but power, and power required that he unify people of different races into a single large machine. For power politics, the natural units are not nations or races, but continental blocs. Hence the ideology of "North Americanism" was born.

Third, because the intended targets of resurgent American imperialism were naturally skeptical of North Americanism, they had to be given something bigger to fear: the world's sole superpower, China. Thus North Americanism presented itself not as another form of imperialism, but instead as an anti-imperialist movement, in solidarity with other anti-imperialist and anti-colonialist movements around the world, all of them unified by their fear of China.

How can the small countries of North America resist Chinese imperialism? Why, through unifying themselves with the rump of the United States. Not, of course, in a reborn American Empire. But merely in a defensive North American Confederation. But the North Americanists tip their hand when their proposed Federation starts looking exactly like the old United States, and their geopolitical outlook clones American ambitions down to the smallest warm water port. Would members of this new Confederation be allowed to secede? Because it started to sound like an "unbreakable union." You can check out any time you like, but you can never leave.

Fourth, since the reborn American Empire requires not just the unification of different racial groups, but also the unification of different religious groups—including large numbers of Muslims whose religion requires the establishment of a Muslim theocracy—the North Americanist ideology also embraces elements of Traditionalism. Traditionalism teaches that all religions are ultimately founded on the same esoteric truths, regardless of their exoteric differences. But if religions differ only on exoteric and thus less important matters, this offers the prospect of religious tolerance, particularly a politically neutered Islam, which would serve the larger interests of power politics. The aim is to install Traditionalists at the top of all religious organizations, then have them implement the policies of their Unknown Superiors. Talk of Traditionalism also serves a dual purpose, since it appeals to many New Right identitarians who find the Traditionalist critique of modernity compelling.

What would New Rightists and identitarians around the globe make of the ideology of "North Americanism"? On the one hand, they would find its rhetoric and stated goals very appealing. They would approve of its critique of modernity and liberalism, its identitarian language, its critique of globalization and colonialism, its warnings about the dangers of a unipolar world under Chinese hegemony, its engagement with Traditionalism, its frequent references to such writers as Nietzsche, Heidegger, Schmitt, Benoist, Faye, etc. It is *designed* to be appealing in precisely this manner.

But ultimately New Rightists would reject "North Americanism" on ethnonationalist grounds. We regard racial and ethnic identities as more fundamental than any others, including religious and regional ones. Our goal is to preserve our race and our distinct ethnic identities by creating racially and ethnically homogeneous homelands.

We are not interested in joining with other races into empires which serve the interests of small elites at the price of the destruction of distinct peoples. We do not wish to rule over other peoples or to be ruled by them. We regard colonialism and imperialism as bad deals for all involved: first, for the conquered, but then for the conquerors as well, who also lose their identities in the end.

We regard Traditionalism as a way of understanding how different paths might lead to the same truth. We do not think of it as a mechanism whereby religions can be neutralized and controlled from the top by political elites.

New Rightists would eventually see North Americanism as a manufactured ideology. Its intellectual murkiness and inconsistencies would suddenly become intelligible when it is seen as merely a tool to promote a new version of the race-denying, race-destroying imperial power politics that we so rightly reject.

Counter-Currents/*North American New Right*
November 8, 2013

THE MUSLIM PROBLEM

In the United States, many white Americans who fear being ethnically swamped by non-white immigrants are not willing to actually say so, for fear of being called racist. So instead they object to *illegal* immigration.

But fixing illegal immigration does not fix the real problem, for illegal immigrants can simply be legalized by the government, and even if all immigration were halted, whites would still be demographically displaced by the fast-breeding non-whites who are already among us.

The lesson here is: You can't solve a problem if you won't accurately name it.

But, on the other hand, if illegal immigration is the first thing to wake up white Americans to our demographic crisis, we should welcome that fact, then try to explain the full nature of the problem and what must actually be done to fix it.

In Europe too, many whites are worried about demographic displacement by non-white immigrants. But instead of objecting to non-whites as such, they prefer to complain about *Islamization*. But this contains traps as well:

❖ Are non-whites OK if they are not Muslim? In that case, there are billions of other non-whites to choose from: Christians, Hindus, Buddhists, etc.

❖ Isn't the problem Islamic "extremism" or "fundamentalism," rather than people who are merely nominally Muslim? If so, then the solution is to secularize the extremists who are here and be more selective about future immigrants, so we only get nominal, secular Muslims. In fact, there are plenty of secular-minded nominal Muslims, the Kemalist movement in Turkey and the Baathist movement in the Arab countries being the best examples.

❖ Attacking Islam invites a host of distracting distinctions and quibbles. What about the Sunni vs. Shia? What about the Sufis? What about Bosnians and Albanians? Are they not European? Are Maronites and Armenians and Georgians European because they are Christian? None of these issues matter if we properly identify the problem as demographic displacement by non-Europeans.

❖ Attacking Islam does not sit well with European secularists, who fought long and hard for religious tolerance. They think that Islam can be made tolerant as well. It took hundreds of years, of course, and many wars, but Europe managed to de-fang Christianity. Today, most whites are nominally Christian and *de facto* liberals, which is the true civil religion of the West. So it is completely conceivable that Islam can be de-fanged as well. Of course, it would be salutary to review the history of the Enlightenment in Europe, as some might blanch at the prospect of turning Europe into a battle-ground for three centuries or so just to "enrich" ourselves with nominal Muslims.

❖ Attacking Islam allows Christians to frame European identity politics as a clash between two universalist religions, Christianity and Islam. But we are not fighting for Christendom, which is now more non-white than white. We are fighting for the white race, regardless of religion.

❖ Attacking Islam plays into the hands of the principal enemy, the organized Jewish community, which is happy to reroute white anti-Muslim sentiment into fighting Israel's enemies abroad, rather than fighting Islam in the streets of Europe. Indeed, when Israel destroys strong Muslim regimes in its neighborhood, this sends new waves of Muslim refugees to destroy white countries, killing two birds with one stone (a stone that we ourselves provide).

Again, we can't effectively fight enemies and fix problems if we do not accurately name them.

On the other hand, if Islamic barbarism, intolerance, violence, and frank declarations that they intend to assimilate us actually *wake up* some of our people, we should be glad of that. But we should work to make sure that they see the *whole* problem and the *necessary* solution, not get sidetracked by half-truths and half-measures.

The problem is the destruction of the white race by non-whites, through demographic swamping, miscegenation, and outright genocide. The solution is White Nationalism: the creation of ethnically homogeneous white homelands through moving borders (partition, secession) and/or moving populations.

In every political struggle, as in every war, we must decide who is "us" and who is "them," the enemy. We are whites—not Christians, not conservatives, not Westerners, etc., although those categories somewhat overlap with the white race—and our enemies are those promoting our racial destruction, namely non-whites and traitorous whites.

But the hard core of the coalition that opposes us is the organized Jewish community. That makes Jews the *principal* enemy, because we cannot set our house in order without defeating them. The role of Jews in creating the present crisis is an interesting but largely academic question, because political change is ultimately about the future, not the past. And there is no question that organized Jewry *today* is opposed to every policy necessary to save our race, and they are the organizational and financial linchpin of the entire anti-white coalition. And since Jews have a record of subverting movements that oppose them, we cannot risk trusting even those Jews who express sympathy for our cause, because that is exactly what Jewish subversives would say.

That said, it is a mistake to dismiss the Muslim problem as simply an expression of the Jewish problem, or as a distraction from the race problem, because *Islam is an independent variable*. If we solved the Jewish problem, and if we solved the race problem, there would still be a Muslim problem. Islam has been at war with the rest of humanity since the days of the prophet. It has brought war, death, slavery, and racial and cultural annihilation to millions. This is not, moreover, a departure from "true" Islam but an expression of it. The establishment of Islamic rule would mean the death of white civilization and the white race.

Islam was a threat to whites before today's Jewish hegemony, and it will be a threat when Jewish hegemony is ended. Islam is not just a problem because it is practiced by non-whites. Islam makes non-whites far more militant and destructive of white civilization. As one commentator pointed out, this may be providential, because without Islam, it would be possible for many Europeans to believe that a multiracial, multicultural society might actually work.

Making an issue of Islam also reveals intellectual confusions and smokes out false friends in our ranks:

- ❖ One-track anti-Semites bristle when Islam is attacked, because they fear it inevitably "plays into the Jews' hands." But it is not an either/or: both Jews and Muslims are problems, and they are problems on their own as well as in concert with one another.
- ❖ Those who put anti-Semitism over race reject criticism of Islam because they hope for an alliance.
- ❖ People who put "tradition" (large or small "t") before race sympathize with Islam and bristle when it is attacked.
- ❖ People who put patriarchy (and, let's be frank, misogyny) before race sympathize with Islam.
- ❖ People who put machismo, bellicosity, and barbarism before race sympathize with Islam.

What, then, should be the White Nationalist solution to the Muslim problem?

- ❖ If non-whites, including Jews, leave white homelands for their own, Islam would become predominantly a question of foreign policy toward the Muslim world, the *ummah*, including its European outposts Bosnia and Albania.
- ❖ Whites would be completely free to convert to Islam. But since Islam is a political religion, and thus a threat to white political orders, such converts would be sent to the *ummah* destination of their choice.
- ❖ White countries would maintain cordial relations with the Muslim world, but our own security dictates that we prefer secular, nationalist Muslim regimes.
- ❖ Wherever our racial interests dictate, we would side with peoples who are resisting Muslim expansion.

❖ The Jewish homeland of Israel would exist alongside a Palestinian homeland, in the sights of a thousand nuclear missiles, so the Jews behave themselves.

In sum, white policy toward the Muslim world would no longer be dictated by Jews, but by our identity and interests. This would eliminate the causes of virtually every current war and intervention in the Muslim world. And that's it. It would be a world we can all live with.

But we are not going to get there from here unless we attain some intellectual clarity about fundamental values and distinctions. That is the purpose of metapolitics. It is particularly important to White Nationalists, since in the present world, our only ally is the truth, and our greatest asset is honesty and credibility.

Unfortunately, politics makes liars of us all. Two cases in point are Marine Le Pen's and Guillaume Faye's reactions to the *Charlie Hebdo* massacre in Paris.

On January 18, 2015, an editorial by Marine Le Pen, "To Call this Threat by Its Name," appeared on the Op-Ed page of the *New York Times*.[1] What her appearance in the *Times* means in terms of world Jewish opinion and strategy is a topic for another time. I wish to focus here on what she said.

Miss Le Pen begins with a quote attributed to Albert Camus: "To misname things is to add to the world's unhappiness." Then she proceeds to misname the problem in terms essentially identical to the line George W. Bush took after 9/11:

> Let us call things by their rightful names, since the French government seems reluctant to do so. France, land of human rights and freedoms, was attacked on its own soil by a totalitarian ideology: Islamic fundamentalism. It is only by refusing to be in denial, by looking the enemy in the eye, that one can avoid conflating issues. Muslims themselves need to hear this message. They need the dis-

---

[1] http://www.nytimes.com/2015/01/19/opinion/marine-le-pen-france-was-attacked-by-islamic-fundamentalism.html?_r=0

tinction between Islamist terrorism and their faith to be
made clearly.

Yet this distinction can only be made if one is willing to
identify the threat. It does our Muslim compatriots no favors to fuel suspicions and leave things unspoken. Islamist
terrorism is a cancer on Islam, and Muslims themselves
must fight it at our side.

What France needs is to become French again. That means
the departure of millions of non-French, most of them non-
whites, most but not all of them Muslim, most but not all of
them non-fundamentalists. Thus, by claiming that the problem
is simply Muslim fundamentalism, the vast majority of the problem is left out of the picture. Furthermore, Le Pen does not
breathe a word about sending even fundamentalist Muslims
back to the *ummah*, although she makes a quite radical proposal
of stripping jihadists of French citizenship, the natural sequel of
which would be expulsion.

Miss Le Pen basically spoke the maximum amount of truth fit
to print in the *New York Times*. Because, with the Right, the more
truthful one's discourse, the smaller the audience Jews allow
you to reach. But even this mealy-mouthed mush is radical
compared to what the French establishment will admit. So Le
Pen's editorial still represents a step forward, the start of a wider
conversation about Islam and France, an opportunity that we
should plunge into and try to lead in our direction.

Guillaume Faye has criticized Miss Le Pen's moderation and
economy with the truth.[2] But Faye too is a politician of sorts and
thus dishonest in his own way. His strategy is to focus on Islam
and avoid the Jewish problem. I am sure he thinks that he can
gain a bigger audience this way. I am sure he thinks that Islamic
immigration is a more pressing problem. I am sure he thinks
that it would be advantageous to posture as an anti-anti-Semite
in the hope of splitting the Jewish bloc and thus reducing their
opposition to French nationalism.

---

[2] https://www.gfaye.com/islam-immigration-integration-marine-
et-valls-meme-utopie/

Not only do I understand his position, but I can even condone it *in a qualified sense*, namely that I think that *some* of our
people should stake out this position and cultivate it intensively,
because it brings some people from the mainstream closer to the
truth. And as long as people like Kevin MacDonald exist, some
of those people can be brought the rest of the way to the truth.

But to bring them the rest of the way, we have to keep up a
steady pressure. That entails taking the Fayes of the world to
task for their omissions. And frankly, in the final section of his
essay, "Jihadist Carnage in Paris," it seems like Faye is setting
himself up for just such a critique.[3]

Because if he is going to use the heading "Designating the
Enemy is the Central Problem," and if he is willing to pull back
from contemporary events to speak of an ancient war, going
back to the 7th century, between Islam and the rest of the world,
that fairly cries out for correction.

For if we are going to name the principal enemy of whites, in
the dual sense of (1) who has done more to cause our present
demographic and cultural decline and, more importantly, (2)
who is the hard core of the opposition to fixing our problems,
the answer has to be the organized Jewish community. And Jewish enmity against the rest of humanity is far older than Islam,
which is only an offshoot of the Abrahamic religious tradition.

Faye pooh-poohs the idea of "good" and "moderate" Muslims because he wants the whole community gone. But in fact he
does recognize that there are such Muslims who are our objective allies against Islamic fundamentalism. He even alludes to
three of them: Bashar al-Assad, Muammar Qaddafi, and Saddam Hussein, all of them nominal Muslims who were committed to secular law and a good deal of religious tolerance. I want
these sorts of Muslims to flourish, but outside of European
lands, with all the rest of their co-religionists.

Faye, however, wants us to believe that there are good and
bad Jews. And he has never uttered a peep about sending either
group away. My attitude toward Jews is exactly analogous to his

---

[3] http://www.counter-currents.com/2015/01/jihadist-carnage-in-
paris-part-2/

views about Muslims: there are good and bad Jews, but such distinctions should not distract us from the overriding necessity of freeing European lands from Jewish power, and that means separating ourselves from the whole community. I want good and moderate Jews to flourish, but in Israel, with the rest of their people.

Faye won't say it, because he is engaged in political maneuvering rather than truth-telling. That's why I cleave to metapolitics: I want to speak the whole truth as I see it. And, in the longest World War of all—between the seed of Abraham and the rest of humanity—telling the truth is also the only practical thing to do, since, as Faye says, we must name the enemy. We cannot fight an enemy we cannot name.

Faye clearly does not want to be the enemy of the Jews. But what Faye wants does not matter, as his quote from Julien Freund implies: "Even if you do not choose the enemy, the enemy chooses you. . . . As long as he wants you to be the enemy, you are. And it will prevent you from tending your own garden."

It takes two to make friends, only one to make enemies. And the Jewish community has marked Faye as the enemy, along with all the rest of us. Whites are slated for extermination by the kinds of genocidal policies that Jews refuse to accept in their own country while imposing them on ours. Since Jews are more aware of what promotes genocide than any other people, it is folly to think that they are unaware or ashamed of this double standard. They consciously intend to destroy us as a race, and all non-white immigrants, not just the most militant and obnoxious among them, are just Jewish biological weapons of mass destruction.

Until we treat the Jews as enemies in turn, and defeat them, we are never going to be left alone to cultivate our garden.

Counter-Currents/*North American New Right*
January 27, 2015

INNOCENCE OF MUSLIMS, GUILT OF JEWS, INTERESTS OF WHITES

Beginning on September 11, 2012, US embassies and other facilities in the Muslim world have been targeted by angry mobs protesting American policy and influence. Protests have also cropped up in countries with large Muslim minorities, including India and such white nations as Australia, the UK, Germany, Denmark, Belgium, and France.

As of this writing, 79 people have lost their lives (including the US Ambassador to Libya, J. Christopher Stevens), more than 600 have been injured, and the costs of property damage and policing are running into untold millions of dollars. The violence continues, and the world is still debating the causes.

The emerging liberal consensus is basically this:

* ❖ The film *Innocence of Muslims* was a vile provocation but protected by freedom of speech.
* ❖ The Muslim world could stand to use some more freedom, democracy, and tolerance. To Muslim ears, this kind of talk should sound like an air raid siren.
* ❖ But the protests and violence were not spontaneous expressions of fanaticism and intolerance by mainstream adherents of the "Religion of Peace" (lest we fear the Muslims who are flooding into white countries and breeding like rodents).
* ❖ Instead, the protests and violence were orchestrated by small groups of extremists, including Al-Qaeda.

Among White Nationalists and others in the Rightist milieu, the debate is whether to blame the Muslims for being intolerant fanatics or the counter-jihadist Jewish neoconservatives who apparently created *Innocence of Muslims* and used it to provoke the mobs.

If we take a step back from these arguments, it seems clear to me that whatever side one chooses in debating the question "Do we blame the Muslims or the Jews?," whites really can't lose, because in the end, we want to free ourselves of *both* groups.

And that's my purpose here: to look at this question from the point of view of white interests. I want to argue that, in terms of white interests, the current violence and polarization between Muslims and the West is not a bad thing. It is in the interest of our race that:

- ❖ Muslim immigration into white lands be stopped and reversed
- ❖ Turkey and other Muslim nations be kept out of the European Union
- ❖ All other attempts at economic and political union between European and Muslim nations around the globe be thwarted.

And mobs of angry, violent, alien-looking Muslims attacking American and European embassies, consulates, and other installations can only work in the long term interests of whites. Yes, I deplore the loss of white lives and property at the hands of Muslim mobs. But we need to balance this against the greater good of our race, namely to prevent white homelands from being swamped and destroyed by Muslim immigration and the religious and cultural imperialism that comes with it.

Thus, besides dethroning Ed Wood as the supreme schlock-*auteur*, the creators of *Innocence of Muslims* might just contribute to the salvation of the white race. Frankly, I hope that 100 more pranks like it are in the works. With additional judiciously applied provocations, the Muslim street could awaken Europeans to the danger of Muslim colonization and bring globalization to an end.

If I had discovered that a White Nationalist had been behind *Innocence of Muslims*, I would, frankly, be pleased. So why go on the attack when it appears that the Jewish-led counter-jihad movement is behind the film?

The answer is simple: Jews are our enemies too. Thus I am not going to pass up an opportunity to comment on Jewish perfidy. Beyond that, I am sick of Jews being at the wheel and whites merely being along for the ride, even when, from time to time, our interests coincide. Whites need to wrest control of our nations from Jewish interlopers and begin pursuing our own interests and destiny, leaving Jews and Muslims to their own devices.

Whites have had our destinies controlled by non-whites for so long that we find it difficult to even *think* in terms of our own interests anymore. So in this debate, some of us end up being more pro-Muslim and anti-Jewish than pro-white. Others tend to be more anti-Muslim and pro-Jewish (or at least anti-anti-Jewish) than pro-white.

But we don't have to pick *either* Jews *or* Muslims. It is not an either/or. We don't have to take sides in their fights. We need to take our own side and recognize that white interests differ from those of both groups.

PRO-MUSLIM/ANTI-JEWISH BUT NOT PRO-WHITE

In an ideal world, we would not have any quarrels with Muslims. They would have their part of the world, and we would have ours. That is certainly the kind of world I want to live in, for the New Right promotes the idea of ethnostates for everyone as the path to global peace and good will.

In such a world, the Jews behind *Innocence of Muslims* would be simply and unambiguously evil, because they are stirring up trouble where no trouble need exist in order to use white-Muslim enmity to advance the interests of Israel.

In the real world, however, there are 60 million Muslims in white countries, reproducing at more than four times the rate of whites. So there is a real clash of civilizations already underway, regardless of the machinations of the counter-jihadists.

Of course Jews wish promote tensions between Muslims and whites to exploit them for their own interests, using Muslims to dilute and destroy white nations while using whites to destroy hostile Muslim regimes.

But whites can also promote and exploit the same tensions for our own interests. There is no reason to think that Jews will always be able turn such tensions to their advantage—unless whites simply refuse to even *try* to promote our interests.

Tender-hearted whites cannot help but sympathize with Muslims who are oppressed and vilified by Jews. I sympathize with Palestinians, because I too live under Zionist occupation. Many whites work against Zionism and for Palestinian rights but ignore the fact that our own homelands are increasingly under occupation by Palestinians and other Muslims, who are hostile to our culture and threaten to swamp us demographically.

There is something absurd about whites, who are losing their own homelands to Muslims, working earnestly to ensure a homeland for the Palestinians. Of course this does not mean that the Palestinian cause is any less just. Indeed, if the Palestinian cause is just, then the cause of European nationalists is also just. And since it is *our own* cause, shouldn't whites give it priority over the Palestinian cause?

Whites with a strongly anti-Semitic cast of mind are drawn to the Palestinian cause because it is a politically correct disguise for their anti-Semitism. Many whites get so caught up in this mentality that they actually would applaud the destruction of the state of Israel, regardless of the fact that presumably most Israeli Jews would end up in white countries. From a pro-white viewpoint, however, that would be a disaster. Thus one could fairly accuse such anti-Zionist whites as hating Jews more than they love their own people.

From a White Nationalist point of view,[1] if Israel did not exist, it would have to be invented so that we could send our Jews there, for whites will never regain control over our own destinies without breaking the power of the Jewish diaspora and sending them slouching toward Bethlehem, to borrow a phrase.

I am convinced that some of the Right-wing rage over *Innocence* is simply the inability to abide the sight of Jews winning at anything, even when it might accidentally serve white interests as well. But, again, this is an instance of hating Jews more than one loves one's own people.

Whites with a reactionary, anti-liberal, anti-modern cast of mind naturally admire Muslims. They admire their patriarchal

---

[1] See my "White Nationalism and Jewish Nationalism" in *New Right vs. Old Right*.

families and high birthrates, their intense religious piety (and concomitant intolerance for blasphemy, relativism, subjectivism, and liberal mush), and their willingness to kill and die over ideals. By comparison, the liberal West is devitalized, decadent, and degenerate.

This admiration is particularly strong among Traditionalists, many of whom followed the example of René Guénon in converting to Islam. Guénon, however, converted to Islam because he ended up living in Cairo; when in France, he was a Catholic; if he had ended up in India, as he had intended, he would have been a practicing Hindu. But he remained a Traditionalist regardless of the external faith to which he adhered. Guénon's decision to follow the dominant religion of whatever land he inhabited was, in short, a deeply socially conservative gesture, whereas the decisions of his European followers to convert to Islam *within European societies* has turned Traditionalism into a vector of subversion.

As gallant as it is to admire one's enemies, however, we cannot lose sight of the fact that Muslims are our enemies. In the abstract we may admire their willingness to kill and die for their religion. But we should not forget the concrete fact that they are willing *to kill us to impose their religion.* Furthermore, their religion can only be implemented through the destruction of our civilization. Finally, given the racial panmixia of the Muslim world, Islam would be even more destructive of the integrity of our race than Christianity and liberalism. Muslim societies may resemble healthy white societies of the past and future, but our race will never be able to regenerate itself unless we first preserve it, and Islam is one of the major opponents of white self-preservation.

Politically realistic whites with a low tolerance for liberal cant are appalled by the idea of a private cabal loyal to a foreign regime scheming to force the hand of American foreign policy while hiding behind the First Amendment. Religious dissent is protected, but treason is not. A serious country would simply arrest and try the people behind *Innocence of Muslims* for treason. That would go a long way to dispelling the anger in the Muslim world and would do far more to repair relations than pious rot about tolerance. (Of course when you start arresting Jews for treason, it is hard to know where to stop.)

But let's face it: America hasn't been a serious country for a very long time. We are led by a rotating elite of selfish plutocrats (Republicans) and pathological altruists (Democrats), none of whom are concerned with the common good of the nation. With leaders like that, it was child's play for their senior partners, the organized Jewish community, to subordinate our nation to theirs.

In such a context, the piecemeal application of the conservative instinct to preserve "the system" merely perpetuates the power of our enemies. Political realism, in this context, is the purest form of idealism, since it is detached from the principal truth about the system: *it is no longer our system.*

It is time to stop promoting policies as if this were still our country. It is not. It is *their* country now, and we need to divest ourselves of it emotionally and in every other way. We need to stand aside and let them run it into the ground, not propose sensible policies as if this were still our country and we still had a stake in its long-term survival.

If this were still our country, kicking the Muslim hornet's nest would be a bad thing. If this were still our country, war with Afghanistan and Iraq would be a bad thing. If this were still our country, overthrowing Gaddafi and Mubarak and Assad would be a bad thing. If this were still our country, going to war with Iran would be a bad thing. If this were still our country, America's confrontational stance toward Russia would be insanity.

But this is not our country. We are just along for the ride. And whites are more likely to gain control over our destiny in North America, Europe, and the rest of the world if America's present rulers run it into the ground. Yes, they will create untold suffering for millions of people. Yes, it could all be avoided if they would just listen to reason. (As if that were realistic!)

If you pride yourself on your realism, then let's be realistic. Once America's economy collapses due to imperial overreach, immigration, globalization, and the financial racket, Europe will have a fighting chance. Once America's corpse grows cold, the lice will abandon it for fresh blood, and whites in North America will have a chance to build something better. Sadly, since people only seem to learn by suffering, that is the best option for our people.[2]

In general, all these pro-Muslim/anti-Jewish lines of thought have a tendency to excessive idealism: they advance positions and policies formulated for a better world than the one we actually live in. My own thinking systematically inclines toward this error, so I constantly have to ask myself whether my reactions are based on the world as it actually is or the world as I would like it to be.

As we shall see, the anti-Muslim/pro-Jewish side tends toward the opposite extreme of an excessive pragmatism, fixating on the most immediate and easily grasped threat, namely Muslims, and failing to grasp the more fundamental Jewish threat to the point of actually countenancing alliances with Jews.

ANTI-MUSLIM/PRO-JEWISH BUT NOT PRO-WHITE

If I think that counter-jihadist provocations like *Innocence of Muslims* can serve white interests, does that mean that I would consider alliances with Jews, as such European Nationalists as Nick Griffin, Guillaume Faye, Geert Wilders, and others have done? Absolutely not, for the following reasons.

Jews are our enemies too. Moreover, Jews may be a less visible enemy than Muslims, but they are a more fundamental enemy. The Jewish role in opening white countries to non-white immigration is substantial, although of course it varies from country to country. What does not vary, however, is the fact that the organized Jewish community is *the primary opponent of any form of European nationalism*, including attempts to halt and reverse non-white immigration. There is no way out but through the Jews. Thus it is superficial to focus on Muslims and ignore Jews. It focuses on the symptoms, not the cause. It focuses on the symptoms, but ignores the primary impediments to actually curing the disease.

The very idea of a good faith alliance between White Nationalists and Jews is absurd on the face of it. First of all, nobody

---

[2] See my "'Worse is Better,'" in *New Right vs. Old Right*.

makes an alliance with the powerless, and White Nationalists have no political power. Second, Jews are the most powerful nation in the world. If they really wanted to change the immigration policies of European countries, it would happen virtually overnight. They would not need the assistance of marginal White Nationalist groups to do it, either. Instead, immigration reform would immediately become a mainstream issue endorsed by all parties.

If White Nationalists are pretty much politically powerless, then why do some Jews make overtures to White Nationalists? What is in it for them? I think that they have two aims here.

First, although White Nationalists have no political power, we do have one asset that the mainstream political parties lack: the truth about race and the Jewish question. Nationalists who form alliances with Jews, however, are compelled to cease speaking the truth about the Jewish question and instead work to obscure or excuse the Jewish role in white dispossession. This silence or collusion advances the Jewish agenda and impedes white liberation.

Second, the Jews have attained hegemony over white societies by infiltrating, subverting, and transforming the whole political spectrum into defenders of Jewish interests. Thus, in terms of vital Jewish interests, it really does not matter which party attains power. It is sheer folly to think that Jews will not seek to do the same thing to all forms of European and White Nationalism. Since there is no sure way to tell a sincere Jewish sympathizer or ally from a mere agent of subversion, we simply must exclude all Jews and go it alone.

Thus it simply does not matter if a Jewish counter-jihadist or would-be White Nationalist protests that he is genuinely concerned to promote white interests, because *that's what any infiltrator would say*. And we need not fear hurting the feelings of any sincere Jewish well-wishers. They will understand our mistrust and refusal to work with them, since they know their people better than any of us could.

WHAT LINE SHOULD WHITE NATIONALISTS TAKE REGARDING JEWS AND MUSLIMS?

Neither group has any place in our societies. Thus our aim is the most complete separation possible from Jews and Muslims.

However, we need to deal forthrightly with the sticky question of how these groups are defined. Islam is a religion, thus anybody who thinks of himself as a Muslim is a Muslim, including white converts. White Muslims, however, have to be seen as vectors of Islamization and thus excluded. By the same token, though, we should have no problem with genetically white Muslim apostates.

With Muslims, the essential issue here strikes me as one of consciousness, rather than ancestry. There are groups that we recognize as European that have some Near Eastern admixture. We should have no more problem, then, with non-Muslims with some Near Eastern Muslim ancestry as we have with any other whites with some Near Eastern ancestry.

The issue is different with Jews, because they are not a religion but a nation. This nation has an ethnic genetic core as well as a national consciousness that takes both religious and non-religious forms. This national consciousness has extended beyond the Jewish ethnic-genetic core to assimilate other groups into the Jewish collective. Thus genetic non-Jews can become functional Jews, e.g., by converting to Judaism or becoming Christian Zionists, Marxists, neocons, Straussians, Libertarians, Objectivists, etc.

But if non-Jews can become Jews, can Jews become non-Jews? Since Jewish identity is not merely a matter of religion, Jewish apostasy cannot be simply a matter of changing religions. Lawrence Auster, for instance, is a convert to Christianity, but his primary loyalty is still to the Jewish nation. One can, however, renounce one's nationality. Pamela Geller, for instance, could get splashed with some holy water and then solemnly swear that she has renounced her "citizenship" in the Jewish nation. But we'd be fools to believe her. So whites should never accept such Jewish apostates as "us," even if they might be genetically no more Near Eastern than your average Greek.

There is, however, a form of Jewish apostasy that whites should recognize: In the past, Jews have married out of the Jewish religion and national community and into the white race.

Thus there are whites today who have some Jewish ancestry but no Jewish ethnic or religious consciousness. Genetically, they may be no more Near Eastern than many Greeks or Italians. A white ethnostate might wish to know who these people are and keep an eye on them, but unless they choose to identify as otherwise, it seems reasonable to consider them whites, not Jews.

Recognizing that some whites might have some non-European ancestry is not, of course, an argument against rigorously preventing any more such hybridization. As a general rule, I think we should be less focused on the race that we have been and more focused on the race we wish to become. If it really bothers us, someday we will be in the position to edit out alien genetic code. But we will never reach that day unless we halt miscegenation in the here and now, the sooner the better.

It is possible that white nations might have amicable relations with Jewish and Muslim communities. It is possible for whites to feel sympathy for the suffering of Muslims and Jews (indeed, all too much). It is possible that Jewish and Muslim interests might overlap with white interests from time to time, in delimited ways. Such commonalities of interests can be the basis of limited, mutually beneficial political alliances.

But not today. Not in this world. There should be no talk of amicable relations, sympathy, or political alliances with Jews or Muslims *as long as they are occupying our nations, oppressing our people, and threatening our long-term biological and cultural survival.*

First, we must attain separation. Only then we can talk about good relations. If, however, out of excessive idealism or pragmatism we entangle ourselves with our enemies, we will never be able to separate ourselves. Thus White Nationalists should do everything in our power to encourage polarization between whites on the one hand and Muslims and Jews on the other.

Counter-Currents/*North American New Right*
October 1, 2012

THE "GAY MARRIAGE" CONTROVERSY

Both the promoters and opponents of homosexual marriage share a common false premise: that the legalization of homosexual marriage overthrows "heteronormativity," i.e., the idea that heterosexuality is normal and other forms of sexuality are not. But the idea that changing marriage laws can change heteronormativity is simply false.

What do I mean when I say that homosexual behavior is abnormal? I don't mean that it is unnatural, since it exists in nature. It is even found in many species besides man. I don't mean that it is a sin, i.e., something that displeases God. The idea of sin pretty much paralyzes the ability to think rationally about morals.

For me, the issue of abnormality all boils down to homosexuality being a non-reproductive, recreational form of sex. And if *everyone* had non-reproductive, recreational sex all the time, the human race would perish. Heterosexual behavior is normal, because only heterosexual sex can perpetuate our species, provided conception is not blocked by birth control.

So the real issue is not even homosexual versus heterosexual, but reproductive versus non-reproductive sex. That's all there is to it.

Homosexual behaviors and tastes are older than the human race, but the idea of homosexuality as an *identity* is a rather recent phenomenon. People with exclusively homosexual tastes are a tiny minority in any society, no matter how permissive and decadent. Thus it stands to reason that no society has ever ceased to exist because the tiny homosexual minority doesn't reproduce. Societies decline demographically when the heterosexual majority doesn't reproduce, primarily due to birth control. Thus if non-reproductive sex is a problem because it does not perpetuate the human race, the bulk of the blame falls on selfish, hedonistic straight people.

Proponents of marriage for homosexuals think that heteronormativity is simply a social construct, a convention that can be changed through legislation, education, and relentless media brainwashing. But heteronormativity is based in nature, not in convention. Sexual reproduction has existed before human beings formed languages and conventions. Indeed, sexual reproduction existed before mankind evolved. The birds and the bees do it too. So heteronormativity is not a social construct and cannot be changed by society. It can only be covered up, lied about, and ignored — at society's peril.

It is easy to understand why homosexual marriage proponents believe they are overturning heteronormativity. It is harder to understand why the opponents of homosexual marriage agree with them on this point. Yet the opponents of heterosexual marriage claim that legally defining marriage as the union of a man and a woman is the key to preserving the institutions of marriage and family life.

This makes no sense for two reasons.

First, if heteronormativity is based in nature or divine commandment, not in law, then it cannot be changed by changing laws. (Human laws can, of course, strengthen natural laws by adding additional punishments and incentives to follow nature.)

Second, the institutions of marriage and family life have been pretty much destroyed already. But during the whole period that marriage and family life have been decaying, homosexuals have not been allowed to marry, and marriage has been defined as a union of a man and a woman. In other words, marriage and family life have declined with their heteronormativity entirely intact. Therefore, heterosexuals bear the primary blame for the decline of marriage and the family.

Since homosexuals are a tiny minority, and only a tiny minority of that minority wish to marry in any case, I think that homosexual marriage opponents owe us an explanation as to how, exactly, such a small group of people could mess up marriage any more than straight people already have.

If one really wanted to defend marriage and strengthen the family, one should do the following.

1. End no-fault divorce

2. Criminalize adultery
3. Criminalize alienation of affections
4. End child support for unwed mothers
5. Establish a legal presumption that unwed mothers are unfit mothers, so that giving up illegitimate children for adoption is the norm
6. End adoption by unmarried individuals
7. Institute positive incentives for high-quality individuals to marry and have families
8. Institute tax incentives for people to marry/disincentives to stay single

These policies would significantly strengthen the bonds of marriage and family life. And the burdens and benefits of these measures would fall on the heterosexual population, where they belong.

But none of our pro-family politicians and moral crusaders shows any interest in such measures. And that, to me, is the sign that the whole anti-homosexual marriage campaign is just another phony Right-wing con job: (1) scapegoating homosexuals for the mess that heterosexuals have made of marriage and the family, (2) and channeling the discontent, energy, idealism, and money of a certain segment of the Right (albeit a pretty hopeless segment, from my point of view) into just another dead end, a battle that, even if it were won, would do *nothing* to halt the demographic decline of our race.

I used to think that these mainstream Right-wingers were merely stupid and/or deluded. A lot of the rank and file are. But they are generally far better than their leadership. The ones on top are so consistently wrong-headed and ineffectual that it is hard to resist the conclusion that they are agents of the enemy, working to misdirect and dissipate Right-wing dissent lest it give rise to a genuine populism that would threaten the hegemony of our ruling coalition of Jews and raceless, rootless plutocrats. I think that the purpose of their campaigns may be to run out the clock until whites are a minority and there is no hope of change within the present system.

The only political issue that matters is whether the white race will continue to exist on this planet in 200 years. White Americans are increasingly aware of, and alarmed by, our demographic decline. But frank appeals to white racial interests are still taboo on the American Right. Instead, the mainstream Right at best offers us race-neutral proxies for racial interests (opposition to "illegal" immigration, libertarian individualism, etc.) and at worst promotes distractions (opposing gay marriage and flag burning, or promoting school prayer) or outright demographic suicide (opposing abortion). Thus I think that White Nationalism will never move forward until the mainstream Right is thoroughly defeated and discredited. I just hope that, by that time, it is not too late to save our race.

I have argued that homosexual marriage is an unimportant issue from the point of view of white demographics. The most important thing to do to increase white fertility and improve white parenting is to strengthen marriage and decrease non-reproductive sex among heterosexuals. I have also argued that the gay marriage issue is being promoted by the phony Right as a distraction from far more important issues. But I am not going to deal with the merits of demerits of homosexual marriage as a policy, because I need to devote more reading and thought to the matter. I do, however, want to end this piece by at least raising the possibility of a society that combines "heteronormativity" with tolerance.

The only real way to maintain high standards is to recognize that people will fall short of them in some ways. That means a certain amount of latitude and tolerance.

A society that cannot tolerate deviation from its norms will inevitably lower its standards to make it easier for more people to comply.

And the end of that process is complete nihilism, for if integrity to one's values is the *highest value*, in the end, it will be one's *only value*. For the easiest way to insure perfect integrity and to make hypocrisy impossible is to value nothing but *being oneself at the present moment*, i.e., to collapse any difference between the real and the ideal, to affirm that whatever happens to be real at any given moment is the ideal.

In short, the only way to always practice what one preaches is to preach nothing but what one practices. And that boils down to doing whatever one feels like from moment to moment, a kind of groundless self-affirmation which is pretty much the moral and cultural dead end toward which liberalism is leading.

Even if one maintains heteronormativity as the social ideal, it is still possible to *like* people who fall wide of the mark. Particularly in a White Nationalist society, where our fellow citizens are also our own extended family.

Why can't we have a society in which parents of homosexual children say, "We're sorry that you are not going to give us grandchildren. It is a misfortune. But we still love you as our flesh and blood, and we know you will still be a good son to us, a good brother to your siblings, and a good uncle to your nieces and nephews"?

Why can't we have a society in which homosexuals accept that they fall short of the norm, rather than tearing down norms merely to feel good about themselves? Why can't we have a society in which homosexuals are grateful to the heterosexuals who gave them life and glad that others are carrying on their families and their race as a whole?

I believe that there are already quite a few people who think this way. But their voices are not being heard.

Counter-Currents/*North American New Right*
June 28, 2013

MARRIAGE:
FIRST & SECOND CLASS

I was surprised to learn that most moderate opponents of same-sex marriage have no problem with the idea of "domestic partnerships," which give homosexual couples many of the legal benefits of marriage. Their thinking is: "If two homosexuals wish to share their lives and fortunes and take care of one another in sickness and old age, why shouldn't they have the legal benefits that straight couples enjoy? Just don't call it 'marriage.'"

It seems a sensible compromise, unless, of course, one simply hates homosexuals and wants them to suffer.

Why not call it "marriage"? Because of a deep conviction that marriage is a more *serious* institution, because it provides the best framework for begetting and nurturing the next generation. Therefore, marriage should enjoy a higher dignity and status than mere domestic partnership.

Gay marriage advocates have a ready reply to this: straight people who cannot have children, or who choose not to have children, are allowed to marry. So marriage is not about reproduction.

There is no real reply to this argument. Yes, some anti-natal couples may change their minds and choose to have children. But that is not possible for sterile couples, who still can marry.

Gay marriage advocates also point out that sterile straight couples can still have families by adopting children or using surrogate parenting—and so can homosexual couples, which opens a whole new can of worms.

One can argue that homosexual couples are not optimal for the psychological development of children, which would be better served by parents of both sexes. But proponents of gay adoption could grant that argument and still retort that even suboptimal parents can give children better care than the staff of an orphanage—many of which, by the way, are staffed by people of only one sex, particularly those run by religious orders, which are not exactly magnets for red-blooded heterosexuals either.

Homosexual marriage advocates demand marriage equality on the grounds that their couplings are not relevantly different from straight marriages, as long as sterile straights are allowed to marry for companionship, and to have families through adoption or surrogacy.

This argument cannot be dismissed as an example of modern one-size-fits-all egalitarianism run amok. For even Aristotle defined justice as treating equal cases equally—and if sterile straight couples can marry, then why not sterile homosexual couples? And if sterile straights can have families through adoption and surrogacy, then why not sterile gays? Why should homosexuals accept second-class status?

It strikes me that the only way to preserve marriage as an exclusively heterosexual institution is to deal squarely with the issue of straight people who cannot or will not reproduce. In the past, when the causes of sterility were poorly understood, it was always possible to believe that a miracle baby would come along. Furthermore, shorter life spans and higher standards of taste and dignity prevented marriages between people who are simply too old to conceive. Finally, the facts that celibacy leaves a lot to be desired and that birth control was unreliable made it very unlikely that fertile couples would never produce children, even if they did not want them. Thus it made sense to think of marriage as simply the union of heterosexuals—the kind of people who, *prima facie*, can produce children—and just treat the instances where that did not happen as negligible. Marry 'em all, and let God sort it out.

But modern medicine has changed everything. Today, when effective birth control (including sterilization) is widely available and fertile couples can confidently avoid conception; when individuals can know for certain that they are irreversibly sterile; and when men and women routinely live long beyond when they can have children, one has to ask: Is gay marriage any more a mockery of the institution than two octogenerians pushing their walkers down the aisle to tie the knot? Is marriage between homosexuals any more a mockery than marriage between straights who cannot or will nor have children, even through adoption or surrogacy, either from medical misfortunes or simply out of selfishness, hedonism, and immaturity?

If the opponents of homosexual marriage are willing to accept a "second class" institution—domestic partnership—for infertile couplings, then why not extend that to straight couples who cannot and will not reproduce? Indeed, why not make "second class marriage" the *default* status for all married couples, granting first class status only upon the birth or adoption of the first child?

Of course we are talking about legal marriages here, marriages recognized by the state. People are—and would remain—free to celebrate religious or spiritual marriages of their own design and definition. But the state need not recognize all of them.

In such a system, the existence of homosexual marriage would be entirely contingent on whether it is deemed desirable to allow homosexual couples to adopt children, avail themselves of surrogacy, or raise the children of one partner's previous marriage. None of these arrangements strike me as optimal conditions for raising children if heterosexual alternatives are available.

Exploring the idea of limiting marriage only to couples who have children, while reserving domestic partnership for the rest, has benefits far beyond reframing the debate about homosexual marriage, which is a minor issue compared to the demographic and cultural problems caused by the decline of heterosexual marriage and the heterosexual family.

Even if homosexual marriage were not an issue, the distinction between marriage and domestic partnership allows us to refocus and recenter the institution of marriage on the sole function by which it merits special social and legal status: the procreation and nurture of the next generation. Such an arrangement would uphold the heteronormativity and reproductive purpose of marriage while giving options to those who fall short.

Counter-Currents/*North American New Right*
July 3, 2013

CONFESSIONS OF A "TRANSPHOBIC"

I never had a chance to read Gavin McInnes' article "Transphobia is Perfectly Natural,"[1] since *Thought Catalog* has taken it down. (But we can read outraged reactions from around the web.)[2] McInnes has apparently been hounded out of his job as chief creative officer of something called Rooster, which I am too unhip to have heard of.[3]

I am sure McInnes' article is somewhere out there on the web, and I am sure someone will send it to me eventually. But I don't want to read it until I have written my own take on the matter. Frankly, I am jealous that McInnes wrote on this first, since I have been kicking a similar idea around for years. I did not write it out, because up until May of this year, I was living in San Francisco, and the trannies there are far scarier than the antifa. Like the lesbians of Berkeley, they can reduce a man to a skeleton in under 30 seconds.

"Transphobia," like "homophobia," is an inherently dishonest term. "Phobia" derives from the Greek "*phobos*" or fear, and phobias are by definition *irrational* fears. But transphobia is neither irrational nor a fear. It is an emotion, of course. But it is a completely natural, normal, and healthy emotion. Which is as rational as any emotion gets.

Specifically, transphobia is a perfectly natural feeling of *revulsion* at men who have their dicks chopped off and women who have their tits chopped off—among *many, many* other things—in order to "change their sex." Of course, one's sex is determined by one's chromosomes, so "sex changes" do not change any-

---

[1] http://thoughtcatalog.com/gavin-mcinnes/2014/08/transphobia-is-perfectly-natural/

[2] http://thoughtcatalog.com/thought-catalog/2014/08/media-roundup-gavin-mcinnes-transphobia-article/

[3] http://www.adweek.com/news/advertising-branding/rooster-cco-gavin-mcinnes-asked-take-leave-absence-159536

one's sex. They merely transform a man into a butchered simulacrum of a woman, or a woman into a butchered simulacrum of a man.

Again: sex-changes are *futile*, because one cannot change one's chromosomes. One can only butcher and drug one's body to look like someone of the opposite sex. And when many transsexuals finally awaken to the horror and futility of what they have done, they kill themselves.

The revulsion I feel toward transsexuals is not based on "meanness" or "ignorance" as liberals would have it, but on *sympathy*. When a healthy person sees another in pain, he recoils in horror because he *feels the pain of others* (which is the literal meaning of sympathy — *suffering with* others). I love my penis, and the thought of losing it fills me with horror. And when one sees *self-inflicted* suffering, it is natural to feel loathing and anger as well, because it didn't have to happen. And by hurting themselves, self-mutilators hurt the rest of us as well. I am a bit overly sensitive, perhaps, but I even cringe at the sight of tattoos, partly in pity, partly in revulsion.

The kind of people who don't feel sympathy and horror at radical forms of self-mutilation are, frankly, sick. They lack elementary sympathy for the pain of others. They may even take pleasure in the pain of others. Or, like most liberals who champion trannies as the next great minority crusade, they take pleasure in the discomfort that sexual mutilation causes "those people" — conservatives, Christians, rednecks, hicks, etc. — the hated others of the liberal loveys. Trannies and other freaks are just tools in the culture war. But in this case, the enemy is not the Right side of the culture, but nature herself — mental and moral health, which apparently drives today's Left to paroxysms of sadistic rage. Because they're evil, of course.

After a healthy person feels sympathy-based revulsion at sexual self-mutilation, the first thought that pops into his mind is, "These people must be crazy." But let's just withhold judgment for a bit and ask the transsexuals themselves what they think. Interestingly enough, they too claim to suffer from mental illness, namely the feeling of being a man trapped in a woman's body, or vice versa. So the real issue here is not *whether* these

poor people suffer from a mental illness—they admit it themselves—but rather what sort of *treatment* they should seek. Self-
mutilation is not the cure for mental illness, but just another
symptom.

If a man thinks he is Jesus, we do not crucify him. If a man
thinks he is Napoleon, we do not crown him emperor. If a man
thinks he is a woman, why then should we go along with it?
Shouldn't we try to help him get over his desire to mutilate himself, just as we help anorexics to stop starving themselves, and
cutters to stop carving themselves?

And since when is it consistent with the Hippocratic oath—
the "First, Do No Harm" part—for doctors to mutilate healthy
bodies and turn them into parodies of the opposite sex?

What would I do with transsexuals? First of all, let me say
that I have actually *known* two people who have embarked upon
this path. To all appearances they were good-looking heterosexual men who dropped out of sight and then re-emerged as not-
so-good-looking women. But all their likable traits and shared
interests were disconcertingly intact. So transsexuals are not
some abstract other. They are very real to me. This is me being
real: having a real reaction to real people undergoing real, drastic transformations. I feel compassion and revulsion toward the
transsexuals themselves, and righteous indignation toward the
people who enable and exploit them.

So what would my policy be?

First, I would simply say "No." Every decent society should
provide healthcare for the mentally and physically ill. When
people are mentally ill, they cannot make responsible decisions
for themselves. Thus a decent society needs to exercise paternalism in the interests of the mentally ill. And the primary interest
of the mentally ill is to get better, to triumph over their delusions, not to be humored in them, much less aided in radical and
futile forms of self-mutilation. Again, self-mutilation is a symptom of mental illness, not a cure. Compassion and responsibility
require that we simply say "no."

Second, the mutilation of healthy bodies is contrary to the
proper aim of the medical profession. Thus every doctor who
performs sex change operations should be stripped of his license

and drummed out of the profession. Sex changes should be outlawed, and any doctor who performs them should be jailed. Indeed, the same treatment should be meted out to doctors who perform any and all forms of genital mutilation.

Third, we must keep a sense of perspective. I don't hate transsexuals. (I am rather proud of my book *Confessions of a Reluctant Hater*, so if I did hate them, I would have no problem admitting it.) Transsexuals aren't evil or threatening. They are not "sinners." They are simply sick people who should be cared for, not hated or harmed.

The truly evil people are those who exploit these unfortunates for gain: the doctors who mutilate them for money and the Leftists who use them as the latest totems of diversity, progress, and enlightenment—thereby revealing that their true enemy is not injustice or inequality but nature, health, and sanity. Craziest of all, though, is a society that consents to be ruled by such monsters.

Counter-Currents/ *North American New Right*
August 20, 2014

FURTHER CONFESSIONS OF
A "TRANSPHOBIC"

Drama, self-mutilation, and suicide are par for the course with transsexuals, so the recent death of would-be transgirl Joshua "Leelah" Alcorn, who threw himself in front of a semi truck, is less of a news story than the subsequent reactions of the Left, who have taken up his challenge to change society so nobody like him will ever shed another emo-tear.

Modern liberalism is basically a crusade against any ideals, norms, or standards that make botched, subnormal, alienated, or just slightly odd individuals feel bad about themselves. To make the Leelahs of the world safe, all we need do is throw overboard nature, religion, morality, and common sense. And the tears of those who resist? To the social justice crusader, all of them put together are not worth one of Leelah's fake fingernails.

The fact that transsexuals are the latest politically-correct totem group is further proof that liberalism really is a mental disease. Lunatics know their own. And unfortunately the lunatics are running the asylum. My hypothesis is that Leftists are physiologically addicted to righteous indignation, which they arouse by adopting simple and absolute values as the focus of moral fanaticism.

The fact that one-dimensional moralism is destructive of other values actually counts in its favor to the addict's mind, just as sacrificing babies to Baal underscored and elevated the god's sanctity. And just as drug addicts require ever higher doses to achieve the same effect, Leftists always require new, more extreme and radical crusades. This is how the history of liberalism has been reduced to a long, glorious march from the tyranny of dashing dictators and divinely-anointed monarchs to the tyranny of sniveling neurotics.

Another reason for today's trans-lib initiative is that homosexuals regard trannies as human shields, reasoning that if normals say "no" to transsexuals, homosexuals will be next.

The LGB community regards the medical mutilation of Ts as a small price for other people to pay to consolidate its recent social gains.

Bain Dewitt argues, however, that the Alcorn affair is not just an embarrassment to the Left but a challenge to the Right.[1] What would a healthy White Nationalist society do about people like Joshua Alcorn? For a racial community presumably has a commitment to all its members. As long as the Leelahs of the world are arrayed against us, it is easy to just mock and dismiss them as well as their enablers and exploiters. But what would be do in our ideal societies if one of our tow-headed youths declared that he was actually a pig-tailed maiden trapped in a boy's body?

My first instinct is simply to dismiss this as a delusion. It *is* a delusion. But simply to label it as such does not make it go away. One could say that virtually any mental illness is delusional, but that label does not make them any better.

We know that a small percentage of people are born physically "intersex," meaning that they have more or less developed traits of both sexes. It is at least *conceivable* that people are born with a mismatch between their physical sex and their psycho-sexual self-image. For convenience, I will refer to these as "trans" people, since they feel "transposed" into the wrong kind of body.

The question is: what to do about such people?

The first thing to make clear is that there can be no sensible solution unless we recognize the normative status of heterosexuality, monogamy, and the roles of men as protectors and providers and of women as mothers and care-givers. We also need to recognize that a society in which these norms are upheld and institutionalized secures the happiness of the overwhelming majority of individuals and the propagation and upward development of the race as a whole. These ethical and political norms are grounded in human biology. White Nationalism, as I conceive it, is about restoring the biological integrity

---

[1] http://www.counter-currents.com/2015/01/virtual-reality-part-2/

of the race and must address sexuality and sex roles as well as demographics.

But although nature provides us with sexual norms, she also provides us with exceptions like intersex individuals and "trans" people. A society in which sexual norms are clearly understood and institutionalized is not threatened by the existence of such people, so we should simply make reasonable accommodations for them. We should add them to the list of different human possibilities and allow them to *be themselves*, as long as it does not undermine norms or infringe on the rights of others.

A key value here is authenticity. People are happiest when being themselves. Authenticity is inseparable from the idea of self-actualization or becoming oneself. And setting aside people like sociopaths and pedophiles, who cannot be themselves without harming others, a White Nationalist society rooted in biological realism should promote self-actualization. Indeed, my central rationale for ethnonationalism is that it is the political philosophy that best allows different races and nations to live in accordance with their own identities.

Unfortunately, the preferred way of dealing with intersex and "trans" people has nothing to do with authenticity. Indeed, it is the epitome of inauthenticity, since in both cases, cosmetic surgery and hormone treatments are used to make such people into simulacra of males or females. Surgery and hormones cannot, of course, give intersex people a particular sex, or transform one sex into the other, for sexual identity is ultimately determined by chromosomes. These treatments are not "cures." They are simply cosmetic.

For intersex individuals, the goal is simply to change their appearance to fit in with the binary male/female norm, so they can "pass" as one sex or the other.

In the case of transsexuals, however, the usual goal is not to "pass" for the opposite sex. Instead, the typical transsexual wishes to be *socially accepted* as a transsexual. They do not wish to be *taken* as a man or a woman, but to be socially accepted and affirmed as a transman or transwoman. In such cases, transsexualism is connected with a significant dimension of histrionic "drama queen" narcissism combined with immense bitterness and aggression. And when the visceral revulsion, religious scruples, and moral qualms of the rest of humanity do not part like the Red Sea for transman's or transwoman's triumphant turn on the catwalk, their anger and hatred turn inwards and large numbers of end up killing themselves. (Do they also feel phantom tingles in their discarded genitalia? That can't help much either.)

In the case of congenital abnormalities that are purely cosmetic, like a harelip or vestigial tail, it makes perfect sense for parents to correct them surgically as soon as possible, so that the afflicted children can live normal lives. So it is natural for parents of intersex babies to think that subjecting them to surgery and hormone therapies as soon as possible might let them pass for normal and lead more or less normal social lives.

Unfortunately, it does not seem to work. It is cosmetic treatment for a problem that is not cosmetic and cannot be fixed cosmetically. Furthermore, many intersex individuals bitterly resent the painful surgeries and mind-bending hormone treatments to which they were subjected as children. If given the choice, they would have preferred to remain intact and ambiguous, the way they came from nature (or God, as some believe).

So, at the very least, in the case of intersex individuals, a decent society should say, "Not yet" to cosmetic surgery and hormone treatments. Parents should not be allowed to mutilate the genitalia of their children. This is analogous to another form of childhood genital mutilation, e.g., circumcision, which should be banned. The operative value here is autonomy: people should not have permanent, life-changing cosmetic alterations forced upon them as children.

But bodily integrity is also a value, which in some cases should trump even the desire of adults to make radical cosmetic transformations of their bodies. We have to ask which is better: to alter the body to meet social expectations or to alter social expectations to preserve the integrity of the body? Do we sanction radical cosmetic transformations of the body so that intersex people can *merely pass* as male or female? Or do we expand our sexual categories, simply recognize that such people exist, accept them as they are, and make sensible social accommodations (e.g., in toilet facilities and gym classes)? I think the latter solution is most consistent with the values of authenticity and bodily integrity. Furthermore, such a change in attitudes no more threatens sexual norms than the recognition of dwarfism threatens height norms.

Why are intersex individuals campaigning against subjecting minors to cosmetic surgeries and hormone treatments, while it is a progressive shibboleth that parents should be able to subject sexually confused "transsexual" minors to the same hormones? The question, of course, is rhetorical. We are dealing here with evil and insanity.

A decent society should provide for the physical and mental health of all of its members. When individuals are incapable of making decisions for themselves, because of immaturity, insanity, or other mental impairments, a decent society exercises paternalism, making decisions for them. Would-be transsexuals suffer from a mental illness, for which they should receive treatment. But in the name of authenticity and bodily autonomy, we should say "No" to "sex changes." Indeed, I would ban all such procedures as violating the basic medical principle that physicians should "do no harm" to healthy bodies. We should also say "No" to people who think they can change their sex simply by saying so.

Only a small percentage of people who imagine that they are gluten intolerant actually are. And if there really are people who are born feeling they are transposed into the wrong body, what are the chances that everyone who thinks he suffers from this now-fashionable malady actually does? Some might just be seeking attention. Others might be mistaken in their self-diagnosis. Still others might simply be self-hating homosexuals. (I suspect that is true in a lot of cases.) Some might just outgrow it. All these false positives will be sorted out in time, and any genuine cases can simply learn to live with their condition, perhaps with some stoic dignity rather than narcissism, self-mutilation, and suicide.

Again, we should prefer to alter social expectations to preserve the body's integrity rather than mutilate the body to conform to social expectations. Again, the solution is to expand people's sense of what is psychologically possible so that discontented individuals do not feel any pressure to mutilate themselves. In this case, we are talking about a handful of people with an invisible malady. It is not even clear if any objective accommodations are required. We already accommodate far larger groups suffering from far more socially disruptive maladies. (Consider the costs of cigarettes and alcohol abuse alone.) There will always be assholes, but the vast majority of white people would neither know nor care about the inner Leelahs of the world.

There are norms, and there are exceptions. When the norms are secure, exceptions are no threat. But when the exception becomes the norm, and all standards must be overthrown to spare the feelings of every special snowflake, then healthy people will naturally conclude that the machine of civilization must be lubricated with tranny tears.

Counter-Currents/*North American New Right*
January 19, 2015

DOES THE MANOSPHERE
MORALLY CORRUPT MEN?

For several years now, the website I read more than any other has been Chateau Heartiste, formerly known as Chateau Roissy. I also read Roosh V. from time to time. Both men are highly intelligent, and Heartiste is also a brilliant stylist, with a wicked sense of humor.

But, for all the pleasure and knowledge I have derived from these and other manosphere writers, I am increasingly drawn to the view that the net result of the manosphere is to morally corrupt men.

Paradoxical though it may seem, I also think the manosphere is actually a mechanism by which *women* morally corrupt men. The manosphere is touted as a way for men to emancipate themselves from the tyranny of feminism, but in reality it functions as a subtle instrument of female domination.

No normal, healthy man would want his daughter or sister to be emotionally manipulated and sexually exploited by a man who is narcissistic, sociopathic, and Machiavellian—or just a garden variety jerk.

However, the manosphere informs us that science, history, and copious anecdotal testimony show that when women are allowed complete choice in the sexual realm—particularly if they can have sex without the threat of pregnancy—they do not simply gravitate toward biologically and mentally healthy men with "alpha" traits but also to a whole range of "false positives," ranging from emotionally aloof and unavailable men to jerks and cads to men with severe "dark triad" personality disorders: narcissism, sociopathy, and Machiavellianism.

A healthy, well-ordered society punishes jerks and cads. Ideally, it should simply weed out people with severe personality disorders by preventing them from reproducing. Thus, emancipated female sexual choice morally and psychologically corrupts men. Not because sex is evil or "sinful," but because emancipated women reward anti-social behaviors and pathological personality traits with sex. Furthermore, emancipated female sexual choice harms the women who fall victim to jerks and sociopaths. Finally, since a great deal of personality is genetically determined and thus heritable, emancipated female sexuality is dysgenic, because it helps perpetuate jerk genes.

To correct these problems, we need to roll back sexual liberation by reestablishing social shaming for female promiscuity and, most importantly, involving the family—particularly fathers and brothers—in the process by which women choose suitors and husbands. Involving the family in her deliberations can expand a woman's awareness and sharpen her judgments by bringing other perspectives into play. Men, furthermore, are better than women at discerning good men from evil ones, and, as I said above, no decent man wants his sister or daughter to be exploited and victimized by bad men. (For all the same reasons, mothers and sisters should involve themselves in the process of selecting suitors and mates for the young men in their families.)

Now, I suspect that manosphere gurus like Heartiste and Roosh are actually with me so far, even agreeing basically with my conservative political agenda.

So why do I think that the manosphere works as a tool by which feral feminine desire corrupts men? Because the manosphere simply takes emancipated female sexuality as a given. Then it teaches young men to adopt the behaviors and mimic the traits that appeal to such women. Young men not only learn about healthy masculine traits but also admiringly analyze "jerkboy" game and "dark triad" cads.

In sum, my concern is that the manosphere teaches young men to emulate anti-social and pathological traits. Women then reinforce these traits with one of the most powerful inducements of all: sex. And, over time, otherwise good men become the kind of men they would never allow around their own sisters and daughters. This is moral corruption. Namely, moral corruption by teaching men to conform to emancipated female desire rather than to correct it.

The manosphere provides the New Right with all the *theoretical* premises necessary for a patriarchal sexual counter-revolution that reinstitutes traditional and—it turns out—biologically sound norms and institutions to govern sexuality, thereby promoting the individual happiness of men and women and the common good of society and the race in general.

But in *practical* terms, the manosphere does not promote such a restoration, but instead urges an ethic of "riding the tiger" (or perhaps the cougar), i.e., to personally wallow in—and thus to amplify and advance—the decadence that we are supposed to combat.

Counter-Currents/*North American New Right*
February 25, 2015

BE YOURSELF?

Andy Nowicki's Counter-Currents article "In Defense of 'Squares'"[1] has prompted a reply from Ferdinand Bardamu, "Can You See the Real Me?"[2] Both articles raise important questions about identity in connection with the "game" or "PUA" (pickup artist) phenomenon.

Nowicki argues that the gamesters are right about female psychology, namely that women are primally attracted to "alpha" male traits. Gamesters teach beta males to mimic alpha traits to get laid. Nowicki's objection is that betas pretending to be alphas is fundamentally false, inauthentic, and self-alienating. Nowicki, who describes himself as a proud beta, instead counsels men to be more concerned with discovering and being themselves, as opposed to pretending to be somebody they are not in order to conform to female expectations and desires.

Bardamu's reply does not really address the essential premises of Nowicki's argument, namely that there really are alpha and beta males, and that betas pretending to be alphas is just that, namely pretending, and is thus inauthentic, self-alienating, and fraudulent.

Instead, Bardamu argues that the advice to "be yourself" is an excuse for complacency when self-improvement is in order. As an example, Bardamu tells of his own transformation from obese nerd to fit, socially-competent hipster. He claims that if he followed Nowicki's advice to be himself, that transformation never would have happened. (Now that we know that Bardamu is Matt Forney, we know that this transformation actually never took place.)

Justifying your unwillingness to improve your life by

---

[1] http://www.counter-currents.com/2012/03/in-defense-of-squaresa-response-to-jack-donovan/

[2] http://www.inmalafide.com/blog/2012/04/02/can-you-see-the-real-me-a-response-to-andy-nowicki/

claiming to be "authentic" or "being yourself" is just a lie you tell yourself to protect your ego. . . . *his argument is fundamentally a loser's argument.* You almost never hear this kind of argument coming from anyone who's accomplished anything real in life. You don't hear it from athletes, you don't hear it from musicians (real musicians, not kids living on trust funds), you don't hear it from international travelers. You hear it from fat girls, feminists, and nerds. "Have another Snickers bar, you gorgeous girl, you!"

This is a good argument so far: If you take "be yourself" to mean "remain as you are at any given time," then self-improvement is not necessary. It is not a reply to Nowicki's argument, but it is a good argument nonetheless.

But then Bardamu adds a very questionable metaphysical statement:

Here's the truth — *there is no "real" you.* You don't have an inviolable, unchanging identity that defines you from the day you're born to the day you die. Your identity is just who you are at this particular moment in time. You're not the same person you were ten years ago, and you won't be the same person ten years from now. You won't even be the same person six months from now. Oh sure, you may have the same name and see the world through the same set of eyes, but events in and out of your control permanently and slowly change you. Getting married and having children, losing your job, moving abroad, graduating from college, the death of your parents — all these and other events leave lasting marks on your soul. Game, along with self-improvement methods like the Paleo diet, are nothing more than ways of guiding your intellectual development in productive directions, taking charge of your life instead of just letting things happen to you.

In other words, being yourself is impossible, because there

is no fixed self. Being the real you is bad advice, because there is no real you. Bardamu denies that there really are alpha or beta males. There are just alpha and beta performances. And if one performs the same role long enough, it becomes "nature":

> A funny thing happens when you do something over and over again—you get good at it. In fact, you eventually get so good at it that it becomes second nature. You no longer think about it consciously; you just do it without thinking or hesitating. If you practice the guitar for fifteen minutes a day, every day, eventually you'll be able to play "Smells Like Teen Spirit" from memory. If you eat soup and tap water for dinner every night and jog/walk three miles a day, eventually you'll be skinny and fit. If you play the part of an asshole consistently and convincingly, *eventually it stops being a persona and becomes who you are.*

He goes on to add, "There was nothing fake about me . . ." Which follows from his basic premises: There is nothing fake about him, simply because there was never anything real about him. He cannot betray himself, because he has no real self to betray.

Now this is a very common viewpoint. Indeed, it is the deep metaphysical presupposition of modernity. The modern worldview sees man as the master of nature, which requires that nature be malleable to the human will. This means that all fixed and immutable natures must be discarded as impediments to human power.

This is the metaphysical presupposition of modern egalitarianism, for instance. There are no inherent, immutable differences between the sexes and the races, because such differences would frustrate the egalitarian project. Therefore, all racial and sexual differences must be socially constructed and socially mutable in the direction of equality. There are no objective standards of beauty. They are all socially constructed and mutable, so ugly people can feel good about themselves too. (But the differences that the Left wish to maintain or excuse, such as homosexuality or fatness, are genetic and cannot be changed.)

One can, however, preserve Bardamu's essential argument—and harmonize it with Nowicki's—by dropping this false metaphysical presupposition.

Bardamu is assuming a false dichotomy: either the self is what is *actual* at any particular moment—or there is no self. The third possibility is Aristotle's view of nature as *potentiality*. For Aristotle, everybody has a self, but it is not necessarily the person one is right now, for one's self can be more or less imperfectly actualized.

For the couch potato, "be yourself" translates as "remain as you are now, in your degraded, unhealthy state." For Aristotle, "be yourself" is equivalent to "actualize yourself," which, for the couch potato, translates as: turn off the television, stop eating chips, and start exercising. Bardamu's story of self-transformation is completely consistent with an Aristotelian metaphysics of self-actualization.

Aristotelian self-actualization is, moreover, consistent with the acquisition of various abilities through the repetition of certain actions until they become "second nature." But for Aristotle, second nature is grafted onto "first nature," the nature one is born with, and for the graft to take, the two natures have to be compatible. You can practice guitar or piano all you want, but if you lack innate musical talent, you will never rise above mediocrity.

This brings us to Andy Nowicki's concern with honesty and authenticity. For an Aristotelian, there is a self, thus it is possible to be true or false to oneself. Being true to oneself means actualizing oneself: living in accord with one's potential for excellence. Being false to oneself means living in a way that is indifferent to one's true nature or in conflict with it. Health, mental and physical, can be defined as a life in accordance with one's nature. Ill health, mental and physical, can be defined as a life in conflict with one's nature.

To adapt an example from Schopenhauer, imagine two men, one brawny but not bright, the other brainy and weak. The brawny man would be most satisfied with a physically active life, say being a lumberjack. The brainy man would be most satisfied with an intellectually active life, such as being a math professor. Now switch the two men's professions. Send the math professor out to cut down trees, and put the lumberjack in the classroom. Both men would be miserable, because they would be required to live in a way that conflicts with their natures. And even if, through a massive act of will, it were possible for both men eventually to perform the other's job competently, they would still be miserable, because they would be constantly going against rather than with the grain of who they really are.

Nowicki's concern is this: If there is a real self, then there must be negative psychological consequences to pretending to be somebody one is not. If there are alpha and beta males, then there must be negative consequences for betas pretending to be alphas. Yet that sort of fundamental falseness is being sold by the PUA community, as well as such pop-Nietzschean swill-mongers as Tony Robbins and his ilk, who promise success — defined in the basest materialistic terms — in exchange for what is often fundamental self-betrayal. I think Nowicki's concern is completely valid and defensible.

My own concern with "game" and allied phenomena — as well as the metaphysics of the will that often accompanies them — is that they appeal to and empower pathological narcissists, pathological liars, and sociopaths.

A pathological narcissist is a person whose identity and self-worth are not anchored in the reality of his own nature and achievements. Indeed, he may be profoundly alienated from himself. He may even believe that he has no real self, just shifting desires.

A narcissist is a fundamentally dependent, parasitic personality. To satisfy his desires, the narcissist does not change reality, he manipulates others. The narcissist's identity exists in his reflection in the minds of others.

The narcissist spends his time acting — projecting a persona — in front of an audience in order to manipulate them into satisfying his needs. When others believe his act and reflect his persona back to him, he feels a sense of self. When they approve of his persona, he feels a sense of self-worth. When they question or dislike his persona, he feels rage. Thus narcissists are pathological liars and manipulators.

The most successful narcissists are also untroubled by their parasitic, manipulative relationships with others because they have no conscience. They are sociopaths or psychopaths, incapable of human empathy even as they are highly astute at reading and manipulating human psychology.

For such men, "game" is merely another tool of manipulation that they can use to get women into highly vulnerable situations.

Of the first three men I met who were really into game, two of them were narcissists, pathological liars, and possible sociopaths. I would feel a lot better about the ethics of the game "community" if it not only offered men advice on how to pick up women, but also offered women advice on how to see through and avoid narcissistic sociopaths who are trying to bed them, or worse.

Counter-Currents/*North American New Right*
April 3, 2012

THE END OF GLOBALIZATION

The market is an inherently global institution. The market is non-racist, non-nationalist, and non-religious, for as long as decisions are made solely in monetary terms, the race, nationality, and religion of buyers and sellers simply do not matter. Often, they are completely unknown.

I know the ethnic identity of the owners of the Armenian rug shop and the Chinese restaurant down the street. But what is the race, ethnicity, or nationality of the Coca-Cola Corporation? Its stockholders, employees, and customers have every identity in the world. But the corporation has none. It is global, cosmopolitan. As its famous jingle tells us, it wants to teach the world to sing in perfect harmony, meaning that it wants a pacified planet where people have relinquished all boundaries and identities that might impede the sale of Coke.

Globalization is the process of making the inherently global, cosmopolitan potential of the marketplace actual by breaking down racial, national, religious, and cultural barriers to the market, such as protectionist laws, religious prohibitions on usury, ancient enmities between peoples, and sentimental attachments to one's community, tribe, homeland, etc.

For consumers in the First World, globalization starts out as a good thing. They can take their First World wages and buy lots of cheaper goods manufactured in the Third World. For capitalists based in the First World, it is an even better thing, for they can make enormous profits by selling Third World goods at only slightly lower prices than goods manufactured at far greater expense in the First World—and pocket the difference.

For example, to use arbitrary numbers, when shoes were made in America, a pair of shoes retailing for $100 might be manufactured by a worker being paid $10/hour, 40 hours/week + overtime pay, plus benefits, plus vacation time, in a factory regulated for health, safety, and environmental impact.

Sure, it sounds like a lot of bother. But it never prevented American shoe manufacturers from becoming millionaires.

And when such a manufacturer left his factory at the end of the day, his luxury car would share the road with the modest cars of his own employees. He would pass through a bustling downtown where the wives of his employees shopped; he would pass the school attended by the children of his employees; he might even attend the local high school football game and cheer the sons of his workers; he would drive through neighborhoods with neatly painted houses and manicured lawns, where his employees lived. And when he arrived at his columned mansion, he would simply pull off the road into his driveway. There would be no security gates and guards to protect him.

With globalization, however, a similar pair of shoes retailing for $95 might be manufactured in Indonesia by a half-starved wretch making a fraction of the wages, with no overtime, no vacation, and no benefits, in a factory with no regulations for health, safety, or environmental impact. And the shoe manufacturer pockets the difference.

Even if the American owner of an American-founded, American-based, American-staffed shoe manufacturer had a sentimental attachment to his nation and his employees, he could not compete with rivals who had no such ties. In the end, he would have to close his factory: either to ship his jobs to the Third World or simply due to bankruptcy. Thus the globalization process selects for and rewards rootless cosmopolitanism and anti-national, anti-patriotic, anti-communitarian sentiments.

In the long run, globalization means one thing: the equalization of wages and living standards over the whole globe. That means that First World living standards will fall a great deal, and Third World living standards will rise a little bit, until parity is achieved. In other words, globalization means the destruction of the American working and middle classes. It means a reduction of their standard of living to those of Third World coolies. Globalization means the reversal of the progress in living standards since the industrial revolution.

Specifically, globalization means the reversal of the genuine progress made by the Left. Gone will be the higher pay, shorter work days, and benefits won by the labor movement; gone will be the health-care plans, safety regulations, welfare programs, and old age pensions created by liberals and social democrats (programs that do not exist in the Third World); gone will be the environmental protections won by ecologists (which are only imposed on the Third World by the First World, which will no longer have that luxury).

But globalization also affects the rich. First of all, those who have grown rich by selling things to the working and middle classes of the First World will disappear along with their customers. There will no longer be a market for riding lawnmowers or camper trailers. The rich who remain will produce either for the global super-rich or the global proletariat.

The lives of the rich will be dramatically transformed as well. Some people will grow very rich indeed by dismantling the First World. But they will end up living like the rich of the Third World. They will commute from fortified factories or offices to fortified mansions in armored limousines with armed guards past teeming slums and shantytowns. They will socialize at exclusive clubs and vacation at exclusive resorts under the watchful eyes of security guards. Like Marie Antoinette, who liked to play milkmaid in the gardens of Versailles, they might even pretend to be bohemians in million-dollar flats in Haight Ashbury, or cowboys on twenty-million dollar ranches in Wyoming, or New England villagers in million-dollar cottages on Martha's Vineyard—having ridden to the top of a system that has exterminated the people who created these ways of life.

The consequences of globalization are not secret. They are not random and unpredictable. They are not even arcane or controversial. They are predicted in every introductory economics textbook. They are apparent in the stagnation of American working and middle class living standards beginning in the 1970s and the steep declines of the last decade, when 50,000 American manufacturing facilities closed their doors, many to ship their jobs overseas—while millions of immigrants, legal and illegal, came to compete with Americans for the jobs that remain, depress wages, and consume public services for which they cannot pay.

Yet the American middle and working classes were never allowed a choice about globalization, for the obvious reason that they would never have approved of their pauperization. The labor movement, the political parties, the churches, and all other forces that are capable of resisting globalization have been coopted.

Sincere progressives recognize the destructive effects of globalization, but most of them think that the only alternative to global capitalism is global socialism, which is no solution, even if it could be attained.

But if we reject globalization, what is the natural economic unit? This is where White Nationalists are able to address the genuine concerns of the Occupy movement and other progressive critics of globalization. For the boundary where globalization ends is the nation. The United States and every other European nation entered modernity and made most of their economic and social progress by practicing nationalistic economic policies, including protectionism. Prosperity and social justice will return when globalization is replaced by economic nationalism.

Libertarians decry protectionism as benefiting one group at the expense of another (as if globalization did not do the same thing). But this is the wrong way to look at it. Every individual wears different hats and plays different roles: producer, consumer, family member, citizen, etc. Free trade makes us good consumers, but it also makes us bad citizens by undermining social justice and national sovereignty. Protectionism limits our acquisitiveness as consumers, but it strengthens us as citizens. Free trade empowers some businessmen at the expense of the common good, making them bad citizens. Protectionism and other regulations make all businessmen good citizens by making it impossible to profit at the expense of the common good — which leaves no shortage of opportunities to generate wealth in a socially responsible fashion.

But wouldn't the completion of globalization, whether socialist or capitalist, be worth it, if it really could lead to a world without nations, borders, boundaries, and wars? It is this utopian hope that sustains the allegiance of many globalists despite the spreading desolation of the Earth. It is the same hope that sustained Communists despite the oceans of blood they spilled.

There are two basic replies to this. One is to argue that it is not worth it, which the die-hard utopian would never accept. The other is to argue that a world without nations will never be achieved, and the people who are pushing it, moreover, are not even serious about the notion. Globalization is not the overcoming of nationalism, but merely the way that market dominant nations break down barriers to expanding their own economic power. Today's color-coded, Twitter and Facebook powered insurrections in Eastern Europe and the Muslim world are merely the modern version of the empire-building and gunboat diplomacy of centuries past. George Soros is just the Cecil Rhodes of today.

Jews like Soros, of course, are the primary preachers of universalist schemes such as global trade, open borders, racial miscegenation, multiculturalism, and other forms of identity erasure. But they show no signs of practicing these same policies among themselves. What is theirs they keep; what is ours is negotiable. The implication is obvious: their goal is to destroy all national boundaries and racial and cultural identities that serve as impediments to expanding Jewish power. Globalization is not a path to universal freedom. It is the creation of one neck to bear a Jewish yoke for eternity.

It is easy to see why Jews think that the devastation caused by globalization is worth it to them, but it is hard to understand why anybody else wishes to go along with it, except for the alienated, deracinated products of cultural decline. And even these people have to be asking themselves if this is the world they really want.

Universalism, after all, is not really universal. Only whites seem susceptible to it in large enough numbers to matter. But if universalism is merely a racially and culturally European belief system, then globalization will only work by exterminating Jews and other ancient, ethnocentric people like the Chinese,

Koreans, Japanese, Armenians, etc., who refuse to jump into the global melting pot. This means that globalization is not the path to a liberal utopia, but merely a genocidal extension of European imperialism. But given the massive investment in Holocaust propaganda, even the most fanatical globalists don't have the heart for that solution, so in the end, they would have to allow ethnocentric peoples to opt out.

And if Jews and others get to opt out of globalization, then why can't the rest of us? Especially since unreciprocated free trade is regressive, dissolving national sovereignty, undermining social justice, and delivering the destinies of European peoples into the hands of aliens.

The conclusion is clear: Progressive advocates of globalization are either ignorant or they are dishonest shills for a process that will pauperize and enslave the people they pretend to defend. There is a vast constituency in America for a racially-conscious, nationalistic, anti-globalist, protectionist, progressive political party. They are only waiting for leadership.

Counter-Currents/*North American New Right*
December 28, 2011

MONEY FOR NOTHING

Everybody knows you need to work for your money. And if somebody just gives you money, that can only be by the expropriation of somebody else's labor. Money just doesn't grow on trees, after all.

But is this really true? Just because *you* work for your money, did the guy who paid you also work for it? What about the guy who paid him? If you follow the money trail long enough, you are going to find someone who did not work for his money. He simply got it for nothing. He did not even have to go to the trouble of picking it off trees. He just created it out of thin air by bookkeeping. We call this man a banker.

Unlike people who have to produce things of real value before they count them up and enter the number in a book, the banker creates his product simply by bookkeeping operations. The whole panoply of bank services—checking accounts, savings accounts, free toasters, checks with cute ducklings or golden retrievers printed on them—are, arguably, props to disguise the fact that the core of banking is the sheer creation of money out of nothing.

When I was a boy, one of the banks in my hometown gave out free piggy banks to children. Today, that seems a masterstroke of propaganda, fostering the impression that real banks, just like piggy banks, can only give out money that they take in. But banks are not required to keep your deposits on hand. They loan them out. Every dollar in your checking or savings account is loaned out ten times over. This is how bankers simply create money through bookkeeping. And that is just the *beginning* of how bankers create money. And bankers can do it even if they do not operate in buildings with Grecian columns out front and teller windows inside, even if they do not have checking and savings accounts and all the other props we associate with banking.

But even though the money you borrow was created for nothing, you still have to pay it back, with interest. And when you pay it back, *you* can't just create the money. *You* have to work for it. *You* have to provide real goods and services. Thus bankers, by loaning out the money they create for nothing, gain a mortgage on future production of *real world* goods and services.

What is money anyway? Money is a medium of exchange that allows one to covert the fruits of one's labor into easily portable tokens that one can exchange for the fruits of other people's labor. What one chooses for tokens does not really matter. Money can be bits of shiny metal, colorful slips of paper, electronic data in computers, or cowrie shells, just as long as they are accepted by the butcher, the baker, and the candlestick maker.

Money does not need to have any intrinsic value. In fact, it helps if its intrinsic value is next to nothing, otherwise people will hoard it rather than circulate it freely, which would cause an economic hardship known as deflation, in which money is a commodity whose value rises because its supply diminishes. (When money is a commodity whose supply rises and its value decreases, that is called inflation. It is worth asking: Can one avoid both evils if money has no value in itself, i.e., if it is not a commodity that can be bought and sold alongside bricks and butter?)

If the best money has no intrinsic value, then the worst sort of money would be precious metals. The best sort of money would be entirely intangible, just data in a computer. Even paper money can be hoarded, for instance, when the price of toilet paper gets too high. (Perhaps the best way to insure that money is not hoarded is simply to print an expiration date on it.)

Ideally money should be a self-effacing servant of the real economy, which produces actual goods and services. But money has grown into a jealous tyrant that interferes with the real economy. The simplest example is your average economic crisis. In an economic depression, the land does not suddenly go sterile. The udders of cows do not go dry. Men do not suddenly become stupid and lazy. The sun keeps shining; the crops keep growing; the chickens keep laying; people keep working. Goods pile up in warehouses and stores. And on the demand side, people still need to eat. But silos are bursting and people are starving because, for some mysterious reason, there is suddenly "not enough money."

People have no money to spend, or they are afraid to part with the money they do have, because of a climate of uncertainty. After all, half way around the world, a massive swindle has been discovered; a bank has collapsed; a speculative bubble has burst. So, naturally, back in Hooterville, stores are filled with sour milk and rotting vegetables and children are going to bed hungry.

If an able-bodied man were shipwrecked on a fertile island, he would not starve for lack of money. But on this vast and fertile island we call Earth, people starve amidst plenty because we have accepted the dominion of a monetary economy that disrupts the real economy. That is no way to run a planet.

The obvious solution is simply to *increase the money supply*. One must make consumer demand *effective* so the market clears and life can go on. And the simplest way to do that is for the government to print money and give it to people. Remember George W. Bush's 2008 "stimulus checks"? That was money for nothing, handed to people to stimulate economic activity. The effect, of course, was negligible. But it was morally and economically far preferable to the massive "bailouts" and the Obama stimulus plan that followed.

Whereas the Bush stimulus checks went directly to millions of consumers, who injected the money directly into the economy when they purchased goods and services, the bailouts and stimulus spending went to a relative handful of politically connected insiders. It turns out, furthermore, that very little of the money went to stimulate the US economy. Instead, a lot of it was invested overseas. Other recipients of bailouts held onto their cash, hoping that they could buy up real assets for cheap if the economy continued to slide deeper into depression. Moreover, whatever money did go into the US economy came with strings attached: the necessity to repay principal and interest. At least with the Bush stimulus checks, the money went directly into the economy with no strings attached in straight up purchases of goods and services.

But, as we have seen, money for nothing is not merely part of an occasional emergency stimulus measure. It is business as usual for banks.

But if money is being created out of nothing all the time, then we have to ask: Should this be left to the banks, or is there a better way of doing it?

Why not simply have the government create money and send each individual a monthly check, to be spent as he sees fit? This money would stimulate the economy directly, through the purchases of goods and services, whereas money created by banks in the form of loans must be paid back, with interest, creating a parasitic class of people who get a share of real production by loaning at interest a commodity they get for nothing.

Again, every industry that produces real goods and services has accounting and inventory costs, but actual production has to come first. You have to make toys before you can count them. With banks, money is by created simply by bookkeeping operations, e.g., making loans. Bankers "produce" merely by juggling numbers.

But if money for nothing is simply a feature of the modern economy, why not cut out the parasitic "private sector" middlemen and simply have the government create money and distribute it directly to consumers?

Why is the government preferable to the private sector as the creator of money? Because, unlike private businesses, the government is accountable to the public. Its purpose is to secure the common good. Moreover, when the private financial sector is in crisis, the bankers look to the government to bail them out — at the expense of the taxpayers. Time for the government to bail the people out — at the expense of the banks. Let's repudiate all our debts and start fresh with a new financial system.

"But simply creating money and mailing out checks would be inflationary!" some would object. True. But it would be no more inflationary than allowing banks to create money.

Furthermore, there is a deeper issue here: Is inflation or deflation simply a product of the commodification of money? The commodification of money means that money is not merely a tool of exchange, but a commodity that is exchanged, a commodity with a cost of its own (interest). Would it be possible to decommodify money, i.e., to eliminate interest and a secondary market in money, either partially or altogether? Would the creation of money that expires after a while cut down on the commodification of money?

"But money for nothing would be socialism!" others would object. Yes, I am proposing socializing the creation and initial distribution of money. But what people do with the money at that point is their own business. The system I propose is completely consistent with private property and private enterprise. Indeed, it would strengthen and secure them, because it would eliminate a parasitic class of people who steadily mulct the real economy, and occasionally send it into crises, by creating and loaning out money that is free to them and should be free to all.

"But how would businesses capitalize themselves without bank loans?" That is a fair question. Perhaps the best answer is to say that that just as individual consumers could get money for nothing from the state, creditable producers could do so as well. But nothing about my proposal would prevent banks and credit unions from forming to capitalize businesses. But they would not be allowed to create money out of thin air. They would have to attract savings by paying interest, then loan out their deposits — and no more than their deposits — at interest to creditworthy businessmen. To do this, banks would have to offer serious interest for savings and charge serious interest on loans, but it *could* be done. It would definitely be "tight" money, though, which might be a good thing in the long run, since it would discourage speculative investments. Of course if money went bad after a while, it would make no sense to save it. But none of this might be necessary if interest-free state financing is a viable option. It is certainly a question worth exploring.

Nothing, moreover, would prevent businesses from capitalizing themselves by selling shares and paying dividends, either.

"But shouldn't people work for their money?" Yes and no. Money needs to get into circulation. And the modern welfare state gives people money for nothing all the time in the form of unemployment insurance, old age pensions, welfare payments, food aid, healthcare, etc. Why not bundle all these benefits together into a single, flat monthly payment? These payments would be enough to ensure the basic social safety net we all have anyway. It would also be fairer than the present system, which expropriates the fruits of some people's labor to redistribute them to others. It would, in effect, be welfare without redistribution.

But the basic payments I envision would not allow people to live opulently. Thus most people would choose to work. Some might choose to invest their monthly checks. Others might wish to defer them so they can enjoy better old age pensions. But the whole character of work would be changed, because people would not work because they *have* to. They would work because they *want* to. The socialist dream of the "decommodification" of labor would be realized.

Sure, some people might choose to spend their time smoking dope and strumming guitars. But one of them might be the next Goethe or Wagner. And surely we would be better off extending the adolescences of a million bohemians than supporting a thousand scheming Wolfowitzes, Madoffs, and Shylocks along with all their warmonger and pornmonger cousins.

"But this system would create public debt!" some might object. But I am talking about creating money, not borrowing it. Why should the government allow banks to create money and then loan it, at interest, to the government, when the government can create money itself? The very existence of public debt goes back to the time when money was something of intrinsic value (like gold) that banks might possess and that the government could not just make up. A government that can simply create money has no need of public debt.

"But this system will create idleness!" is another objection. Yes, but there is nothing wrong with idleness. In fact, as I see it, the whole point of social and technological progress is to create a world in which *machines put us all out of work*. The goal of social policy should be to create conditions of ever-increasing productivity through scientific and technological progress.

But it would be ecologically irresponsible, indeed catastrophic, if people were to take the gains of increased productivity in the form of more consumer goods or burgeoning population growth. Thus the goal of social policy should be to keep consumption roughly stable and cash out productivity gains in terms of ever-shorter work weeks. As productivity increases, it might be possible to maintain a comfortable standard of living with 20 hours of work per week, then 10, then 5, then 1.

When the work week approaches zero hours, we would be living in a "Star Trek" economy in which scarcity of physical goods is abolished through the invention of unlimited cheap and clean energy sources and the "replicator" which can turn energy into any desired good, simply poofing it into existence. In such a world, the only scarcity would be ecological carrying capacity, which would have to be zealously guarded by keeping populations in check—or sending them out to colonize the stars, terraform dead planets, create galactic empires, etc.

But what to would people do with their leisure? Such a society would be the culmination (and, I would argue, following Hegel, the hidden inner purpose) of all human striving, from the moment man first differentiated himself from the animal and stepped into history. It would obviously be a farce if mankind struggled for millennia only to give birth to a world of indolent, empowered morons. Imagine Homer Simpson poofing donuts and Duff into existence while watching holoporn until he becomes one of the boneless blobs in hoverchairs depicted in *Wall-E*. Utopia would be wasted on such people. Thus along with scientific, technological, and social progress, we would also need to pursue cultural, spiritual, and genetic progress to create a race worthy of utopia.

A job is just something you do to make money so you can do the things you really enjoy. A job is just a means to doing things that are ends in themselves. Once machines put us out of work and the lollygaggers and lotus-eaters are bred out of the gene pool, people can busy themselves doing the things they find intrinsically rewarding: raising children, writing books, playing and composing music, writing software, inventing machines, playing sports, tending gardens, perfecting recipes, advancing science, fighting for justice, exploring the cosmos, etc.

It will be a realm of freedom in which the human potential to create beauty, do good, and experience joy will be unhampered by economic necessity.

This is the stuff of science fiction and other utopias, staples of the American imagination. Yet the dominant political paradigm in America and the rest of the white world is profoundly regressive and dysgenic. While whites dream of the Space Age, our system is headed toward to the Stone Age, worshiping Negroes as heroes and gods (Morgan Freeman has been typecast as God) and placing a product of dysgenic miscegenation in the highest office of the land.

If we are to resume the path to the stars, we will have to begin by addressing four principal evils: dysgenics, economic globalization, racial diversity (including non-white immigration), and finance capitalism.

What do we call this alternative economic paradigm? Ultimately, I would call it National Socialism. But the little florilegium of economic heresies I have assembled above is drawn primarily from the Social Credit ideas of Clifford Hugh Douglas (1859–1952) and Alfred Richard Orage (1873–1934), partly by way of Alan Watts, who was my first introduction to these ideas, and Ezra Pound, who is the most famous exponent of Social Credit.

It is my conviction that the North American New Right, if it is to provide a genuine alternative to the existing system, must break with all forms of "free market" economic orthodoxy and work to recover and develop the rich array of Third Way economic theories, including Social Credit, Distributism, Guild Socialism, Corporatism, and Populism. This essay is my naïve attempt to start a conversation in the hope that it might draw in other writers who are more qualified to construct a critique of capitalist orthodoxy.

Creating an ideal world will cost us, and our enemies, a great deal in real terms. But the first step toward freedom, namely the act of imagining it, is free.

THOUGHTS ON DEBT REPUDIATION

In Ancient Athens, debtors who were unable to pay their creditors lost their land and were reduced to serfs who had to give their landlords one sixth of their produce in perpetuity. If the debt exceeded the debtor's total assets, he and his family were reduced to slavery. A debtor could also become a slave by pledging his personal freedom for his debts.

By the 6th century BC, serfdom and slavery had become so widespread in Athens that the small landowners and militia men who were the backbone of Athenian society were disappearing. Wealth and power were becoming concentrated in the hands of a few families through the black arts of usury. Athens was thus in danger of losing the freedom guaranteed by its large, landed middle class, which was increasingly unable to resist the power of the rising plutocratic elite.

Thus to preserve republican government, the Athenian lawmaker Solon (c. 638 BCE–558 BCE) instituted the *Seisachtheia*, from *seiein*, to shake, and *achthos*, burden, i.e., to shake off the burden of debt. Solon's debt repudiation cancelled all outstanding debts, emancipated all slaves and serfs, and returned all property seized by creditors. Solon also instituted a legal limit to property size, to prevent the concentration of land into the hands of a few wealthy families.

Similar forces were at work in the Roman Republic. Debtors who defaulted could lose their property, their freedom, and even their lives to usurers. This led to the concentration of power and property in the hands of the few and the decline of the small farmers and legionaries who were the foundation and strength of the Republic.

Rome, unfortunately, lacked a statesman with the vision of Solon. There was no wholesale debt repudiation, but some palliative measures were passed. For example, one of the provisions of the Lex Licinia Sextia of 376 BCE was the distribution of captured lands to establish small farms. The Lex Poetelia

Paprina of 326 BCE abolished debt bondage (*nexum*).

But, as Brooks Adams summarizes so compellingly, the un-relieved march of usury — along with deflation and cheap slave labor — was one of the chief causes of the destruction of Roman freedom.

Debt repudiation is also described in the book of Leviticus, where it is instituted on a 50 year cycle. In Leviticus 25:10, it is commanded: "Consecrate the fiftieth year and proclaim liberty throughout the land unto all the inhabitants thereof: it shall be a Jubilee unto you — and you shall return every man unto his own clan, you shall return every man to his family." This is taken to mean the abolition of debt slavery and indentured servitude.

The Jubilee is also connected with land reform. In Leviticus 25:23 we read: "The land must not be sold permanently, for the land belongs to me. You are only foreigners, my tenant farm-ers." In Leviticus 27:21 we read: "When the field reverts in the Jubilee year it shall become holy unto the LORD, as a field set apart; and it shall become owned by the priests."

The purpose of the Jubilee seems to be the prevention of the concentration of land (the primary form of wealth in pastoral and agricultural societies) in the hands of a few families through usury, which results in the loss of land and liberty for debtors who cannot pay. Presumably, after the Jubilee, when land reverts to God (under the administration of the priests), it is again divided up among small farmers, including newly freed slaves and indentured servants. The idea that all men are tenant farmers of God means that no men should be tenant farmers of other men, which is a strong affirmation of the idea of a society of small, independent farmers. (It is ironic that the ancient Jews argued against usury and debt slavery and in fa-vor of agrarian populism, given the economic profile they later assumed as urban money-lenders, traders, and professionals. Apparently Jews had become an overwhelmingly urban and non-agrarian people by late antiquity.)

The common assumption of the Solonic *Seisachtheia* and the Biblical Jubilee is that freedom is a high political value. Free-dom, moreover, is best secured by a society in which as many men as possible are free and able to support themselves on their own land. Freedom requires private property that is widely distributed. Over time, however, debt and foreclosure lead to the concentration of wealth and power into the hands of the few, leading to the loss of freedom. Thus the preservation of freedom requires wholesale debt repudiation

The fate of debtors has become easier over the centuries. Debt slavery and serfdom are no more. Debtors' prisons were abolished in the United States beginning in 1833 and in the United Kingdom in 1869. Bankruptcy laws allow people to escape crushing burdens of debt.

The moral premise of bankruptcy laws is that individuals should not have their lives and prospects ruined by financial mistakes. Society as a whole is better off if a man can shake off his debts and focus on the future: pursue an education, start a family, create a business, etc.

But if it is right for individuals to shake off their own debts, then it is certainly right to shake off the debts imposed upon us by others, including people who are long dead, i.e., public debts. Life is lived forward. Ascending life should not be shackled by the dead weight and accumulated mistakes and debts of the past.

Debt may no longer lead to slavery or prison. But debt still corrodes freedom is subtler ways. Those who are self-employed have more liberty of thought and action than employees, who are pressured to conform to the opinions and tastes of their employers. For the same reasons, property owners are freer than renters. And debt and foreclosure are the major factors in turning the self-employed into employees and property owners into renters. Thus if we wish to reestablish a society with a large middle class of self-employed farmers and businessmen, we need to revisit the idea of debt repudiation.

America's national debt is now beyond $15 trillion and counting. The debt now approaches $50,000 per American citizen, $135,000 per taxpayer. Unless we have radical change, it will only get bigger. And in addition to paying those debts, taxpayers will also have to fund Social Security, Medicare, and Prescription Drug liabilities approaching $120 trillion and counting. That means that every white baby born today is saddled with $1.2 million in federal debts and liabilities (provided that he becomes a producer not a parasite). And this does not include state and local government debts.

But ask yourself: when a pregnant Mexican sneaks across the border to drop her "anchor baby," is she bringing America another taxpayer to assume $1.2 million in debts and liabilities run up by Gringo politicians? Or is she here to add to the burdens that must be borne by white children?

Remember this when the eyes of immigration apologists grow moist describing the travails of hard-working people from around the globe who only wish to "contribute" to the great American experiment. Are they here to contribute more than $1.2 million apiece? Obviously not. They are coming to take, not contribute. They are coming to add to our burdens, not share them. Ultimately, they are coming here to replace us and our posterity. And when they are the majority, they are not going to go on laboring to feed and medicate old white people. They are going to pull the plug and take care of their own.

In addition to public debt, Americans also have trillions of dollars in personal debts, primarily in the form of credit cards, home mortgages, and student loans, some of them accruing interest at ruinous rates.

Nobody seriously thinks that all of these debts will be repaid. It is not a question of whether they will be repudiated, but how. The most likely method will be the devaluation (inflation) of the dollar. Someday, you might have the choice of paying $100,000 to pay off your student loans or to buy a cup of coffee. And since we'll always be able to buy a cup of coffee, maybe hyperinflation would not be such a scary prospect, except that it creates economic and social chaos.

Beyond that, inflation is deeply unfair. When the currency is inflated, it is not all devalued at once. Instead, huge amounts of money are handed over to politically connected insiders. When they spend this money, it has the purchasing power of the previous day's non-inflated currency. But with every subsequent transaction, as the value of the money is discounted, its purchasing power drops. So the first man who gets to spend a $100 bill can buy a nice dinner for two, but the last man who spends it can't afford a taco. That can only lead to further concentration of wealth in the hands of parasites.

From a White Nationalist point of view, the most important thing is to accomplish debt repudiation with a minimum of interference in the real economy, particularly the core biological functions of the economy: the preservation and reproduction of our race. We cannot have bursting silos and empty stomachs. We can't have creditors seizing real assets for merely notional debts.

But before we deal with practical questions, we need to deal with the moral question of the *rightness* of debt repudiation.

Two points of clarification: First, I am not arguing for the wholesale repudiation of debts between individuals or businesses. Sometimes such debts need to be repudiated, but this can be handled with existing bankruptcy laws.

Second, I am not arguing for the wholesale repudiation of Social Security, Medicare, and other such entitlements. I believe that these sorts of programs ought to exist in some form. The existing programs should simply be improved, not abolished.

What I specifically wish to establish is the morality of repudiating *government* debts and all private debts *to banks*.

Ultimately, only the ends justify the means, and in this case, debt repudiation is justified as the means to restore and preserve a society with widely distributed, securely held private property, which is the foundation of a large and powerful middle class. Aristotle argued that such a society best equips the majority to resist the tyranny of elites, although Aristotle could not have imagined the ultimate in tyranny: an elite so wicked that it would work for the destruction and replacement of its own people.

But debt repudiation would not merely help preserve our people. It would also simultaneously strike a blow against our enemies, who are deeply invested in the financial sector of the economy.

Let's deal with government debts first. The moral principle behind public debt is that governments, acting in the common good of the people, can create collective obligations, such as laws, treaties, or debts. Although one can question whether many government policies really are in the common good, I accept the underlying principle that there are collective goods that can justify collective obligations.

My question is: Why do governments need to go into debt in the first place? Why do governments have to borrow money at all when they can either (a) print it, or (b) raise it through taxation?

In the past, currency consisted of scarce bits of shiny metal. If the government needed more of these bits than it could raise by taxation, it had to go to people with hoards of coins and borrow them at interest.

But in today's world, in which governments can simply *print* money, why is there any need to borrow it from banks? Particularly when the banks themselves just make up the money they lend out.

Thus my argument is simply that public debt is wrong because it is not necessary. It is, therefore, fraudulent to justify public debt in the name of the common good. Public debt is actually a way of making the society as a whole—specifically, the taxpayers—subservient to private interests (banks) and even to alien peoples (market dominant minorities, foreign governments).

But a free people should serve its own interests—and, I would argue, the higher interests of life—not foreign interests or private interests. Such debts should, therefore, be repudiated.

As for the foreign governments holding US bonds, we should offer them the following compensation. They can keep all the factories that American businesses have built over there, and they can use them for domestic production. Because debt repudiation should go hand in hand with the restoration of economic nationalism, including tariffs on imported manufactured goods. So businesses that wish to sell products in the United States should have to manufacture them here.

As for the repudiation of debts to banks: this is necessary, because existing debts can never be repaid, and it is moral for the reasons already laid out above. Beyond that, it is morally absurd to hold that banks, which create money out of nothing, have a right to demand the repayment of their principal plus interest. In the end, however, the case for the repudiation of bank debt rests on the existence of a viable alternative financial system, some elements of which I have sketched above in "Money for Nothing."

The repudiation of government and individual debts should be a political imperative for White Nationalists. When White Republics emerge, we will of course repudiate the debts of predecessor states. But even within the present system debt repudiation should be stressed by White Nationalists, for it would prove a very popular political plank. Debt repudiation would also be useful to break White Nationalists away from the dead ends of Republican conservatism and "free market" economic orthodoxy.

Of course the primary aim of White Nationalism is to secure the existence of our people and a future for white children. But if that does not get people's attention, then promising to cancel their credit card, student loan, and home mortgage debts definitely will.

Counter-Currents/*North American New Right*
February 6, 2012

BROOKS ADAMS ON
THE ROMANS

Peter Chardon Brooks Adams, 1848–1927 was an American historian and a classical republican/agrarian/populist critic of capitalism.

Brooks Adams was from an immensely accomplished family. He was a great-grandson of President John Adams, a grandson of President John Quincy Adams, a son of diplomat Charles Francis Adams, and the brother of Henry Adams, the philosopher and historian whose own theory of history was influenced by Brooks.

Brooks Adams' greatest work, *The Law of Civilization and Decay: An Essay on History* (1895), is an essential document for understanding Third Way economics, specifically the classical republican/agrarian/populist critique of capitalism in the name of preserving freedom and private property.

In his *Politics*, Aristotle argues that a society that wishes to preserve freedom needs a large middle class. By a middle class, he specifically meant people who owned property and were self-employed rather than employed by others. From Aristotle's time to the 20th century, most human beings were involved in agriculture. Thus the middle class consisted primarily of small farmers. Consequently, the problem of preserving freedom was inevitably framed in terms of agrarian economics. The lessons still apply, however, to middle classes in post-agrarian societies.

In chapter 1, "The Romans," Adams illustrates how capitalism ruined Rome. The backbone of Rome's strength was its yeomanry: its small farmers and militia men, the legionaries who carved out antiquity's greatest empire. Adams establishes a number of striking conclusions.

Adams argues that Rome never had an aristocracy in the strict sense of the term, meaning a ruling elite chosen for their excellence in virtue, valor, and statesmanship. Instead, the Roman elite from the beginning was oligarchic or plutocratic, defined by wealth. When the populace held the power of the oligarchy in check, Rome's yeomanry made her the mistress of the world. However, the oligarchical forces ultimately triumphed, which led to the destruction of the Roman middle class, then to the destruction of the Empire, and ultimately to the destruction of the oligarchs themselves.

The economic devices by which the Roman oligarchy destroyed the Roman farmers are threefold: (1) usury, (2) deflation, and (3) cheap labor.

Farming is a perilous profession, since a farmer can be ruined by bountiful as well as bad harvests. (Bountiful harvests can cause prices to fall below the costs of production.) Thus farmers tend to borrow. In ancient Rome, however, moneylending was usurious: interest was high, which made defaults more common, and when defaults did take place, the debtor could lose not just his property but his life and that of his family, for debtors and their heirs could be reduced to slavery to repay loans.

The problem was confounded by deflation. In ancient Rome, gold and silver coins served as currency. As Rome's empire grew, immense amounts of gold and silver were brought back as war booty from the East. However, most of this gold and silver began to flow back to the East in exchange for luxury goods like silk, spices, glassware, and perfumes. This money did not return to Rome, for Rome exported very little, and its ultimate destinations, such as China and India, were too far away to be conquered.

As the amount of currency in circulation declined, the value of money began to rise, which meant that prices denominated in the currency began to fall (assuming that production stayed constant). Deflation makes it difficult to pay back loans, for every year one must work harder and harder to make the same amount of currency to service one's debts.

To deal with deflation, the Romans constantly debased the value of their currency. Eventually, they repudiated their silver currency altogether and went to a pure gold standard, which had devastating consequences. The gold standard tends to be deflationary, since the gold supply usually does not grow quickly, and gold has a tendency to be taken out of circulation in the form of jewelry, religious offerings, and hoards.

Before the invention of modern fiat currency, the gold standard was the preferred monetary instrument of money-lenders, since they are benefited by deflation. This is the basis of the 19th-century populist advocacy of bimetallism: gold and silver currency. Charlemagne established the pound sterling—literally a pound of silver—as the European monetary stand-ard, reversing the deflationary tendency that had existed in the West since the silver *denarius* was repudiated in 220 AD.

Furthermore, the successes of the Romans as legionaries led to their undoing as farmers. Rome's victories led to the en-slavement of entire nations. These slaves provided cheap labor, which allowed large landowners to undercut the prices of small farmers. When Egypt was added to the Empire in 30 BC, its impossibly fertile land tilled by wretched *fellaheen* spelled doom for the Roman farmer. Adams describes how entire dis-tricts of Italy were depopulated. Farmers starved to death, abandoned their lands and drifted to the cities as paupers and proletarians, or simply failed to reproduce themselves.

But as Adams reveals, the Roman system did not merely ex-terminate the Roman middle classes. It also destroyed the plu-tocrats as well. As early as the reign of Augustus, many of the great Roman families were becoming extinct. The life of mon-ey-making and pleasure-seeking increasingly absorbed their energies. There was little interest in child-rearing. By the end of the second century, Rome's Emperors were no longer Romans. None of the great Roman families seemed to have survived the end of the Empire in the West. All of them were extinct in By-zantium by the beginning of the 8th century.

Rome was never really a people, never a nation. It was merely a system, a machine. From the very beginning, accord-ing to its own founding myths, Rome populated itself by open-ing its gates to refugees from other cities and by abducting the Sabine women. Obviously somebody had to be there to open the gates, and a common Roman religion, culture, and identity emerged. But the Roman machine liquidated this founding stock and replenished itself with foreign blood until it became too weak to assimilate new peoples. Eventually the Germans in the West and the Muslims in the East kicked over the table and started something new.

In the late 19th century, Brooks Adams saw clear analogies between ancient Rome and America. The analogies have only grown stronger, and Adams' work has never been more relevant.

In ancient Rome, as in modern America, the economic system and its imperatives are treated as absolute and fixed, whereas the people are treated as liquid and fungible. Nationalism represents a complete reversal of these priorities. For the nationalist, a people and its interests are absolute and non-negotiable. The economic system must be subservient. Thus for nationalists there are no economic absolutes.

Capitalists tend to treat private property, markets, rights, trade, etc. as unconditional goods that trump all national interests. For the nationalist, however, the only unconditional good is the interest of the nation. Markets, private property, rights, etc. are good only on the condition that they serve the people. When they fail to serve the common good, they must be corrected.

The Tea Party and Occupy Wall Street movements are drawing upon a deep discontent with America's plutocracy. Adams shows where such plutocracies come from, how they sustain themselves, and how they eventually perish. *The Law of Civilization and Decay* should be required reading for those who wish to create a better society.

Counter-Currents/*North American New Right*
October 27, 2011

THE AUSTRIAN ECONOMIC APOCALYPSE

Back at the beginning of 2012, I stuck my neck out a bit by writing an article on economics, "Money for Nothing," in which I offered my take on Social Credit theory. The subsequent discussion thread, as well as private communications with Social Credit experts, convinced me that I was on the right track. So every once and a while, I am emboldened again to offer some economic heresies for discussion. Today is one of those days.

One does not have to lurk very long at Lew Rockwell's site, or read many articles by Paul Craig Roberts, without encountering the ideas that I will dub the Austrian theory of economic apocalypse. These ideas are not confined to Austrian school economists, but they are certainly concentrated among them. The theory has the following premises.

1. "Sound" money is good. "Fiat" money is bad.

2. Sound money is currency whose value is derived not from its usefulness as a medium of exchange for all manner of goods and services. Instead, what makes money sound is its exchangeability for a hoard of goods, most often precious metals, held by a bank. The amount of sound money is limited by the amount of the hoard of goods backing it up.

3. The value of fiat money, by contrast, is not determined by its exchangeability with a fixed hoard of goods, but rather by its exchangeability with the whole world of goods and services. As long as fiat money is accepted as a means of exchange, it has value.

4. The amount of fiat money is not limited by a fixed hoard of precious commodities, but by the entire economy of goods and services. And the amount of fiat currency can be increased proportionate to the growth of the entire economy without any negative consequences.

5. Money is a commodity, which is subject to the laws of supply and demand, like any other commodity.

6. Money also has a price, which is interest.

7. When the supply of money increases while other things remain equal, the value of money will go down. This is called inflation. Inflation manifests itself in the rise of prices for goods and services, as more currency chases the same amount of goods. But not every price increase is due to inflation.

When the supply of money decreases while other things remain equal, the value of money will rise. This is deflation. Deflation manifests itself in falling prices, as less currency chases the same amount of goods. But not every price decrease is due to deflation. The falling price of computing power, for example, is not due to currency deflation but to technological progress. (Propositions 5 to 7 are orthodox monetary theory even outside Austrian hard money circles.)

8. If a society dramatically increases the money supply while economic productivity remains the same, there will be inflation. However, while in the last decade, the supply of US dollars and Zimbabwe dollars has dramatically increased, there has been hyperinflation in Zimbabwe, not the United States. This seems to be a clear empirical falsification of orthodox monetary theory.

9. To explain this discrepancy, economists appeal to the status of the US dollar as the world reserve currency. After World War II, the US was in a position to dictate that international trade be priced in dollars, which creates a demand for dollars among foreign governments and individuals. Hard money economists claim that this demand is so immense and insatiable that the United States has been able to create immense amounts of fiat currency without hyperinflation.

10. However, if the dollar is no longer the world reserve currency, then, the hard money advocates insist, the economic apocalypse will arrive, and America will be devastated by hyperinflation.

11. Those given to conspiracy theories argue that the United States resorts to wars and assassinations to prevent political leaders from dumping the dollar in favor of other currencies. Saddam Hussein and Qaddafi, it is alleged, were destroyed because they entertained the idea of pricing oil in currencies other

than the dollar. Iran, it is alleged, is a target for the same reason. (Such *Judenrein* explanations for US foreign policy in Israel's neighborhood should be automatic cause for suspicion.)

12. Hard money advocates are constantly looking for signs of imminent economic apocalypse. It is, for example, routinely predicted that China and Russia will abandon the dollar for the euro. It is even alleged that the Chinese are buying up vast amounts of gold to put the yuan on the gold standard. (Google it if you don't believe me.)

13. If any of these things happens, the dollar will crash and American political and economic hegemony will be destroyed, so we are urged to protect ourselves. Sound money advocates are happy to take your soon-to-be-worthless fiat currency off your hands in exchange for precious metals—even though their own theory would seem to predict the exact opposite behavior. Am I the only one who thinks this is a blatant swindle?

This all looks rather different, however, from a Social Credit point of view.

Social Credit advocates the creation of a pure fiat currency that has absolutely no intrinsic value and is not backed by a fixed hoard of goods. Instead, currency's sole value is as a medium of exchange. It is "backed" by the entire realm of economic goods and services for which it is exchangeable.

Social Credit seeks the complete decommodification of money. Under a Social Credit system, money would have no price, i.e., there would be no interest. And decommodified currency would not be subject to the laws of supply and demand like other commodities. That is to say, there would be no inflation or deflation of currency.

I wish to suggest that the reason that the US dollar has not gone the way of the Zimbabwe dollar is simply that it is functioning as if it were a decommodified pure fiat currency on the Social Credit model. Yes, the US dollar is still a commodity, because it is loaned out at interest. But the reason that it is not massively discounted like the Zimbabwe dollar is that international markets will not treat it like a commodified currency as long as it serves as a universal medium of exchange.

It seems exceedingly unlikely that any country or group of

countries can replace the dollar as world reserve currency, even if they wanted to.

Logically, the dollar could only be replaced with a soft currency or a hard currency.

If any country tried to replace the US dollar as the world medium of exchange with a soft currency of its own devising, the likely result would go the way of the Zimbabwe dollar, i.e., it would be discounted/inflated to worthlessness. Because there would be no compelling reason for the whole world to trade a known soft currency for an unknown one.

And if someone tried to replace the dollar with a hard currency—such as gold or euros—particularly for trading petroleum or agricultural commodities, the result would be the curse of deflation. And no sensible government would accept the reality of deflation to avoid the mere possibility of inflation. Of course some governments might still be irrational enough to follow hard money policies. But the consequences would eventually argue for their repeal.

If the US system does collapse, it will probably not be due to the collapse of the dollar. The US economic system might well be able to continue indefinitely producing only currency. Americans might be able to consume the bounty of the globe simply because we get to spend dollars first. White Nationalists who pin their hopes on the collapse of the US dollar might be guilty of irrational optimism. Larger social forces are still on our side—particularly the social consequences of dysgenics and race replacement—but the dollar apocalypse is not among them.

Along with writers like Kerry Bolton, the North American New Right is doing its part to recover the rich tradition of Right-wing alternatives to capitalism, including Social Credit, Guild Socialism, Populism, and Distributism. The Right, particularly in the United States, desperately needs to break away from free market economic orthodoxy.

Counter-Currents/*North American New Right*
October 28, 2014

5 TO 9 CONSERVATISM

Years ago, the friend who had the most influence on my awakening on race and the Jewish question offered a quite clarifying distinction between "9 to 5" and "5 to 9" conservatism.

The 9 to 5 conservatives take their name from the standard 9:00 a.m. to 5:00 p.m. work day. These conservatives focus on the economic realm. They wish to preserve economic freedom from government interference. They also focus on cutting taxes and resisting new taxes, so that productive people can keep more of the fruits of their labor. 9 to 5 conservatism, in short, is just economic liberalism. Its most ideologically pure advocates in America today are libertarians and the Tea Party.

5 to 9 conservatives take their name from the rest of the day. They focus on preserving the non-economic realms of life: the family, civil society, religion, culture, history, the environment, etc.

Many 5 to 9 conservatives are actually political liberals. For instance, environmentalists, historical preservationists, and promoters of walkable communities, mixed-used development, human-scale architecture, and public spaces are all objectively conservatives of the 5 to 9 variety (regardless of any genuinely liberal positions they might also hold). But politically they tend to be left-of-center and at odds with the commercial interests championed by 9 to 5 conservatives.

There is good reason why the two kinds of conservatives are at loggerheads. Unlimited economic freedom tends to corrode the other realms of society. The best way to appreciate this is to consider working hours. In America today, we do not have a 9 to 5 economy. We have a 24/7 economy.

As a bohemian intellectual, I can't complain about this. I find it very convenient to be able to go out at 4:00 a.m. to buy a carton of milk from a meth-zombie. Americans living in Germany are shocked that most stores are closed by 6:00 p.m. and are not open at all on weekends. It forces them to actually plan ahead, one of the many faculties that American life has allowed to grow slack.

The reason why Germany and other countries regulate the hours of businesses is not because they are "socialists" or "liberals." It is because they are 5 to 9 conservatives. They realize that shop clerks have friends and families and communities. Work days are regulated so that more people can spend the 5 to 9 hours, and weekends, with their families and friends. Yes, such laws inconvenience us insofar as we are consumers. But we are more than consumers. We have families, friends, communities. Or we *should* have them.

Why does the government have to get involved? Say that there are no laws regulating the hours of retail establishments. If one firm decides they will extend their evening hours to increase their market share, others will be pressured to follow. Eventually, through the magic of the marketplace, we will compete our way into a 24/7 economy, in which there will be entire industries where the entry level jobs often taken by young people who have children (or should have them) are on aptly-named "graveyard" shifts.

From a social point of view, this is a profoundly destructive development. And from an economic point of view, it is destructive too, *since the same amount of milk is sold in a 24 hour day as would be sold in a 10 hour day*, yet all are forced to keep the lights on and the buildings manned 24/7 lest they lose their market share.

F. Roger Devlin uses an excellent analogy to illustrate the nature of destructive competition.[1] Imagine you are seated at a sports event. It might be to your advantage to stand up to see an exciting play. But if one person stands, then others will be forced to stand as well. Eventually, everyone will be standing, so the advantage to any individual of standing will be erased. Everyone will have just as good a view of the game as when they started, but they will all be less comfortable . . . because they are standing. The only way to stop this sort of destructive competition is for people in authority to legislate and enforce rules

---

[1] F. Roger Devlin, *Sexual Utopia in Power: The Feminist Revolt Against Civilization* (San Francisco: Counter-Currents, 2015), 141.

against it. The same goes for the economic realm.

The idea of 5 to 9 conservatism is useful to White Nationalists, because we are 5 to 9 conservatives ourselves. After all, we
are concerned to preserve our race, and we are willing to do battle with the 9 to 5 conservatives who are destroying us by importing non-white labor to take white jobs, or exporting white
jobs to non-white countries.

The distinction between 5 to 9 and 9 to 5 conservatism is also
helpful for envisioning new political alliances—and breaking up
existing ones. In America today, the major political parties are
coalitions, both of which include significant numbers of 5 to 9
conservatives.

Among Republicans, the 5 to 9 conservatives tend to be religious conservatives and traditionalists. Among Democrats, the 5
to 9 conservatives tend to be environmentalists, consumer advocates, historical preservationists, new urbanists, and the like.

In both parties, the 5 to 9 conservatives tend to be overwhelmingly white. Furthermore, in both parties, 5 to 9 conservatives are exploited by party leaders for their votes. Finally, in the
end, 5 to 9 conservative interests are vetoed by the leaders of the
major parties, because their primary focus is the promotion of
socially corrosive ideologies: economic liberalism for the Republicans, social liberalism for the Democrats. It would be enormously subversive/productive if 5 to 9 conservatives could free
themselves from the corrosive ideology of liberalism, whether of
the Left or the Right.

It would be interesting to bring together 5 to 9 conservatives
from across the political spectrum to begin a dialogue. I think
they would discover that they have a lot more in common than
they think. It is a conversation in which we White Nationalists
need to take part. We need to be there to help bring their implicit
whiteness to full consciousness. We must show them that their
values are the products of homogeneous white communities and
cannot be preserved without them. We need to explain to them
that the leaders of the major parties are exploiting and betraying
them. And we cannot neglect to explain to them why both parties pursue Jewish interests at the expense of white interests.

It is also important to help them understand that before the emergence of the modern aberrations of economic and political liberalism, the mainstream of Western political thought from Aristotle through the American Founders recognized that a free society requires private property broadly distributed and stably possessed, and that to achieve this end, a certain amount of economic regulation is necessary.

In the end, White Nationalists are more than mere conservatives, for although a lot of what we want can be captured by the idea of 5 to 9 conservatism, it is not enough. From my Nietzschean/Spenglerian point of view, mere conservatism is not really an alternative to decadence. Instead, it is a form of decadence, for a healthy organism does not merely preserve or repeat the past, but carries it forward and transforms it creatively. But politically speaking, conservatism comes first, since our race needs to survive before we can worry about the luxury of self-perfection.

Counter-Currents/*North American New Right*
October 19, 2011

HOW ABOUT FASCIST MEDICINE?

Most productive Americans hate the idea of socialized medicine since they think that they will pay more into it than they will get out of it, and they are right. Americans who take care of their health—i.e., exercise and avoid smoking, junk food, excessive drink, and recreational drugs—should also hate the idea of socialized medicine, since they will be paying for the cancer treatments of chain-smokers, the triple bypasses of lard-asses, the venereal diseases of the oversexed and impulsive, and the diabetes, cirrhosis, dialysis, obesity, etc. of the overfed and overindulgent.

Is it any wonder, then, that productive, health-conscious people prefer the present semi-private system to socialized healthcare? They would need mental healthcare if they thought otherwise.

But, crazy though it may sound, I want to argue that healthy, productive Americans should prefer a socialized healthcare system to what we have now.

First, they are already paying for socialized medicine without reaping any of the benefits, because we have a sneaky, hypocritical form of socialized medicine anyway.

Second, a socialized healthcare system need not exploit the health-conscious to coddle the sickly and self-destructive. One could also award health-conscious people certain benefits and penalize people who do not take care of their health appropriately, so perhaps they would take better care of themselves.

Before we go into the details, however, we have to confront honestly why we do not have a completely capitalist, free-market healthcare system. Such a system would mean that the only health care one could get would be what one can pay for by oneself (or persuade others to pay for).

Yes, there would be charity hospitals for the indigent in such a society, as long as some people did not completely embrace the libertarian ethic of selfishness. But there would be no "safety net": no government guarantee that everyone who needs healthcare gets some care, no matter what.

In a completely capitalist system, there would be people who suffer and die of easily preventable diseases simply because they lack money (or the ability to persuade others to foot their bills). Not enough people want that sort of society, whether from religious conviction, altruistic sentiments, or simple rational self-interest (since anyone can have a run of bad luck). So we already have a form of socialized healthcare.

If you have private health insurance, you still pay taxes for Medicare and Medicaid and emergency room care for the indigent. And private health insurance is also a form of redistribution. The healthier you are, the less medical care you use. The people who really benefit from private insurance are those who have serious medical problems.

In the past, healthy people with private insurance could at least count on a modicum of protection from this because their insurers could turn away people with serious health problems or at least refuse to cover pre-existing conditions. But today, thanks to our government, they can't. So the healthy are forced to contribute to the health care of smokers, fatties, drunks, druggies, AIDS patients, and others who can join your "private" health plans.

But it gets worse. Many health-conscious and responsible people pay such high premiums with high deductibles that they postpone visits to the doctor and important checkups and tests, while hypochondriacs clog the waiting rooms. This often leads to serious medical problems that could have been easily prevented if decent people were a little more inclined to be crybabies and mooches. Where is the justice in that?

In our current system of semi-socialized medicine by stealth, disproportionate benefits go to the improvident, undisciplined, and irresponsible — paid for by the productive, disciplined, and responsible. Given that, productive and health-conscious people might actually be better off with outright socialized healthcare.

Socialized healthcare is merely the logical extension of the commitment that our society has already made not to allow anybody to go without necessary care. I believe that commitment is fundamentally right.

But a socialized healthcare system need not be run by malevolent egalitarians out to penalize the healthy and responsible and coddle the sickly and irresponsible. Instead, one could have a set of incentives that reward healthy lifestyles and penalize unhealthy ones.

First of all, let's divert all the monies raised from cigarette and liquor taxes to the healthcare system, so that people who smoke and drink subsidize their own care.

Second, let's tax junk food for the same purpose. Let's make corn syrup more expensive than caviar. Let's return to a society where obesity is a rare sign of great wealth rather than a common sign of poverty, as it tends to be today.

Throw in hefty taxes on TV, golf carts, ride-on lawn mowers, leaf-blowers, drive-throughs, and everything else that promotes laziness and unhealthy living.

Conversely, give tax breaks for healthy lifestyle choices: joining gyms, taking yoga classes, quitting smoking and drinking, etc. Change zoning laws to mandate mixed-used development and walkable communities.

These are just a few suggestions, but they suffice to illustrate the basic idea. We need to create incentives to encourage healthy living and personal responsibility rather than penalize them.

But what about freedom? It's overrated, but still a value to be preserved. Under my plan, nobody would be forced to do jumping jacks. Nobody would be prevented from eating Twinkies. I do not propose turning society into a vast boot camp or making fat farms mandatory.

But people who abuse their health will have to pay the full cost of it, since their little indulgences will be taxed to pay for treating the illnesses that follow from their lifestyle choices. (I do, however, think that individuals whose drug and alcohol problems prevent them from carrying out their personal and social responsibilities should be forcibly dried out.)

Should people have the freedom to opt out of a socialized healthcare system altogether? Yes and no.

No, people should not be able to opt out of paying for a basic healthcare system, even if they say that they are willing to suffer the consequences. First of all, most of them would come running to the emergency room anyway. But beyond that, some individual choices are foolish and should not be honored. A certain amount of paternalism is necessary in a decent society.

But although people should not be free to opt out of the standard healthcare package available to all citizens, they should be free to pursue additional healthcare if they can pay for it. The rich, after all, will always be with us, and as long as they can travel abroad, they will seek out whatever healthcare they can afford. So there is no reason to eliminate a private healthcare sector in addition to a socialized sector. Furthermore, it would probably be more efficient if most healthcare providers were private enterprises. The government would merely be the biggest customer.

Of course, the biggest barrier to socialized healthcare in America is not that people think it is immoral, impractical, or undesirable. The problem is a deep division and distrust within American society. Most white Americans correctly believe (1) that the Left would end up administering any system of socialized medicine, and (2) that the American Left is deeply hostile to the interests of white Americans.

There is also a racial dimension of this anxiety. Whites instinctively know that blacks and browns would take more from the system than they contribute, with whites paying the bills. Moreover, the old are disproportionately white, the young disproportionately non-white. Thus it makes political sense for the Democrats, as the party of non-whites, to want to bump off old white people to divert their healthcare dollars to the Democrats' younger, non-white constituency.

As Harvard professor Robert Putnam's studies have shown, racial and ethnic diversity are profoundly destructive of social solidarity and civic mindedness. Thus America will never have a Scandinavian-style welfare state unless and until we have the racial and ethnic homogeneity Scandinavia used to have. (Specifically, we would need a homogeneous society of intelligent, industrious, conscientious people.)

We're never going to have a fully private healthcare system. The present semi-socialist system is immensely costly and inherently unjust. Maybe somewhere down the line, when the White Republic is established, we should consider replacing the socialism of the sick with the fascism of the healthy.

Counter-Currents/*North American New Right*
October 24, 2011

THE BOOMERANG GENERATION:
CONNECTING WITH OUR PROLETARIAT

The stereotype of White Nationalists is that they are white male "losers" who have no jobs, live with their families, and spend all of their time on the internet. As it turns out, under Obama, such "losers" are one of the fastest growing segments of the US population: the millenials are now becoming the "Boomerang Generation."

For instance, in New Jersey, 25% of adults between 18 and 31 are living with their parents, 42% of them 24 or older.[1] These are not high-school dropouts, either. A very high percentage are college graduates who cannot find work in their field, who have tens of thousands in college debts (if not more than $100,000), and who are unemployed or underemployed or employed at jobs where they are overqualified (Starbucks, Trader Joe's, Whole Foods).

White Nationalists, of course, are always bemoaning the lack of young people in our movement, especially middle-class, college-educated young people—the people who were brought up on the idea that they were "tomorrow's leaders." We are also, of course, given to bemoaning the fact that our best people are systematically coopted by the system. Their careers, families, and mortgages discourage them from taking unpopular stands.

Well, the system is no longer coopting an astonishing number of young, middle-class, college-educated white men and women. White dispossession has worked its way to their demographic group too. They are intelligent, educated, and ambitious. They are also unemployed, idle, angry, and searching for answers. For White Nationalists, they are a vast, increasingly receptive audience, for we are the only ones offering honest explanations of what is happening to them and realistic, long-term solutions.

Boomerang discontent did feed the Occupy movement for a

---

[1] http://www.breitbart.com/Big-Government/2013/08/20/Census-At-Least-25-of-New-Jersey-Adults-Moving-Back-Home-with-Parents

while, but Marxism, Political Correctness, and the "Progressive Stack" rapidly wore thin for those looking for real answers. The fact of the matter is that Boomerangs are not victims of Adam Smith's "Invisible Hand" but of the all too visible hand of systematic white dispossession.

While whites are graduating from universities hobbled with tens of thousands of dollars of debt, affirmative action students come out debt free. While white job applicants face systematic discrimination, affirmative action applicants have unfair advantages. While native-born white Americans are struggling to find jobs, the country is being flooded with immigrants, who are taking disproportionate numbers of jobs and driving wage scales down even as college costs—and debts—balloon.

College-educated, middle-class whites are not "tomorrow's leaders." Tomorrow's leaders consist of a largely Jewish oligarchy, surrounded and protected by layers of non-white and alienated white allies. Since Jews are few in number, they cannot fill all leadership and middle management positions. But it is imperative that whites *not* fill these positions. If non-whites cannot be found, white women, homosexuals, or miscegenators will have to do. Anything but straight white men married to white women and reproducing the white race. Hence the necessity of affirmative action and non-white immigration, to lower white wages and raise white unemployment.

White Nationalists are the only people who offer real upward mobility to the Boomerang Generation. We will end affirmative action. We will end immigration for non-whites and start repatriation. We will reinstitute protectionism and rebuild America's economy. We will cancel all student loan debts, as well as all other private and public debts to banks. We will make affordable family formation a national priority. We will create a society in which white people feel at home and have real hope for the future. White Nationalists often lament that our message falls on deaf ears. Well, the Boomerang Generation have ears to hear us. We just need to hone and deliver our message.

Counter-Currents/*North American New Right*
August 27, 2013

OUR STRUGGLE TOO:
PROPAGANDA & ORGANIZATION

I find it astonishing that many of today's younger White Nationalists have read Saul Alinsky's *Rules for Radicals* but not Adolf Hitler's *Mein Kampf*. I do not wish to denigrate Alinsky's book, which should be required reading for all political activists and organizers. But Hitler was a formidable political organizer as well, and he recorded the insights he gained from his first four-and-a-half years of activism in *Mein Kampf* (*My Struggle*), which he wrote in prison in 1923–1924 and published in two volumes in 1925 and 1926.

The best place in *Mein Kampf* to begin appreciating Hitler the political organizer is volume 2, chapter 11, "Propaganda and Organization," which contains a number of deep political insights formulated in lapidary aphorisms. The chapter falls into two parts, the first dealing with the relationship of propaganda to political organizing, the second dealing with the reorganization of the NSDAP under Hitler's leadership. I will discuss only the first part here.

POLITICS & METAPOLITICS
In "Propaganda and Organization," Hitler deals with the relationship of metapolitics to politics, for propaganda refers to communicating the intellectual preconditions of political action, and organization refers to creating the institutional framework of political action—two essentially metapolitical activities.

Hitler begins by emphasizing the priority of metapolitics over politics: "Propaganda had to run far in advance of organization and provide it with human material to be worked upon"[1] (Mannheim trans., p. 578). Hitler explains that, "I devoted myself to propaganda in the first period of my activity in the

---

[1] Adolf Hitler, *Mein Kampf*, trans. Albert Mannheim (Boston: Houghton Mifflin, 1943), p. 578.

movement" in order to "gradually fill a small nucleus of men with the new doctrine, and so prepare the material which could later furnish the first elements of an organization" (p. 581). One cannot create a political organization out of men who are not of *one mind* about who they are, what they are doing, and why.

Hitler declares himself "an enemy of too rapid and too pedantic organizing" (p. 578). Organizations necessarily congeal into hierarchies, and the people at the top naturally resist challenges from below. It is crucial to avoid premature organizing, and rigid (*pedantisch*) structures, lest inferior people be placed in positions of responsibility and prevent superior people from rising to replace them. Thus, "It is more expedient for a time to disseminate an idea by propaganda from a central point and then carefully examine the gradually gathering material for leading minds" (pp. 579–80).

Hitler also cautions against using superficial criteria for judging the individuals drawn in by propaganda efforts: "Sometimes it will turn out that men inconspicuous in themselves must nevertheless be regarded as born leaders" (p. 580).

Hitler's aim in the early years of the National Socialist movement was to create a vanguard, an elite that would lead the National Socialist German Workers Party and eventually all of Germany. To create that elite, he needed to attract likeminded people and convert others to his way of thinking by articulating and disseminating his worldview, i.e., through propaganda. Once these outreach efforts bore fruit, the party had to recruit people with leadership potential, then train them to ever higher levels of awareness and competence.

THEORISTS, ORGANIZERS, & LEADERS

Hitler rejects categorically the notion that "a wealth of theoretical knowledge" is "proof for the qualities and abilities of a leader." Indeed, "The opposite is often the case" and "great *theoreticians* are only in the rarest cases great *organizers*." The virtue of a theorist is to produce systems of "abstractly correct laws," but the organizer marshals human material to put these laws into practice. Thus the organizer "must primarily be a *psychologist*." Organizers are also pragmatists, who must take human beings as they are in the present, with all their flaws and weaknesses, and turn them into "a formation which will be a living organism, imbued with strong and stable power," which will serve as the vehicle and instrument for realizing the ideal (p. 580).

If theorists rarely overlap with organizers, then they almost never overlap with a small category of organizers, namely *leaders*: "*For leading means: being able to move masses*," which is something that can be achieved by agitators and demagogues gifted with psychological tact, even in the absence of correct theoretical knowledge.[2]

Regarding the relationship of fundamental ideas to politics, Hitler dismisses as "quite useless" to argue about "which is of greater importance, to set up ideals and aims for mankind, or to realize them. Here, as so often in life: one would be utterly meaningless without the other" (p. 580). Ideals that are not realized in action are empty. Action that is not directed by ideals is blind.

The theorist sets the aims of a movement. The organizer creates a machine to pursue and realize those aims. The leader guides the machine to its goal. Hitler asserts that "the combination of theoretician, organizer, and leader in one person is the rarest thing that can be found on this earth; this combination makes the great man" (pp. 580-81).

SUPPORTERS & MEMBERS

When a movement's propaganda begins to attract people, they must be divided into supporters and members. The distinction is simple: "A supporter of a movement is one who declares himself to be in agreement with its aims; a member is one who fights for them." Being a supporter "requires only a passive recognition of an idea" while membership "demands active advocacy and defense." Being a supporter requires only "understanding" of a doctrine, while membership requires both understanding and "the courage personally to advocate

---

[2] At least in this chapter, Hitler does not explain what differentiates leaders from other organizers.

and disseminate what has been understood." All members are supporters, but not all supporters are members. Only members are part of the movement organization. Since the courage to fight for ideas is rarer than the ability to passively support them, "to ten supporters there will be only one or two members" (p. 581).

Propaganda is directed to the public at large, and to subgroups within the public, but it is still directed to men *en masse*, not at individuals, whereas organizers have to be concerned with carefully evaluating the character and abilities of the individuals who are potential members.

Propaganda directed to the general public makes them "*ripe for the victory of [an] idea*," while "*organization achieves victory*" by mobilizing those supporters who will fight for the idea's realization.

Hitler also points out that the victory of an idea comes more quickly the broader its dissemination and acceptance in society, and the more "*exclusive, rigid, and firm the organization which carries out the fight in practice.*" Thus, "*the number of supporters cannot be too large, but . . . the number of members can more readily be too large than too small.*" Moreover, if "*propaganda has imbued a whole people with an idea, the organization can draw the consequences with a handful of men*" (p. 582).

In other words, there is an inverse relationship between the breadth of propaganda's success and the necessary size of an organization. The more successful the propaganda, the smaller the organization needs to be. The more supporters there are in the general public, the fewer members are necessary. The less successful the propaganda, the larger the organization needs to be. The fewer the supporters, the more members are needed.

Hitler emphasizes that ultimately, the aim of both propaganda and organization is political power. Thus although the first task of propaganda is to attract people, and the first task of organization is to create a vehicle for more propaganda, both propaganda and organization ultimately have to challenge and replace the existing system: "The second task of propaganda is the disruption of the existing state of affairs and the permeation of this state of affairs with the new doctrine," and "the second ask of organization must be the struggle for power, thus to achieve the final success of the doctrine" (p. 583).

TWO EXTREME POSSIBILITIES

The inverse relation between breadth of propaganda and size of organization points to two extreme possibilities.

First, if propaganda becomes so widespread that it penetrates all the institutions of a society, then a single specifically political (as opposed to propaganda) organization fighting for the realization of the idea would no longer be necessary simply because *all* institutions of society would now fight for the realization of the idea.

This essentially describes present-day Jewish intellectual hegemony in white societies. While there is a formidable array of specifically Jewish organizations working to maintain Jewish hegemony, all other institutions—government, academia, the churches, business, the culture industries, etc.—are so permeated with Jewish propaganda and subversion that they are now *de facto* organs of Jewish power as well.

And if white racial consciousness becomes equally hegemonic, then White Nationalism can be achieved by means of propaganda alone, for a fighting White Nationalist organization is redundant if all of society's organizations are fighting for White Nationalism as well.

The other extreme is a society in which propaganda has minimal diffusion and acceptance, in which case the organization becomes, in effect, an invading army seizing control of a hostile population by force.

When faced with overwhelming Jewish intellectual hegemony, such Old Right-style National Socialists as William Pierce and Harold Covington have conceived their struggle essentially along the lines of a conquering army. The North American New Right aims at the opposite extreme, on the principle that present-day Jewish hegemony should be fought on its own terms. Bad ideas must be combated with good ideas, institutional subversion with institutional renewal.

I do not deny that it may be necessary for political organizations to actually struggle for power. (I simply have no talent for or interest in politics.) But I do believe that such organizing is premature before propaganda delivers quality human material, and if propaganda is wildly successful, White Nationalism may not need to create new institutions, simply because it can capture the existing institutions by capturing the minds of those who control them.

KEEP PROPAGANDA TRUTHFUL

One of the most important lessons to draw from Hitler's discussion of propaganda and organization is the necessity of keeping one's propaganda truthful — even when the truth hurts or seems scary and "radical." One must direct one's propaganda to the general public and all subgroups within it. One must find ways to appeal to everyone. But this pertains only to the *form* of one's propaganda, the different media one employs, the different ways one pitches it to different audiences. In these matters, one should be maximally pragmatic, flexible, and innovative.

But one must not, under any circumstances, alter the *content* of one's message merely to appeal to weak and squeamish people. Such tactics may increase the number of nominal supporters and members. But they are not worth the costs they impose. Under normal circumstances, associating with people who do not fundamentally agree with one's platform necessitates that one spend time wrangling with them rather than pursuing one's long-term aims. One ends up fighting one's "friends" rather than one's enemies. And in emergency situations — when one has to count on an organization acting with one mind and will — the squeamish will sheer off and abandon you when you need them most. So, in terms of what is most important — namely, the achievement of one's ultimate goals — moderation at the expense of truth gains one nothing.

The North American New Right, for example, has been advised to "soften" its stance on a number of issues — as if we were peddling seat cushions rather than proclaiming crucially important truths. We have been urged to soften our take on the Jewish problem to appeal to the squeamish. We have been urged to soften our stance on biological race to appeal to religious obscurantists, petty nationalists, etc. We are constantly asked to make our movement more friendly to women by censoring certain male writers. (I have given a platform to female writers, but they have lost interest quickly.) Finally, we are constantly prodded to censor honest religious dissent to pander to Christians.

Ironically, the positions I have outlined on these matters are as "soft" as one can reasonably go—meaning that I concede to facts and reasonable arguments, not to dogmas, feelings, and folly. But there is no advantage in compromising our intellectual honesty merely to associate with people who will at best slow us down and, at worst, abandon us in a crisis.

Hitler shows us that we can ignore all this "clever" and "practical" advice and still win. Sometimes the clever thing is not the smart thing to do.

KEEP ORGANIZATIONS UNITED

Just as it is more important to keep one's propaganda truthful than appealing, it is more important for one's organizations to be radical and united than large, flabby, and inclusive. The purpose of an organization is to fight for the realization of its guiding ideas. To do this, an organization must have strength, which requires both numbers and unity. But strength does not lie merely in numbers, since growth that is too rapid or indiscriminate can weaken unity, "since only a small fraction of mankind is by nature energetic and bold, a movement which endlessly enlarges its organization would inevitably be weakened someday as a result" (p. 584). Thus one must manage growth to maintain unity, so additional numbers strengthen rather than weaken the organization.

Truthful propaganda makes unified organizations possible, as Hitler explains:

As director of the party's propaganda, I took many pains not only to prepare the soil for the future greatness of the movement, but by an extremely radical conception in this work, I also strove to bring it about that the party should obtain only the best material. For the more radical and in-

flammatory my propaganda was, the more this fright-
ened weaklings and hesitant characters, and prevented
them from penetrating the primary core of our organization. . . . The movement, they said, was so radical that
membership in it would expose the individual to the
gravest difficulties, nay, dangers and we shouldn't take it
as amiss if the honest, peaceable citizen should stand
aside for the present at least, even if at heart he was entirely with the cause. And this was good. (p. 586)

Although Hitler would have preferred a small but radical
party to a large and centrist one, he understood that this was
not the only alternative. His aim was a very large, very radical,
and highly unified party, which he created in the end by stick-
ing to his principles from the beginning.

Hitler understood the importance of getting things off to a
good start. He understood that with time, correct principles —
or small deviations from such principles — have dramatically
different results. He had faith in the truth of even his most unpopular and discomfiting ideas. Thus he aimed to change the
public mind rather than merely pander to it. So he was unwilling to dilute truth with ignorance and error in order to win
short term gains at the expense of long-term victory.

In the end, Hitler's problem was not too few followers and
members, but too many of them:

The greatest danger that can threaten a movement is a
membership which has grown abnormally as a result of
too rapid success. For, just as a movement is shunned by
all cowardly and egoistic individuals, as long as it has to
fight bitterly, these same people rush with equal alacrity
to acquire membership when the success of the party has
been made probable or already realized by develop-
ments. (p. 584)

Thus, as soon as the party began gaining momentum, Hitler
blocked new enrollments, then added new people only slowly
and after the most exacting process of scrutiny. His aim was to

"preserve the core of the movement in unvitiated freshness and health" (p. 585). He also restricted the leadership of the party to this core alone. This measure not only protected the leadership from penetration by opportunists, but also by enemy agents, who would target the party for subversion as soon as it became a threat.

OUR STRUGGLE TOO

I believe that Hitler's *Mein Kampf* is relevant to our struggle too, because White Nationalism in the United States is in a position analogous to the early years of that National Socialist movement. This will be a galling statement to some, given the decades of White Nationalist efforts behind us. Yet those efforts have to be judged a failure, either due to the lack of a coherent worldview, or the inability to propagate one, or the failure to recruit a genuine vanguard—or some combination of the above.

Ideologically, the movement has been most compromised by conservatism, mainstreaming, the failure to confront the Jewish problem, and a general lack of seriousness about the role of ideas in politics.

In terms of communications, the movement has been most compromised by incompetence and bad taste.

But the greatest failures have been in terms of cadre building. We have simply failed to attract and cultivate quality people. Because of premature populism,[3] we have attracted people who are average or below average in intelligence, taste, moral character,[4] and moral seriousness.[5] Because we lack confidence in our message, we are content to coddle cranks and kooks, even though each one repulses 100 superior people.

Because of superficiality and confused motives, competence and character frequently take a back seat to looks, bonhomie, "clubbability," bourgeois respectability, pandering to Chris-

---

[3] See my "Premature Populism" in *New Right vs. Old Right*.

[4] http://www.counter-currents.com/2014/04/on-the-necessity-of-a-new-right/

[5] See my "The Moral Factor" in *New Right vs. Old Right*.

tians, and even such bizarre fixations as gender parity. Movement groups have been modeled on churches, cults, historical societies, fraternities, scout troops, Masonic lodges, businesses, historical reenactment societies, the Republican party, etc. It is only for lack of women that they have not yet been modeled on ballroom dancing clubs. Some of them have even been modeled on the NSDAP, 1919–1945, in complete defiance of historical context. Every model, really, except a machine for realizing our ideas in the 21st century.

But before we organize, we must have people. And to attract people, we need propaganda. But before we engage in propaganda, we need a message. We need to figure out who we are, what we want, and why. That brings us back to metapolitics and the project of the North American New Right.

Counter-Currents/*North American New Right*
May 20, 2014

Vanguardism, Vantardism, & Mainstreaming

The perennial debate between White Nationalist "vanguard-ists" and "mainstreamers" is raging again at *Alternative Right*[1] and *The Daily Stormer*.[2] I think the discussion would be clarified by introducing a third category: "van*tard*ism," which is a com-bination of "vanguard" and "retard" and refers to stupid, counter-productive forms of vanguardism—a vanguardism that holds us back rather than leads us forward.

Vanguardism comes from the word "vanguard" (French *avant-garde*), which refers to the leading edge of a military for-mation. In White Nationalist terms, vanguardism is the com-mitment to *lead* our people to a White Nationalist society, to pull the political mainstream in our direction. It requires both metapolitics and straightforward politics: changing how people think and changing the political leadership of society.

But the core of vanguardism is metapolitical, meaning that vanguardists hold that certain political *principles* and *goals* are absolute and non-negotiable. And because we will not budge on these principles, we will have persuade the rest of society to think like we do. A rational minority must accept our princi-ples as truths; a broader minority must accept them as articles of faith; the majority must accept them because we will consist-ently deliver prosperity, security, and peace; and a sullen mi-nority of dissidents must accept them because they simply have no choice.

For me, there are four political absolutes.

First, Europeans constitute a distinct race, the white race. Thus to be French or German or Swedish or Greek or Italian or Irish is also to be *white*. Therefore, no non-racial form of civic,

---

[1] http://www.alternative-right.blogspot.co.uk/2014/09/andrew-anglins-inverted-ghetto.html

[2] http://www.dailystormer.com/ramzpaul-attacks-hero-robert-ransdell-why/

linguistic, cultural, or religious nationalism is sufficient to defend European peoples. Because non-whites can be citizens of European lands, speak European languages, share in European culture, and profess Christianity, any form of nationalism that cannot distinguish such people from whites cannot save our race.

Second, the white race is threatened with simple biological extinction, compared to which all other political issues are trivial distractions. Only by recognizing the absolute and biological nature of the threat can we define a real solution and create the necessary moral seriousness and urgency to implement it.

Third, the only tenable solution to the threat of white extinction is White Nationalism: the creation of homogeneously white homelands for all white peoples, which will require the alteration of political borders and the mass resettlement of non-whites.

Fourth, Jews are not Europeans. Many Jews have European blood, but they have a distinctly non-European consciousness, which defines their origins, interests, and destiny in contradistinction to Europeans. This means that there is an inevitable conflict between Jewish and European interests and identity. There is, moreover, a long history of Jewish enmity and malevolence towards Europeans, which has sometimes — though not always — been recognized and reciprocated. Finally, although White Nationalists can debate endlessly on the relative responsibility of Jews for the perilous state of white humanity, there should be no debate on the fact that the organized Jewish community is the *principal* enemy — not the sole enemy, but the principal enemy — of every attempt to halt and reverse white extinction. One cannot defeat an enemy one will not name. Therefore, White Nationalism is inescapably anti-Semitic.

That is a rather short list of non-negotiable political absolutes. But if our race is to survive, we cannot abandon these principles, so we will just have to win our people over to them.

In terms of political platforms and propaganda, principle 1, the racial component of European identity, and principle 3, the necessity of resettling non-whites to create white homelands, are the most essential. The constant message should be: "We

[English or Finns or French] are losing our homelands to non-white invaders, and we must send them back."

Neither the threat of global white extinction nor the Jewish problem should ever be denied. They are essential principles, after all. But politically, they are somewhat recondite and eso-teric. They are more touchstones than talking points. They should be trotted out when needed, in the most casual and un-apologetic manner possible. They should be the ever-present busts glowering authoritatively in the background, always vis-ible as the politicians hammer away endlessly on variations of principles 1 and 3.

Mainstreaming is not just the use of slick communications techniques. Nobody objects to that. Mainstreaming is objec-tionable simply because it entails the abandonment of *any* of these core principles. The British National Party under Nick Griffin abandoned repatriation of non-whites and the white-ness of British identity. The National Front under Marine Le Pen has abandoned repatriation and the whiteness of French identity. I am sure both Griffin and Marine would grant that globally, the white race is on the path to extinction. But local-ly—politically—they have given up the struggle for white preservation. And there is no point in even asking people this crooked for straight answers about the Jewish problem, since facing it requires as much courage as the other three issues combined.

What about White Nationalist politics in countries that ban parties that make explicit appeals to racial identity, or explicit calls for repatriation of non-whites, or explicit reference to the Jewish problem?

First of all, such parties may choose to remain silent on these matters for political reasons, but everyone should still know where they stand. And to assure that, they cannot just let *others* accuse of them of heresy. They also need to offer a steady stream of martyrs for the truth.

Second, there should be no question in anyone's mind that such parties intend to change the system by whatever means necessary. If they are allowed to speak freely and pursue pow-er through legal political channels, they will do so. But, lest their enemies consider jailing their leaders or outlawing them entirely, they need to present a credible threat of violence. If forced by the system, perhaps every White Nationalist political party should be ready and willing to follow the example of the Communists and immediately switch to armed struggle. A party that presents a credible threat of disciplined, sustained, and effective violence is less likely to be banned in the first place. Who wants to remove the stopper from the mouth of hell?

I have dealt in detail with the case against mainstreaming elsewhere.[3] In a nutshell, mainstreamers are correct to emphasize that we must communicate with our people as they are now. As a vanguardist, I fully agree that we will never change our people's thinking and pull the mainstream in our direction unless we communicate with them effectively. Thus we need to be maximally flexible and pragmatic in crafting White Nationalist messages that appeal to every white constituency. We need to colonize every shade of the political spectrum with white-friendly alternatives, so that no matter what party wins, white interests are sacrosanct. Our aim is full-spectrum intellectual and political hegemony, in order to move the mainstream toward White Nationalist policies.

But we will never pull the rest of the world in our direction *if we also abandon our direction*, i.e., our guiding principles. The error of mainstreaming is to abandon essential principles in the name of broader political appeal. This is self-defeating, because instead of leading the mainstream, we let the mainstream lead us. And the whole political mainstream is flowing toward white extinction. Why? Because the enemy has a vanguard too—a vanguard which has *not* abandoned its principles—a vanguard which is steadily pulling the mainstream in their direction.[4]

---

[3] See my "White Nationalists and the Political 'Mainstream'" and "Why Conservatives STILL Can't Win," in *New Right vs. Old Right*, and "Implicit Whiteness and The Republicans" in *Confessions of a Reluctant Hater* (San Francisco: Counter-Currents, 2010)

[4] See my "Metapolitics and Occult Warfare" in *New Right vs. Old Right*.

Vantardism accepts the four essential principles outlined above, but fails to communicate them effectively because of two errors.

First, vantards insist on linking White Nationalism to unreconstructed Old Right movements, particularly German National Socialism, which are impediments to persuading our people today. Half a century ago, George Lincoln Rockwell at least had a rationale for such tactics, but with experience, even he was moving away from them at the time of his death.

Colin Liddell is quite eloquent in his dismay with such counter-productive posturing:

> Imagine a scene, if you will: You live in a Northern English town in the run-up to next year's UK general election. Recently UKIP has been making inroads, and the socialist Labour Party is worried enough to go canvassing door-to-door, so you get a knock on your door. Up pops your Labour candidate, but instead of talking about preserving the National Health Service or some other warm and fuzzy vote winner, he starts going on about what a great guy Pol Pot was and how he was right to march all those Cambodian bourgeoisie scum out into the Killing Fields. And, as for those Liberal-Democrat-supporting farmers, he suggests, the best way to deal with them would be to re-enact the Holodomor in the dales of Yorkshire, etc., etc.
>
> He's also got some old WWII-style cartoons, showing Nigel Farage as a diseased rat, and hands you one to post in your window. Now, assuming this is the way he canvases with everybody, how do you think he will do on election night?
>
> If you answered "landslide victory" you are obviously a moron and should immediately put down reality as you might get seriously injured.
>
> This is a mirror image of how nationalists who allow themselves to be associated with the Third Reich appear to members of the public, in other words as complete nutcases living in a particularly dark and sticky corner of

the past. Socialists enjoy their enormous success because they skip lightly over Pol Pot, Stalin, Mao, and Kim Il Sung, and connect their ideas with what they redefine as the basic interests of the people, even though their vision is ultimately a poisonous and destructive one.

White nationalists of *The Daily Stormer* type—and my attack is not just aimed at Andrew Anglin but all those who strive to harness White Nationalism to Hitler's corpse—effectively do the exact opposite. Even though nationalism is the essence of the basic interests of the people, many nationalists manage somehow to step over this strong point and instead connect themselves with the worst excesses of the past. It looks like a clear defeatist strategy, and defeatist strategies always look like deliberate betrayal, or at best stupidity.

Of course vantards can protest that Adolf Hitler did, in fact, agree with our principles. That is true of course, and to Hitler's credit. It is also true of quite a lot of other intelligent whites. But the things we believe are true and good regardless of what any historical figure thought about them, one way or the other. So does harping on Hitler, no matter how factually correct one might be, make it any easier to persuade the people we are trying to save?

In the end, I am more interested in intellectual and spiritual matters than retail politics. I am on a longer journey, so to speak, so I am unwilling to travel as light as Liddell would have it.[5] But I also understand why BUGSters, Identitarians, and others might wish to step over the Old Right altogether. In the end, is any historical fact or figure as essential as the four principles outlined above? There are many paths to the truth, and National Socialism is just one of them.

The second vantard error is to insist on what I call "premature populism," which is presented as an appeal to working class whites but is in fact usually just an appeal to stupid, vicious, and tasteless whites of all social classes (and an implied

---

[5] See my "The Burden of Hitler" in *New Right vs. Old Right*.

insult to working class white people).[6] But our movement should aim to recruit whites of *all social classes* who are *above average* in intelligence, virtue, and taste. At this stage we simply don't need inferior whites, and no special efforts should be made to recruit them. We'll represent their interests just like the rest of our folk, but we would be foolish to trust our racial salvation to them.

Mainstreamers tend to be sophisticated and pragmatic about communicating ideas, but they are also quick to compromise on essential principles. Vantards refuse to compromise on essential principles, but they are wedded to crude and ineffective forms of communication.

Both vantards and mainstreamers are wrong about something very important, but both groups persist in their folly through "negative legitimization," i.e., by rejecting the vices of the other without thereby having any virtues of their own. Mainstreamers like to legitimize themselves by pointing to vantard stupidity, and vantards reject any non-stupid form of vanguardism as just more mainstreamer cowardice and drivel.

The North American New Right stands for a vanguardism that is absolutely dogmatic about core principles but also maximally flexible and pragmatic—and thus potentially effective—about ways to communicate and actualize our principles. Therefore, we combine the strengths of our opponents while rejecting their weaknesses.

For nearly 70 years, post-war White Nationalism has been dominated by conservative mainstreamers and self-marginalizing vantards. The record of failure speaks for itself. It's time we think our way outside that box. Let's try genuine vanguardism—for a change.

Counter-Currents/*North American New Right*
October 9, 2014

---

[6] See my "Premature Populism" in *New Right vs. Old Right*.

VANTARD STRATEGIES

My essay "Vanguardism, Vantardism, and Mainstreaming" was directed primarily at mainstreamers. My goal in distinguishing between genuine vanguardists and "vantards" was to force the mainstreamers to focus on the substance of the vanguardist position, which I think is entirely defensible, rather than on the non-productive strategies of the vantards, which I characterized in two ways: (1) as needlessly linking White Nationalism with German National Socialism and the Holocaust, and (2) as embracing "premature populism."

Colin Liddell sent his initial salvo in this debate, "Andrew Anglin's Inverted Ghetto,"[1] to Counter-Currents, but I did not want to run it. Liddell was responding to Anglin's response[2] to RamZPaul's attack on Robert Randsell. (See how complicated this gets? And this was just the beginning.) I told Liddell that I want Counter-Currents to stay above this kind of web drama because it is wearisome and usually unproductive.

I particularly objected to Liddell's suggestion that Andrew Anglin is working for the enemy. My gut tells me that Anglin is sincere—but then so is bad poetry. Moreover, I think that we should presume that people are sincere until proven otherwise. And even counter-productive behavior can be quite sincere. Too often one has occasion to ask: "If so-and-so *were* working for the enemy, would he be doing anything different?"

I thought RamZPaul's attack to be pointless, because evidently he wants people like Randsell to shut up and go away, and they never will. So one needs to find a way of dealing with them. For instance, if you want to seem more moderate and reasonable, you can always point to someone like Randsell. And if you take umbrage to being linked with Randsell, well, that would not stop even if he did go away. The enemy is not

---

[1] http://www.alternative-right.blogspot.co.uk/2014/09/andrew-anglins-inverted-ghetto.html

[2] http://www.dailystormer.com/ramzpaul-attacks-hero-robert-ransdell-why/

"fair." They would simply play the Hitler canard. So one has to have an answer anyway. Best, then, to focus on honing your own message than calling Randsell a clown.

Anglin then responded to Liddell, prompting Liddell to write a real stylistic and argumentative *tour de force*, "Stormer in a Teacup," which at a stroke elevated the discussion to a level that prompted me to take part.[3] Anglin then responded to both Liddell and me. (And Alex Linder has also chipped in.[4]) Then Liddell responded yet again with "Go Straight to NAZI; do Not Pass Go . . ."[5] To which Anglin—who obviously relishes playing the victim and collecting props from dullards—has now hammered out another response.[6]

This controversy has proved useful, because it has prompted Anglin and Linder to set down some of their presuppositions, which I would like to examine critically.

THEY'LL CALL YOU A NAZI ANYWAY, SO YOU MIGHT AS WELL BE ONE

Liddell's strongest argument is that linking White Nationalism to German National Socialism is self-defeating. Our enemies go out of the way to assert such linkages. They even claim that harmless conservatives like Rush Limbaugh are Nazis. Why do they do that? Because they correctly perceive that linking any Right-wing cause to Hitler stigmatizes it in the minds of most people. Being linked to Hitler, for example, is much more damaging than being linked to the devil himself, which is quite a feat. Why, then, go out of one's way to tie White Nationalism to Hitler, when it is hard enough to get Americans or Swedes or Englishmen concerned with stopping their own ethnic displacement in the here and now?

I think Liddell makes a good point, which I would like to

---

[3] http://www.alternative-right.blogspot.co.uk/2011/09/stormer-in-teacup.html

[4] http://vnnforum.com/showthread.php?t=212845

[5] http://www.alternative-right.blogspot.co.uk/2014/10/go-straight-to-nazi-do-not-pass-go.html

[6] http://www.dailystormer.com/infinite-dramaquest-the-battle-for-the-soul-of-american-white-nationalism-continues/

amplify. I think it is necessary to reject the premise shared by both vantards and the enemies of White Nationalism, namely, that *White Nationalism really, authentically just is National Socialism.* If you really are a National Socialist, then that is true. And if, like me, your intellectual journey took you through the Old Right, there is no point in denying it.

But, in truth, National Socialism is just one path that people take to White Nationalism. It is not the sole path. It is not a necessary path. Why? Because White Nationalism is based on *reality*, which is common to all peoples, places, and times. Because White Nationalism is the only rational and moral response to the white race's ongoing, programmed march to extinction. Because a rational man who had never heard of Adolf Hitler or World War II would still conclude that ethnonationalism is the best political philosophy for all peoples.

Anglin and Linder, in effect, argue that "You're going to be called a Nazi anyway, so why not go 'full Nazi'?"[7] Rejecting the label, they imply, looks weak. Of course in this movement, it is inevitable that they will be accused of being fags, Jews, and FBI informants as well. But for some reason, they don't wish to embrace those identities. Is denying such charges, if untrue, also "weak"?

If one is *not* a National Socialist, then one should indignantly reject the charge for what it is: an attempt to distract people from the present-day reality of our race's demographic displacement. Even if one is a National Socialist, the charge is no less an attempt to distract us from the present justification for White Nationalism. For White Nationalism is justified based on what is happening in America and England and France and Germany and Italy *today*. And nothing that happened in Germany 70 years ago can make it either more or less true.

---

[7] If socialism (welfare statism) is an essential trait of National Socialism, then Linder is not a National Socialist, because he believes in free enterprise. Of course this is also true of George Lincoln Rockwell, who still insisted on calling himself a National Socialist—sometimes a "Free Enterprise National Socialist." I have no idea what Anglin believes on this issue, but he calls himself a National Socialist, so I will accept that at face value.

But one must not, like RamZPaul, think that one will be spared that charge if people like Randsell and Anglin shut up and go away. And it intensely irritates me when our people think it is clever to pre-emptively throw Hitler under the bus to appease public opinion.[8]

But, at the risk of sounding like an old drunk lecturing the youth on the virtues of temperance, I completely sympathize with the Identitiarians, BUGSters, and others who wish to create a case for White Nationalism without reference to Hitler and the Holocaust.

THE "HOLOHOAX" HOAX

Anglin stridently asserts that (1) the Holocaust is a hoax, and (2) this hoax is the foundation of Jewish power today, such that undermining the orthodox Holocaust story will undermine Jewish power.

I think that both claims are false.

First, even if one deducts all the falsehoods and exaggerations so ably debunked by revisionists, there is still Holocaust enough for Jewish purposes. How many Jews died and how? Probably in the millions, by all causes. But whatever the historians determine in the end, we can be reasonably assured that it is enough to be (a) the worst thing that ever happened to Jews, and (b) an occasion for endless moral and financial blackmail directed at whites — until we simply harden our hearts to the sob stories.

Second, as Mark Weber has pointed out, the Holocaust is not the foundation of Jewish power.[9] It is certainly a handy tool of Jewish power, which they will exploit to the hilt. But Jews already had enormous financial, cultural, and political influence in the white world long before the Second World War, and the ability of Jews to capitalize on the Holocaust presupposed existing Jewish power in politics, academia, and the mass media. Even if the Holocaust could be completely debunked — and no sensible revisionist argues that it can — the pillars of Jewish financial, political, and cultural power would still stand.

---

[8] See my "The Burden of Hitler" in *New Right vs. Old Right.*

[9] http://www.ihr.org/weber_revisionism_jan09.html

Fortunately, as I argue in my essay "Dealing with the Holocaust,"[10] even if every jot and tittle of the Holocaust story were true, it does not undermine the validity of White Nationalism.

Anglin and Linder interpret the existence of laws against Holocaust revisionism and "denial" as a sign of Jewish vulnerability. But this does not follow. Such laws may be merely one more expression of overweening Jewish power, self-confidence, and vengefulness. They may not be necessities, but luxuries. Just another boot stomping on a human face, forever.

PREMATURE POPULISM

In his latest, Anglin writes:

> Watch one of the presentations of Richard Spencer or Jared Taylor, and ask yourself: "who exactly it this supposed to appeal to?" Go peruse Counter-Currents—or any of these other "intellectual" blogs—and ask yourself the same thing.
>
> The answer, obviously, is middle class White liberals over the age of 40—precisely the most useless group of people on the face of the earth, as well as the group that is the least likely to have any interest whatsoever in issues of White survival.
>
> That is why virtually no one at all cares about Richard Spencer, Jared Taylor or any of the rest of these people, and no one ever will.
>
> So then, who am I targeting [in America]?
>
> First, I am targeting all disenfranchised and angry White males under the age of thirty, which is where all of the real power lies. This site appeals to members of all socio-economic classes in that age bracket.
>
> Second, I am targeting all age groups of traditional American conservatives, who generally come from the working and middle classes. This is still the core of America . . .[11]

---

[10] In *New Right vs. Old Right*.

[11] http://www.dailystormer.com/infinite-dramaquest-the-battle-

Now, Anglin is mistaken about my intended audience, which is: whites of all social classes who are *above average* in intelligence, morality, and taste. But let's just accept his terms for the sake of argument. Why would one wish to convert "middle class White liberals over the age of 40," whom Anglin disdains as "the most useless group of people on the face of the earth"? Well, because middle class white liberals over the age of 40 have *a huge amount of the power in this society.* And Counter-Currents certainly does not neglect the tastes of the rich, who have even more power.

Every society is ruled by elites. Every revolution is launched by elites. My approach to White Nationalism is to target elites: the existing elite and the elite that we will raise up from all social classes to replace them.

Anglin is also mistaken about his actual audience. He claims that he is appealing to "all disenfranchised and angry White males under the age of thirty" and working and middle class American conservatives. In fact, his site is designed to appeal to whites of all social classes who are *below average* in intelligence, morality, and taste—and, based on a perusal of his comments, he has hit his target. But no society is ruled by the below average. No revolution is made by the below average. Below average people are just historically inert ballast moved around by elites.

Anglin claims correctly that conservative working and middle class people are "the core of America." But they are also politically inert and powerless. Anglin also makes the ludicrous claim that "all of the real power lies" with angry and disenfranchised young white men, who are also politically powerless and inert. Again, these people are mostly just historically inert ballast manipulated by elites.

Average whites, and below average whites, are still our people. We still wish to save them. We still represent their racial interests. But they will not save our race without leadership, and to be effective, the leadership of the white masses must be, on average, *better* than the masses. They must be an

for-the-soul-of-american-white-nationalism-continues/

elite that can outmatch our Jewish and plutocratic enemy elites in brains, will, and ruthlessness. And that sort of elite will be more likely to emerge among the readers of Counter-Currents and *The Occidental Observer* than from the readers of *The Daily Stormer* and VNN Forum.

Counter-Currents/*North American New Right*
October 15, 2014

THE SMARTEST GUY
IN THE ROOM

I recently had an epiphany about how White Nationalists might do a better job of creating a genuine vanguardist movement. Vanguardism, as I never tire of pointing out, is and must always be an elitist strategy. History is made by elites. Whites, however, are ruled by a Jewish and plutocratic elite that is at best indifferent to the future of our race and is at worst intentionally supporting policies that are leading to our simple biological extinction.

To save our race, White Nationalists must depose the existing elite and make white survival and flourishing the highest political priority. But to beat our enemies, our elite has to be *better* than their elite. White Nationalism will never win until our movement becomes an elite capable of giving our people a future again. And that is a tall order.

According to Patrick Le Brun, one principle of doing well in business is "Never be the smartest guy in the room." The same is true of politics. If I were the smartest guy in White Nationalism, we would be doomed. Fortunately, from the start, I was privileged to meet people whom I genuinely admire as superior intellects, Kevin MacDonald and Phil Rushton among the very first. And in recent years, I have been very excited to meet more and more younger people who are frighteningly smart, many of them coming out of the "neoreactionary" blog sphere.

The great puzzle that I face is how to create an intellectual movement that attracts and sustains the interest of people who are much smarter than me. My IQ is 136, heavily tilted toward the verbal. That puts me in the 99th percentile for the general population but at the low end of the spectrum for really smart people. There are at least ten million white people who are smarter than me, and it would be nice to have more of them on our side.

Of course, the problem is not just to attract smarter people, but also people who are more creative, noble, honorable, and brave than average.

THE DOWN ESCALATOR

Now, let's survey the various existing models for creating a vanguard, to see if they are likely to put our movement on an upward or a downward trajectory. Any organization in which, by default or design, the founder ends up the smartest guy in the room has to be judged a failure.

First, there is the guru/religion model, in which a teacher claims to have access to a body of wisdom which he dispenses to his students in a hierarchical course of study. This model never surpasses the founder. It only attracts people who are impressed by the founder's knowledge and aura of wisdom. Superior people are put off.

It does not matter what doctrine the guru preaches, whether it be Traditionalist wisdom or Faustian self-transcendence. The National Alliance is an example of an organization that was ideologically committed to surpassing mankind but could not even surpass its founder, William Pierce.[1]

Second, there is the Gunnery Sergeant Hartmann/drill-instructor/polarization model, in which one subjects the moderate voices and polite websites where the White Nationalist movement abuts the Republican mainstream—*American Renaissance*, *VDare*, NPI, *Radix*, etc.—to relentless vulgar abuse in order to split off some of their followers, who will then gather at other websites and chat rooms to trade fantasies of ultraviolence.

Unfortunately, this strategy only attracts people who are inferior in intellect and self-confidence to the person issuing the harangues. Superior people are repulsed, and the founder ends up bickering in a chat room with grabastic pieces of amphibian shit. (Occasionally, though, things liven up when one of them goes on a killing spree.[2])

---

[1] I discuss the appeal and limitations of this model in more detail in my essay "Metapolitics and Occult Warfare" in *New Right vs. Old Right*.

[2] http://www.counter-currents.com/2014/04/on-the-necessity-

Third, there is the gentleman's club/fraternity model, in which people at least try to *dress* like an elite.[3] This model is the least problematic. It can provide a forum for back channel communication among activists and writers. It can mentor young writers and activists. It can bring donors together with people who need money for promising initiatives. As a model, it is not inherently, constitutionally opposed to an upward trajectory.

But the one such group that I have direct experience of excluded from the start some of the most important people in the movement, people who were bigger than—and thus threatening to—the founders.

Furthermore, the frat model is a poor fit with the movement's most creative people, who tend to have introverted personality types.

Finally, the more conservative a group is, the more likely its ethics are to be bourgeois rather than aristocratic and warrior-like. But the present system has been carefully calibrated to keep bourgeois men placidly working and consuming and playing it safe and smart until extinction. Only an aristocratic, warrior ethic that holds selfishness and safety in contempt has a chance of stopping white genocide.[4]

CLASSICAL VS. BOURGEOIS VIRTUES

Again, if by default or design, any organization ends up with its founder as the smartest guy in the room, it is doing something wrong. One reason this happens is because it is *important* for some individuals to always be the smartest guy in the room. In short, the purpose of too many groups is not really to save the white race, but merely to feed the narcissism of a "great leader." This sort of narcissism is often entwined with a thoroughly bourgeois value system, forming a rope sturdy

---

of-a-new-right/

[3] See James J. O'Meara, "Mad *Männerbund*," in *End of an Era: Mad Men & the Ordeal of Civility* (San Francisco: Counter-Currents, 2015).

[4] For more on the difference between the warrior and bourgeois types, see my essay "The Moral Factor" in *New Right vs. Old Right*.

enough to hang any organization.

In 2009, my friendship with a minor but perennial fixture on the White Nationalist scene took a turn for the worse when he mentioned, quite casually, that one of my biggest flaws is not knowing how to "suck up." "Suck up *to you*," I translated in the privacy of my thoughts. He'd always had a neurotic need for attention. That was clear to everyone. But I never thought his need so desperate that he would voice it, much less be satisfied with the insincere praise that he was inviting. My initial reaction was pity. But he had lost all dignity, and my pity quickly soured into contempt.

"Sucking up" has an entirely pejorative tone. It means insincere flattery as a tool of social climbing. But sucking up is just one tool of unscrupulous ambition, along with slander, blackmail, and fraud. When sucking up fails, the others are not far behind.

In my book, these vices are worse than outright theft, assault, or even murder. An "honest" thief merely takes your property. A confidence trickster takes your property *and* undermines the trust that makes advanced civilization possible. I'd hang every one, from Bernie Madoff on down to the beggar who claims he just needs 50 cents for a bus ticket.

These vices flourish in a bourgeois society, in which financial success is the highest goal, which allows people to wallow in moral squalor with good conscience, as long as they end up "winners."

Advanced, high-trust societies are also hierarchical societies. But hierarchy is one of the main causes of lying, because it is often the first resort of those desperate to retain or raise their status. As one rises in a hierarchy, it is simultaneously more important to have correct information and harder to obtain it, because suck ups will conceal bad news, cherry-pick data to confirm one's prejudices, hail bad decisions, and just feed one's ego.

This is why frankness in speaking the truth is one of the classical aristocratic virtues. This is why magnanimity— "bigness" of soul—is an important feature of leaders. Magnanimity flows from high and justified self-worth, self-esteem that is strong enough to hear the truth, even when it is bad news, even when it is not particularly flattering.

By contrast, the narcissist's need for constant external affirmation, is an aspect of the classical vice of "pusillanimity" or "pettiness of soul." One sign that your boss is a narcissist is that he cannot bear to be corrected and punishes people for bringing him bad news.

One sign of magnanimity is the ability to lose gracefully from time to time, since it demonstrates that an individual's self-worth is not tied to victory in every little contest. (Losing gracefully all the time merely makes one a Republican.)

Pusillanimous people, by contrast, are "competitive." They make contests of everything, even when you just want to relax with your friends. They always *need* to win—or be *seen* to win—because their self-worth depends upon constant external affirmation.

Although magnanimity involves frankness with peers and superiors, Aristotle also claims that magnanimity can license "irony" when dealing with inferiors, irony being a kind of lying. When an inferior makes an honest mistake, the magnanimous boss will downplay its seriousness. "Think nothing of it. These things happen all the time." Magnanimous people don't get angry about such things, because they have realistic expectations of human behavior. And they know that accurate information is both valuable and rare, thus they do everything they can to avoid giving incentives to their underlings to lie or conceal bad news.

THE UPWARD ESCALATOR

How then can we create a movement that can constantly surpass itself, that can constantly attract better and better people? We want a movement in which people are smarter, nobler, braver, and more creative with each passing year. That is the only way we will raise up an elite that will beat the enemy's elite.

First, a heresy: *beware of leaders and the leadership principle.* This flies in the face of the common sense of the movement. It even flies in the face of my own experience, for in the last 10+

years I have met many highly talented individuals who have done practically nothing for the cause because of the collapse of the National Alliance, which supplied them with leadership.

Of course we will need leaders eventually. Just as we will need followers eventually. But just as I think that populism is premature, I think we are not ready for leadership either.

Leaders only attract followers, and followers are generally inferior to leaders. Once a movement finds a leader, its tendency to surpass itself is capped off. Thus I would much rather wait until we have a far higher average before risking that. Instead of seeking followers, seek people you would like to follow. Believe me, when we need leaders, they will emerge. So in the meantime, let's worry about becoming a group that a great man would *want* to lead. Because we are not there yet.

Second, we need to cultivate the classical virtues necessary for an ever-ascending movement. We need to value magnanimity. It takes a certain bigness and self-assuredness to seek out greater men than oneself. I am not paying myself a compliment here. I know that I would *like* to be such a person, that I *need* to be such a person.

We must shun petty-minded, narcissistic men who only want to be surrounded by flatterers and flunkies. If a man is vain, he is needy. If he is needy, he is weak. When weakness is wedded to ambition, intrigues and lies inevitably follow, and the social capital of a high trust society will be consumed as narcissists claw their way up on stage.

We need to cultivate an ethic that causes truth rather than flattery to be the *lingua franca*. We must be humble but frank with superiors, frank and collegial among peers, and gentle and ironic with inferiors.

We need to avoid people who are pretentious, because they cannot spot superiors; who suck up to the people they recognize as superior; who back-bite among their peers; and who tyrannize over people they think beneath themselves. Again, such people inject false information and ulterior agendas into all interactions, depleting the social capital of high trust civilization.

So how do we *organize* this upward intellectual and moral

trajectory? I want to end with one more heresy: *beware of organizations*. One cannot have organizations without leaders, and I already explained my reservations about them. But there is an alternative model to the hierarchical organization, namely the non-hierarchical network.[5]

This means that we start where we are right now—namely situated in a web of virtual and real-world networks—and we must think about how to build them up and make them better. What changes can we make, right now, in our interactions with other White Nationalists to set our movement, and our race, back on the upward path?

Counter-Currents/*North American New Right*
March 26, 2015

---

[5] I go into some detail about the limits of hierarchies and the need for such networks in my "Metapolitics and Occult Warfare."

SPEND YOURSELF, SAVE THE WORLD

Sometime in 2003, I was feeling tired and thinking of knocking off work on a movement-related project. It was 2:30 a.m., and I had not been sleeping well for a while. But then a question occurred to me: "What are you saving yourself for?" Did I really need my beauty sleep? Everything we save has to be spent eventually, because death will take it away in the end. And we will not save the world by saving ourselves. We will save it only by spending ourselves.

So I put in another 90 minutes, then slept soundly and got up the next day with renewed energy and eagerness. For I discovered that sometimes when we ask more of ourselves, we find that we have more to give—more than we ever suspected.

A perennial question debated by American Rightists is why politics continually drifts to the Left.[1] An important factor is simply that the Left is morally stronger than the Right,[2] which gives them a systematic advantage.

Moral strength has two dimensions.

First, Leftists are on average more dedicated, idealistic, and altruistic than Rightists. Meaning that they are willing to work harder and sacrifice more to bring about their ideals.

Second, Leftists and mainstream Rightists both share the same basic egalitarian individualist outlook, but Leftists are truer to their ideals, whereas Rightists are more willing to compromise their ideals out of timidity, greed, and inertia. But other things being equal, a principled man is morally stronger than a hypocrite, so the Leftists always wrangle the Right around in the end.

Many racial nationalists reject egalitarian individualism. We think that individualism and equality are not entirely without

---

[1] See my "Metapolitics and Occult Warfare," in *New Right vs. Old Right*.

[2] See my "Learning from the Left," in *New Right vs. Old Right*.

value. But they are not the highest values of a society. The highest value is the common good: the preservation and flourishing of our people. When equality or individualism conflict with that, the common good must always win out.

But although we reject the moral premises of the Left, destroying one of their moral advantages at the root, we have not yet equaled the Left's other moral advantage: their superior idealism, commitment, and self-sacrifice. And other things being equal, the team that can muster these to a greater degree will win.

In this area, the main stumbling block of the Right is bourgeois morality. As I define it, the bourgeois ethic holds that the highest good is a long, comfortable, secure life. This is in contradistinction to the aristocratic ethos that holds honor as the highest value, to which the aristocrat is willing to sacrifice both his life and his wealth. (Bourgeois man, by contrast, is all too willing to sacrifice his honor to pursue wealth and extend his life.) The bourgeois ethic is also opposed to the willingness of idealists to die for principles, whether religious, political, or philosophical.

The bourgeois ethos was articulated by early modern philosophers like Hobbes, Locke, and Hume, who heap scorn on the "pride and vainglory" of aristocrats and the "superstition and enthusiasm" of fanatics, for these values make men "contentious and quarrelsome," which interferes with the peaceful pursuit of happiness by the "industrious and rational."

In terms of Plato's tripartition of the soul between reason, spirit (*thumos*), and desire, the fanatic is ruled by reason since his highest values are matters of principle; the aristocrat is ruled by spirit since his highest value is honor; and the bourgeois man is ruled by desire, since his highest value is a long, peaceful, and prosperous life.

The bourgeois pursuit of happiness basically reduces human motives to greed and fear: greed for more life, more property, more security — and fear of death, insecurity, and material loss. Over time, the very possibility of other motives — idealism and self-sacrifice — have receded from the bourgeois understanding of psychology.

That pretty much sums up the mentality of American bourgeois conservatives, whose entire ethic is devoted to saving themselves and accumulating wealth rather than expending them on higher values. When he encounters people with higher concerns, bourgeois man either argues that they are merely acting out of a disguised form of egoism, or, when this fails, he clucks disapprovingly about the inscrutable wellsprings and evil consequences of human fanaticism.

The Left mobilizes greater dedication, idealism, and self-sacrifice than the Right simply because it disdains bourgeois man's selfishness and anti-intellectualism. Even Marxism, which has an entirely materialistic value system, in effect "backs into" idealism and self-sacrifice merely by negating the bourgeois ethos. White Nationalism desperately needs to do the same.

Unfortunately, the American White Nationalist movement is thoroughly bourgeois. We have a culture of excuse-making and failure, a "can't do" attitude. I have sat through far too many meetings in which weary old sellouts persuade young idealists to follow the bourgeois path: keep their heads down, keep their mouths shut, pursue their careers, and accumulate money, until . . .

Well, that is never made clear. But the answer is: (1) until they die with their fortunes and mainstream reputations intact, without accomplishing a fraction of what they could have done with a different ethic, or (2) until men who don't take such advice create a movement worth following.

The European movement is far healthier than the North American one, primarily because the United States and Canada are entirely bourgeois societies, whereas Europe still has remnants of a pre-bourgeois ethos. North America was largely peopled by those who preferred the pursuit of economic opportunities over ties to their homeland, whereas those who remained behind faced the same choice and elected to stay. Such preferences continue to matter today.

Even American White Nationalists who reject conservatism still think in entirely bourgeois psychological terms and cannot fathom motives other than greed and fear. But they can't beat our enemies if they can't understand them or ourselves.

There are White Nationalists who deny that morality plays any role in politics at all, since people are entirely motivated by greed and fear. They are unaware that this concept of human motivation is itself a moral code, namely the bourgeois one, and that there are other moral codes that disdain such mean motives.

There are White Nationalists who claim that altruism or idealism are merely masks for purely selfish motives. But they do not explain why, if everyone is really just selfish, so many people bother faking a morality that they claim is practiced by nobody at all.

In biological terms, altruism is any act that decreases the fitness of the actor while increasing the fitness of related individuals, which also helps promote the actor's own genes in those whom he benefits. Parasitism is when an actor works to benefit genetically unrelated individuals, such as when a bird incubates the eggs and feeds the chicks of a brood parasite species.

White dispossession, including white self-destruction or racial suicide, is taking place because our biological altruism has been transformed into biological parasitism. Regardless of who is promoting and benefiting from such behavior, it would not have been possible if whites did not have a predisposition to moral universalism and impartiality, which makes it possible for us to conceive of even dramatically unrelated people as members of a common moral community. It would also not be possible if our sense of high-mindedness did not include a willingness to make moral gestures toward strangers — even at the risk they will not be reciprocated — in the hope of expanding our moral community, and to persist in these gestures again and again, even when they are rebuffed or exploited. A crucial task of White Nationalists is to combat such self-destructive moralism, and to scale our altruism back within biologically functional bounds.

But if the Left is too altruistic, the bourgeois Right is not altruistic enough. Prizing one's individual life above the race is a silly thing. Higher values are objective and persistent, not subjective and fleeting. The individual dies, but the race can live on—if it finds the right defenders. Bourgeois individualists tend to lose sight of the purpose of wealth and reputation, which only make a difference if spent, not saved, and are wasted if death takes them intact.

As a movement, we need to cultivate idealists who take principles seriously and warriors who are willing to fight and, if necessary, die for our people. Only these people have the moral strength to begin pulling the political spectrum back towards the Right.

Our impact on the world is based on what we spend, not what we save. We have to spend ourselves to save the world.

Counter-Currents/*North American New Right*
May 8, 2015

In My Grandiose Moments . . .

One of our readers asked me, ever so gently, if I did not think it a bit grandiose to try to raise $40,000 this year. My answer was simple: compared to our ultimate goals, no, it doesn't seem grandiose at all . . .

There is a poetic moment in Paul Verhoeven's *Starship Troopers* when Johnny Rico, who has just washed out of the Mobile Infantry, is leaving base. Suddenly, he sees people on the parade ground breaking formation and running. And, perhaps out of curiosity, perhaps out of a kind of herding or schooling instinct, he starts running along with them. "War! We're going to war!" one of his former comrades shouts.

The scene beautifully communicates the feeling of being caught up in events, of being a tiny piece of driftwood carried along by the great surge of history. Of course, this is not something that only happens in times of war. Indeed, it happens all the time. It is like gravity, like the air we breathe. It is child's play to put bubble-headed aliens on screen. It takes a masterful filmmaker to make us experience and wonder at what is utterly close and commonplace.

All of us, all the time, are subjected to historical forces we cannot control. We are objects, not agents. Things are done *to* us, not *by* us. Most of our actions are piddling, reactive, and entirely ineffectual—at least if we try to go against the current. Somebody else establishes the pace, and we try to catch up. Somebody else sinks the ship, and we try to tread water. Somebody else tanks the economy, and we end up bailing them out. Somebody else opened the borders, and we just have to cope with the depressed wages and increased crime, corruption, ugliness, and alienation. That's life—for most people, most of the time.

But there are people who exercise power and bear responsibility. The system does not just run itself. What would it be like to be a historical agent, not just one of their pawns? What would it be like to be the master of one's own destiny, rather than a plaything of the powerful? What would it be like to live in a system that advances our individual and group interests rather than subordinates and sacrifices them? What would be like to belong to a people that has a sense of destiny—and is in control of how that destiny unfolds?

The purpose of White Nationalism is for whites to regain control of our destiny as a race, to make us collectively masters of our own fate. We are not egalitarians. We are not individualists. We understand that our powers and responsibilities differ. We understand that not everyone can exercise agency all the time. But our goal is to create a system in which the few govern in the interests of all, in which the limited agency of each individual is amplified rather than smothered by the social order.

It seems like a tall order. But such systems are not utopias. We know they are possible, because they have been actual. They have existed in history. They even exist in the present day in the Far East. We can, of course, improve upon them. But the blueprints already exist. The real question is: How do we get there from here? A related question is: How can one experience, in the present day, the world we are trying to create in the future? Because some of us will never live to see the Promised Land.

Both questions have the same answer: by acting to bring about a White Nationalist society, by participating in the White Nationalist cause in whatever way possible, to whatever extent possible, we can create an ideal world and have a taste of it in the present day.

I am fond of the phrase that those who fight for the Golden Age live in it today. I do not mean this in a merely symbolic sense. It is a very real phenomenon: the world we are fighting for is one in which whites are masters of our fate, in which we have control of our destiny, in which we are agents not objects of history. Acting to create that world *is* taking control of your own destiny and working for the freedom of our people. Each white who moves from being a passive spectator to being an active agent of our cause brings us one step closer to victory. Working to create a White Nationalist society is to participate in some way in the society we wish to create.

But what is to be done?

Counter-Currents has always stood for pluralism. There is not "one right way" to do this. I have consistently argued that our movement will function best if we (1) try new approaches, (2) seek to tailor our message to every different white constituency, and (3) allow each individual to determine his own level of explicitness and involvement.

But, by the same token, I am always encouraging people to become *more explicit* and *more involved*, to get people outside their comfort zones, to become more radical, and not just in the sense of understanding things to their roots, but in the sense of being increasingly active, committed, and fanatical.

The best thing is to be an explicit White Nationalist. We need a lot more of them.[1]

The next best thing is to be a secret agent, working actively within the system to undermine it.[2]

The next best thing after that is to actively support those who are willing to do more than you.

If you are not willing to do any of those things, then please, at least do no harm.[3]

But, for the love of everything good and beautiful in this world, *you have to stop being passive consumers of free information on the internet, or mere kibitzers on online forums.* That was the beginning for most of us, but it is only the beginning, and if it is the end of your involvement, then our race is going to die.

One of the secrets of Communism is that it mobilized enormous energy and dedication from people because its goals demanded them.[4] They promised themselves the world, and they went about delivering it.

Although manic grandiosity and malignant narcissism are the two more destructive personality disorders in our circles, we have to risk grandiosity. We have to put aside our humility,

---

[1] See "Explicit White Nationalism" in *New Right vs. Old Right*.

[2] See "Secret Agents" in *New Right vs. Old Right*.

[3] See "'First, Do No Harm'" in *New Right vs. Old Right*.

[4] See "Learning from the Left" in *New Right vs. Old Right*.

put aside our modesty, and entertain the possibility that *we can become world-historical individuals*: that we can change the course of history, that we can save our race, that we can turn it from the path to extinction and return it to the path of godhood.

And it is not just about saving the white race. It is about saving *all life on earth*—the only life in the cosmos as far as we know—because if our enemies win, this blue planet will someday be reduced to a dead cinder in space. You can save all the other endangered species by saving the most important one, our own.

Yes, this cause is *that important*, and by moving our cause forward, you share in that importance. If your life lacks meaning and purpose, this is where you find them.

There have been times when I wished that I had never gotten involved with White Nationalism. I tend to focus on the negative and forget about the positive. Sometimes I brood over the fact that the craziest, crookedest, most loathsome people I have ever encountered have been White Nationalists—forgetting that the finest people I know are White Nationalists as well.

My complaining finally angered a good friend, a secret agent who does as much as he can for the cause. He told me that I lead an enviable life, that I work full time for the most important cause in the cosmos, that I can speak the truth as I see it for the rest of my days. Then he reminded me of the basic premise of *Buffy the Vampire Slayer*: Buffy has super-powers and is part of a secret initiatic society doing battle with the forces of evil. Night after night, she is literally saving the world. And yet . . . all she wants to be is an ordinary high school cheerleader.

Well, when you put it that way, I choose to fight evil and save the world. Allow yourself a grandiose moment, and then choose to join us.

Counter-Currents/*North American New Right*
September 27, 2013

INDEX

This index lists all occurrences of proper names plus definitions and discussions of important concepts. Numbers in bold refer to a whole chapter or section devoted to a particular topic.

ABOUT THE AUTHOR

GREG JOHNSON, Ph.D. is Editor-in-Chief of Counter-Currents Publishing Ltd., as well as Editor of *North American New Right*, its webzine (http://www.counter-currents.com/) and occasional print journal.

He is the author of *Confessions of a Reluctant Hater* (San Francisco: Counter-Currents, 2010) and *New Right vs. Old Right* (San Francisco: Counter-Currents, 2013). Under the pen name Trevor Lynch, he is the author of *Trevor Lynch's White Nationalist Guide to the Movies* (San Francisco: Counter-Currents, 2012) and *Son of Trevor Lynch's White Nationalist Guide to the Movies* (San Francisco: Counter-Currents, 2015).

He is editor of Alain de Benoist, *On Being a Pagan*, trans. Jon Graham (Atlanta: Ultra, 2004); Michael O'Meara, *Toward the White Republic* (San Francisco: Counter-Currents, 2010); Michael J. Polignano, *Taking Our Own Side* (San Francisco: Counter-Currents, 2010); Collin Cleary, *Summoning the Gods: Essays on Paganism in a God-Forsaken World* (San Francisco: Counter-Currents, 2011); Irmin Vinson, *Some Thoughts on Hitler & Other Essays* (San Francisco: Counter-Currents, 2011); *North American New Right*, vol. 1 (San Francisco: Counter-Currents, 2012); Kerry Bolton, *Artists of the Right: Resisting Decadence* (San Francisco: Counter-Currents, 2012); James J. O'Meara, *The Homo & the Negro: Masculinist Meditations on Politics & Popular Culture* (San Francisco: Counter-Currents, 2012); Jonathan Bowden, *Pulp Fascism: Right-Wing Themes in Comics, Graphic Novels, & Popular Literature* (San Francisco: Counter-Currents, 2013); James J. O'Meara, *The Eldritch Evola . . . & Others: Traditionalist Meditations on Literature, Art, & Culture* (San Francisco: Counter-Currents, 2014); Jonathan Bowden, *Western Civilization Bites Back* (San Francisco: Counter-Currents, 2014); and Collin Cleary, *What is a Rune? & Other Essays* (San Francisco: Counter-Currents, 2015).

His writings have been translated into Czech, Danish, Dutch, Estonian, French, German, Greek, Hungarian, Norwegian, Polish, Portuguese, Russian, Slovak, Spanish, Swedish, and Ukrainian.

www.ingramcontent.com/pod-product-compliance
Lightning Source LLC
Chambersburg PA
CBHW031427270326
41930CB00007B/606